I Can't Breathe

I CAN'T BREATHE

HOW A RACIAL HOAX IS KILLING AMERICA

DAVID HOROWITZ

Regnery Publishing
WASHINGTON, D.C.

Regnery® is a registered trademark and its colophon is a trademark of Salem Communications Holding Corporation

ISBN: 978-1-68451-218-8
eISBN: 978-1-68451-219-5

Library of Congress Control Number: 2021938092

Published in the United States by
Regnery Publishing
A Division of Salem Media Group
Washington, D.C.
www.Regnery.com

Manufactured in the United States of America

10 9 8 7 6 5 4 3 2 1

Books are available in quantity for promotional or premium use. For information on discounts and terms, please visit our website: www.Regnery.com.

To the victims

CONTENTS

PART ONE

AN AMERICAN CATASTROPHE

A SUMMER OF INSURRECTIONS

On May 25, 2020, the death of a black American in the custody of Minneapolis police led to one of the greatest eruptions of lawlessness and violence in American history. The violence was provoked by a disturbing video that recorded the last breaths of George Floyd, a Minneapolis citizen who expired with a policeman's knee pressed firmly on the side of his neck for more than nine minutes.[1] The principal organizer of the protest was a group called Black Lives Matter (BLM), which for seven years had been conducting similar demonstrations against what it called the "systemic racism" and brutality of a "white supremacist" society that targeted black Americans like George Floyd.

The protests and riots that followed Floyd's death were so large and destructive, involved so many Americans, and involved such powerful elements of the nation's culture as to reshape its political alignments, affect a presidential election, and inspire the largest exodus from America's cities ever recorded. An earthquake in the nation's human landscape had altered its political and social fault lines for good.

Studies by Princeton University and the Wisconsin-based "Armed Conflict Location and Event Data Project" revealed that during the first 103 days of the unrest, there were 633 violent protests in approximately 220 locations across the United States, including 48 of the 50 largest American cities, and 74 of the top 100. Black Lives Matter activists were involved in about 95 percent of those violent and destructive incidents.[2] According to the studies, there were also approximately 11,400 so-called "peaceful protests"—which advanced the same Black Lives Matter indictment of America as a systemically racist society—at more than 2,400 distinct locations nationwide.[3]

During the riots, Black Lives Matter leaders issued no condemnations of the violence—in direct contrast to the Civil Rights Movement leaders of the 1960s, who insisted on the principle of non-violence and whose demonstrations were not accompanied by attacks on police and the destruction of local businesses. The peaceful protests associated with Black Lives Matter were staged during the daytime and then regularly morphed into riots under cover of night.[4] By illegally blocking traffic on major roadways, the daytime protests created an atmosphere of lawlessness that not only was dangerous in itself but also contributed to the violence that followed.[5] These facts make it difficult to regard the "peaceful protests" as distinct and separate from the violence, rather than as fraternal accessories to it.

The insurrectionary nature of the Black Lives Matter protests was captured in the principal slogan used by both demonstrators and rioters: "No Justice, No Peace!" This could easily be seen as a thinly veiled threat: "Submit to our views and meet our demands, or face destructive chaos." The chant "No Justice, No Peace!" accompanied by such large-scale violence made clear that the remedy envisaged was not—and could not be—a reform within existing institutions. To make the changes necessary to secure "justice," the system must be dismantled first, and then "reimagined," to use the in-vogue radical verb. The message was clear: the only acceptable solutions were extreme measures. Only a revolutionary force outside the "system" could fix it, even though the systems in cities like Minneapolis and all the other major centers of the violence were entirely controlled by liberal Democrats who had endorsed the Black Lives Matter movement. Apparently, those liberals shared the goals of the radicals but lacked the spine to achieve them.

Six years earlier, Black Lives Matter had instigated similar riots over a similar arrest in Ferguson, Missouri. The principal differences between the civil violence in Ferguson and Minneapolis were scope and scale. The Ferguson street battles, arsons, and lootings were mainly confined to one city and lasted roughly one month. But in the intervening years, Black Lives Matter had grown in number and capability to the point where it could now threaten civil order on a national scale. Its increased power was fueled by tens of millions of dollars donated by tax-exempt foundations; major American companies like Apple, Microsoft, and Amazon; and wealthy individuals on the political left, such as George Soros and LeBron James.[6]

During the 2020 sieges, hundreds of millions of additional dollars in donations from corporate America and celebrities in entertainment and sports flowed into the war chest of Black Lives Matter, making it the most powerful radical movement in American history. Thanks to its increased resources, the wave of Black Lives Matter riots engulfed hundreds of municipalities and brought several major cities, including Minneapolis, Portland, Seattle, and New York, to their knees.

The night after George Floyd's death, thousands of angry demonstrators took to the streets and began a war that would continue throughout the summer and beyond. As in the Ferguson riots, the primary targets were the forces of law and order. It was an insurrectionary movement, directly challenging the civil authority.

Sometime after 6:00 p.m. on the night after George Floyd's death, rioters in Minneapolis vandalized the local police headquarters, spray-painting squad cars and hurling rocks and other projectiles at law-enforcement officers.[7] At the same time Black Lives Matter operatives organized demonstrations and riots in five other U.S. cities, with participants chanting the names of black Americans whom they portrayed as civil rights martyrs who allegedly had been killed merely because they were black, by police officers who were presumed to be white.[8]

In direct refutation of the central claim of Black Lives Matter—that rampant "white supremacy" in America had led to George Floyd's murder—the actions of the arresting police officers were universally condemned across the country. The spectacle of a black man's life slipping away on camera was horrifying to Americans, both black and white. Police chiefs and police unions across the country were as outraged as everyone else about what had happened to George Floyd, describing the incident as "not acceptable," "deeply disturbing," and "absolutely reprehensible."[9] These condemnations came in advance of any autopsy report or formal investigation. Not a single voice was raised in defense of the police, despite the absence of any investigation into the facts. The officers involved were stigmatized as "murderers" and immediately fired from their jobs. Within a few days, the lead officer in the incident was formally indicted for murder and manslaughter while the other three were charged with abetting those crimes.[10]

The consensus over the Floyd killing raised unsettling questions. How could there be "systemic racism" throughout America's criminal justice system if the condemnation was so universal? Many police departments, including Minneapolis's, were headed by blacks. Why were violent demonstrations and threats of "No Justice, No Peace" the only solutions capable of addressing the death of George Floyd if it was so unanimously deplored? In the prevailing atmosphere of outrage, these questions were never asked. Instead, bowing to the political demands of the rioters, the Minneapolis authorities—all Democrats and supporters of Black Lives Matter—ordered their police department not to suppress the violence of what were, in fact, vigilantes, and therefore not to fulfill their oaths of office to ensure civil order and peace.

The Riots

With police standing by or in retreat, some two thousand rioters burned down the Minneapolis Third Precinct police station. It was actually surrendered to the rioters by the Democrat authorities, as the mayor of Minneapolis, Jacob Frey, explicitly ordered his officers to evacuate the station.[11] As the officers fled, the rioters hurled bottles, rocks, concrete blocks, and other debris at them without fear of reprisal. When the officers got into their cruisers to flee the scene, they had to crash through the parking-lot gate which had been padlocked by protesters in an attempt to trap them in a confined space where they would have been easy targets for further attacks.[12]

More ominously, this easy victory for the rioters became an inspiration to radicals in other cities to do the same. The attacks on police marked the beginning of sustained violent assaults that left in their wake the kind of devastation familiar in war zones. During the next several weeks, looters and arsonists destroyed nearly 1,500 businesses in Minneapolis and its twin city, St. Paul, alone.[13] Within a month, the total damage sustained by Minnesota came to more than $500 million.[14]

Many of the destroyed businesses were local shops that served poorer communities. The life savings and investments of the ordinary citizens who owned them were destroyed overnight. One handicapped black woman wept bitterly as she said, "These people did this for no reason. . . . This is ridiculous. These people are tearing up our livelihood. This was the only place I could go to shop, and now I don't have anywhere to go. . . ."[15]

Black-owned businesses that had been thriving in the Trump economy were suddenly wiped out by violent mobs that shattered the dreams of hardworking entrepreneurs as recklessly as they had smashed the windowpanes of their storefronts. Eli Aswan had immigrated to the U.S. from Tanzania and opened a small car dealership in Minneapolis. On the morning of May 27, Aswan went to his dealership and found that the building had been vandalized, his vehicles had been destroyed, and looters had made off with many thousands of dollars in car titles and equipment. "They cleaned out everything," he lamented. "It's really, really sad."[16]

On June 6, twelve days after George Floyd's death, half a million people turned out for Black Lives Matter protests in nearly 550 cities and towns across the United States.[17] By June 9, those demonstrations had spread to more than 2,000 locales in all 50 U.S. states.[18] As spring gave way to summer, in city after city the rioters defaced both public and private property, smashed windows, looted stores, set vehicles and buildings ablaze, desecrated or toppled civic monuments and statues, attacked citizens who opposed them, assaulted police officers trying to stop them, and turned large urban areas into war zones where no one was safe.

By June 3, at least 200 cities had imposed curfews in an effort to quell the mayhem. More than 30 states had activated 62,000 National Guardsmen to help restore order. Law enforcement personnel were among the primary targets of the protesters. By June 8, two policemen had been killed in the nationwide riots, while more than 700 officers in 25 states had been injured, along with 60 Secret Service agents and 40 U.S. Park Police. Fifteen civilians had already died in the riots.[19]

One of the more poignant victims was David Dorn, a seventy-seven-year-old African-American retired police captain who was fatally shot on June 2 by a man who was looting a St. Louis pawn shop where Dorn was employed as a security guard. On the night of Dorn's death, four active-duty police officers in St. Louis were also shot, while many others were attacked with rocks and fireworks, and fifty-five businesses were burglarized, vandalized, or burned.[20]

By the end of June, at least 14,000 protesters and rioters in more than four dozen separate cities had been arrested. So vast was the property damage they had caused, that in terms of losses due to theft, fire, vandalism, and other forms of destruction, the riots triggered by George Floyd's death were projected to be the costliest sustained acts of civil disorder in American history.[21]

Divisions over the Mayhem

Because the Democrat Party had long since formally endorsed Black Lives Matter and considered the organization its political ally, leading Democrats and their advocates in the national media sought to minimize the destruction, claiming that the protests were "mostly peaceful" expressions of a right protected by the First Amendment. An article in *Catholic World Report* summed up their reaction:

> The elites in the mainstream press are at great pains these days to assure us that the violence and mayhem we are witnessing in our country is really only a small by-product of protests which, in the main, are "mostly peaceful." Protesters gather in Portland and attempt to burn down a federal building—with federal employees still in the building—yet, the protest was "mostly peaceful." A few thousand folks burn a police precinct in Seattle and take over a section of the city for weeks. The life's work of the business owners in the area is destroyed, mayhem reigns within the "autonomous zone," a 19-year old is even murdered, yet, the protest was "mostly peaceful." In Wisconsin a state senator is beaten up. Innocent motorists are surrounded and terrorized on city streets. Each morning we wake up to news of cities burning, our emergency rooms clogged with the injured, even dead bodies being hauled to funeral homes, and, yet, we should ignore all this since the protests are, according to our secular press, "mostly peaceful."[22]

Here is how the *New York Times* described the mayhem: "The vast majority of protesters in Minneapolis, like others around the country, marched peacefully, and some tried to intervene to stop the destruction." But even the violence, the *Times* explained, could be seen as "an understandable response to years of injustice at the hands of the Minneapolis police, an explosion of anger that activists had warned was coming if the city did not reform law enforcement."[23]

The eagerness of Democrat partisans in the media to downplay the violence in Democrat cities was dramatized with almost comic clarity in a CNN segment in which correspondent Omar Jimenez reported from Kenosha, Wisconsin, which had been under siege for days. While a massive arson fire was visible in the background of his screen shot, Jimenez said, "What you're seeing is one of multiple locations that have been burning in Kenosha, Wisconsin, over the course of the night.... [T]hese images came in stark contrast to what we saw over the course of the daytime hours in Kenosha and into the early evening, which were largely peaceful demonstrations in the face of law enforcement." While fires engulfed buildings in the distance, a chyron at the bottom of the television screen read: "Fiery but mostly peaceful protests after police shooting."[24]

A Seminal Clash in Washington, D.C.

The contrast between a media sympathetic to the rioters, and the Trump administration, which was calling for law and order, reached a climax following a presidential address on June 1, 2020. Speaking from the White House Rose Garden, Trump condemned the nationwide riots as "acts of domestic terror" and urged governors to use as many National Guard troops as necessary to stop the violence.[25]

Following his speech, Trump's plan was to walk from the White House across the street to St. John's Episcopal Church, a historic building commonly known as the "Church of Presidents." The night before, "protesters" had vandalized the church and set it on fire. Trump had demanded a greater law-enforcement presence in the vicinity of the White House, but the Democrat mayor, Muriel Bowser, was a supporter of the rioters and refused to order it. As a result, the White House was being guarded by U.S. Park Police, the Secret Service, and some D.C. police.[26]

The night Trump spoke, the protesters had again massed in nearby Lafayette Square, broken police barriers, and hurled a variety of projectiles, including fireworks and flares, at the officers as they pressed towards the fence protecting the White House.[27] Alarmed by the violence, the U.S. Park Police decided to clear the area and put up new fencing. A year later, a report from the inspector general of the Department of the Interior established that this was in fact a decision of the Park Police—not President Trump.[28] The police were concerned about the safety of the park and the White House. Trump decided to turn their decision into a teaching moment about public safety and civility. Accompanied by members of his cabinet, Trump was able to cross the street to the church and pose for photographers. It was a stark reminder to Democrat governors and mayors of their responsibilities as civic officials charged with protecting their citizens. When the president reached the sidewalk in front of St. John's, he held up a Bible. It was an obvious symbol of his often-expressed concern for religious liberty as the foundation of all America's liberties, and of his often-repeated reminder that America's motto is "In God We Trust."

The media's response to this gesture was to mock the president for dispersing "peaceful protesters" in order to have a "photo op"—what a *Washington Post* opinion columnist called an "ugly Bible stunt."[29] Trump was even accused of having infringed on the rights of the mob. As a headline in the *New York Times* put it, "Protesters Dispersed with Tear Gas So Trump Could Pose at Church."[30] Former presidential candidate

Hillary Clinton tweeted, "Tonight the President of the United States used the American military to shoot peaceful protestors with rubber bullets & tear gas them. For a photo op. This is a horrifying use of presidential power against our own citizens."[31] (This from a woman whose husband, twenty-five years earlier, had unleashed a government tank attack on the Branch Davidian religious compound in Waco, Texas, incinerating seventy-six men, women, and children—mostly children.) There was no evidence that either tear gas or rubber bullets were used on the D.C. mob, or that the American military was present. House Speaker Nancy Pelosi made up for the deficiency by calling the Park Police and Secret Service officers Nazis: "The use of stormtroopers under the guise of law and order is a tactic that is not appropriate to our country in any way."[32]

Gregory T. Monahan, acting chief of the U.S. Park Police, challenged the claims of the president's opponents. According to Monahan, (a) the area had been filled with many "violent protestors" who were "throwing projectiles including bricks, frozen water bottles and caustic liquids"; (b) "intelligence had revealed calls for violence against the police"; and (c) "officers [had] found caches of glass bottles, baseball bats, and metal poles hidden along the street."[33]

"To curtail the violence that was underway," Monahan explained,

> the U.S. Park Police, following established policy, issued three warnings over a loudspeaker to alert demonstrators . . . to evacuate the area. Horse mounted patrol, Civil Disturbance Units and additional personnel were used to clear the area. As many of the protestors became more combative, continued to throw

projectiles, and attempted to grab officers' weapons, officers then employed the use of smoke canisters and pepper balls. No tear gas was used by U.S. Park Police officers or other assisting law enforcement partners to close the area at Lafayette Square.[34]

In this Washington stand-off, the battle lines of the national conflict were clearly drawn. Four days later, on June 5, Mayor Bowser had the Department of Public Works paint the words "Black Lives Matter" in thirty-five-foot yellow capital letters on 16th Street just north of Lafayette Square, an area that had long been known as President's Park, and named it "Black Lives Matter Plaza." It was a clear gesture of support for the insurrectionists and contempt for the president. The new "Black Lives Matter Plaza" also featured a large painted street mural of the flag of Washington, D.C. The following night, activists removed the three stars from the mural, replaced them with the words "Black Lives Matter," and also added the words "Defund the Police."[35]

In announcing the renaming of President's Park, Mayor Bowser tweeted, "Breonna Taylor on your birthday, let us stand with determination."[36] Taylor was one of the victims that Black Lives Matter claimed had been murdered by police. In a subsequent press conference, Bowser, who is black, explained, "There are people who are craving to be heard and to be seen and to have their humanity recognized. We had the opportunity to send that message loud and clear on a very important street in our city."[37]

Black Lives Matter regarded the riots, the violence, and even the looting as positive achievements. During an August 10 rally, for example, Ariel Atkins, a leading organizer for Chicago Black Lives Matter, defended the widespread looting in her city as a form of "reparations," explaining, "I don't care if somebody decides to loot a Gucci's or a Macy's or a Nike because that makes sure that that person eats. That makes sure that that person has clothes. That's a reparation. Anything they want to take, take it because these businesses have insurance."[38] When asked how she would respond to critics who claimed that the violence was undermining the Black Lives Matter movement's ability to win the hearts and minds of the American public, Atkins replied, "I think that those [critics] are forgetting the way that history has ever worked. The way that history has worked, the way that we've ever gotten wins, has never been through peaceful protests alone, and I will say with quotes, 'peaceful protests.' Winning has come through revolts. Winning has come through riots. . . . The only people that can undermine our movement are the police, our oppressors, and then us when we don't believe in the people that we're fighting with. . . . I don't undermine my movement."[39]

Atkins's "history" is totally detached from reality. Martin Luther King Jr. would turn over in his grave at Atkins's dismissal of the greatest, most successful, and most peaceful protest movement in American history.

Cancelling the Critics

Despite the destruction and lawlessness of the riots, they continued to enjoy the support of the Democrat Party and its constituencies. In June, Stephen Colbert interviewed Senator Kamala Harris. "I know there are protests still happening in major cities across the United States, I'm just not seeing the reporting on it that I had for the first few weeks," Colbert said. "That's right," Harris replied. "But they're not gonna stop. They're not gonna stop, and this is a movement, I'm telling you."[40]

Ten weeks into the riots, Congresswoman Ayanna Pressley tweeted, "You know, there needs to be unrest in the streets for as long as there's unrest in our lives."[41] No dissent was forthcoming from her Democrat colleagues.

In June 2020, *New York Times* opinion page editor and liberal James Bennet resigned from a twenty-year career under pressure from staffers at the paper. His sin? Publishing an op-ed by a United States senator, Tom Cotton, which favored invoking the Insurrection Act and deploying the U.S. military in cities where police were unable to prevent the riots.[42]

Bennet was followed by *Philadelphia Inquirer* executive editor Stan Wischnowski, who was forced to resign over an architecture column headline that read, "Buildings Matter, Too," which was published after the rioters had ravaged many downtown buildings in his city.[43]

When sports announcer Grant Napear tweeted the phrase "All Lives Matter" on May 31, he was fired from his radio show and resigned in shame from his job as the voice of the Sacramento Kings basketball team. In an embarrassing but not atypical apology, Napear confessed to being "not as educated on Black Lives Matter as I thought. . . . I had no idea that when I said 'All Lives Matter,' that it was counter to what Black Lives Matter is trying to get across. . . ." Then he said, "I'm in pain. I'm 60 years old and I still have a lot to learn."[44]

Professor Gordon Klein, who had been teaching at UCLA's Anderson School of Management since 1981, was put through the wringer in June after he rejected a student's emailed request that a final exam be postponed for blacks in his class because of the alleged trauma that George Floyd's death had caused them. In his response to that student, Klein wrote: "Thanks for your suggestion . . . that I give black students special treatment, given the tragedy in Minnesota. Do you know the names of the class-mates that are black? How can I identify them since we've been having online classes only? Are there any students that may be of mixed parentage, such as half black–half Asian? What do you suggest I do with respect to them? A full concession or just half? . . . One last thing strikes me: Remember that Martin Luther King famously said that people should not be evaluated based on the 'color of their skin.' Do you think that your request would run afoul of Martin Luther King's admonition?"[45]

Klein's sarcasm triggered his critics. In response, UCLA senior Preet Bains started a Change.org petition asking the university to fire the professor "for his extremely insensitive, dismissive, and woefully racist response to his students' request for empathy and compassion during a time of civil unrest." Before long, some eighteen thousand people had signed the petition, and Klein was placed on involuntary administrative leave.[46]

Democrats and the Riots

Nearly every major city victimized by riots during the spring and summer of 2020 was governed—and governed almost exclusively—by Democrats. The destruction visited on their inhabitants was made possible by ineffectual officials who were openly sympathetic to the rioters and refused to perform the principal task of government: to ensure the safety of citizens and their property. The political leaders placed limits on the actions their police forces could take to control the violence and also rejected the president's repeated offers to dispatch military personnel who would have quickly restored order. President Eisenhower sent federal troops to Little Rock to integrate the schools in 1957; President Kennedy deployed the military to Mississippi to integrate the schools in 1962; President George H. W. Bush called out four thousand army and marine troops to quell the 1992 Los Angeles riots.[47] But Trump's offers were rejected by Democrats and even members of the joint chiefs of staff as "dictatorial," "unconstitutional," and "dangerous."

A trio of left-wing cities—Seattle, Portland, and New York— were hit particularly hard by the protests. In early June, a mob led by Black Lives Matter activists and the violent Marxist- Anarchist militia known as Antifa—which is an essential mili- tary component of the Black Lives Matter movement—took over the East Precinct of the Seattle Police Department. The mob also occupied Seattle City Hall and announced the estab- lishment of a "liberated" area called CHAZ (an acronym for Capitol Hill Autonomous Zone), which soon was renamed CHOP (Capitol Hill Organized Protest). Drawing a parallel between CHOP and the Occupy Wall Street protests of 2011, which were also lawless, violent, and anti-capitalist, one Seattle observer described the scene in these words: "They bar media from entering and screen people coming in. They are walking around fully armed. Talking about making their own currency and making their own flag. . . . This is just like the Occupy movement. Soon we will have feces and drugs everywhere and people getting assaulted and raped in the encampments." One police officer who had been previously stationed at the East Precinct reported that those in charge of CHOP were "shaking down businesses for $500 for protection."[48]

Seattle's Democrat mayor Jenny Durkan turned a blind eye to the illegal "occupation," the extortion, and the general lawless- ness. Citing the "food trucks, spaghetti potlucks, teach-ins, and movies" present in the zone as quaint indicators of *bon homie*, she hailed CHOP as a place whose "block party atmosphere" heralded a potential "summer of love." Durkan tweeted a defense of the occupation, describing it as nothing more than "a peaceful expression of our community's collective grief and their desire to build a better world."[49]

The CHOP occupiers issued a series of transparently racist ultimatums titled, "The Demands of the Collective Black Voices at Free Capitol Hill to the Government of Seattle, Washington." The demands included the "abolition" of the Seattle police force and "100% of [its] funding"; "a retrial of all People of Color currently serving a prison sentence for violent crime, by a jury of their [nonwhite] peers in their community"; "the abolition of imprisonment . . . especially . . . youth prisons and privately-owned, for-profit prisons"; "free college" for "people of color" in Washington state as "a form of reparations for the treatment of Black people in this state and country"; and the hiring, by hospitals and care facilities in Seattle, of "black doctors and nurses specifically to help care for black patients."[50]

Much like the Occupy encampments of 2011, CHOP quickly degenerated into a quagmire of graffiti, decaying garbage, drug and alcohol abuse, and violent crime. At about 2:30 a.m. on June 20, a crowd inside CHOP blocked police from reaching two shooting victims—one of whom, a nineteen-year-old male, later died, while the other was hospitalized with serious injuries.[51] Nine days later in the same autonomous zone, a black sixteen-year-old was fatally gunned down and a fourteen-year-old was shot and critically wounded.[52] Finally the protesters, unhappy that the mayor wasn't going far enough in her support for them, defiled her home with graffiti. This was a bridge too far. Mayor Durkan responded by issuing an executive order designating the encampment an unlawful assembly, and in one day it was dismantled by police.[53] Inadvertently, this showed how directly responsible Democrat mayors across the country were for enabling the riots.

The Siege of Portland

If one American city could be described as the epicenter of the insurrections, it was Portland. Every night for four months, criminal mobs ranging from hundreds to thousands attacked Portland's downtown area, firing explosives and wielding machetes, terrorizing its inhabitants, setting fire to its hall of justice, smashing public monuments, and calling for the abolition of the United States.

Portland's long nightmare began at about 9:00 p.m. on Friday, May 29, when protesters marched down Martin Luther King Jr. Boulevard, chanting, "Black Lives Matter," "No Justice, No Peace," and "I Can't Breathe." Soon, many of the protesters began vandalizing businesses along the boulevard, shattering windows and spraying graffiti on buildings over an area of approximately twenty city blocks. Without the slightest regard for human life, one protester recklessly fired his gun at a passing car. The bullet grazed one of the people inside the vehicle.[54]

When the demonstrators reached the downtown area, they broke into the Multnomah County Justice Center and started a fire. Other arsonists lit additional fires throughout downtown Portland, torching dumpsters, trash cans, pallets, and automobiles. Portland Mayor Ted Wheeler declared a state of emergency, enacted a citywide overnight curfew, and publicly condemned the violence. But even as he took these actions, he signaled his sympathy for the anti-police sentiments of Black Lives Matter: "I can't stand by and watch our city be destroyed, buildings set aflame. I won't. But nor will I stand silent as men like George Floyd are murdered by the very institutions that are supposed to protect and serve them."[55]

The U.S. Department of Homeland Security described the protesters who descended on Portland as "violent anarchists" who repeatedly blocked traffic, engaged in arson, destroyed and stole private property, and attacked police officers with fireworks, aerial mortars, laser beams capable of causing permanent eye damage, and various projectiles including glass bottles, rocks, golf balls, ball bearings, metal railroad spikes, plastic eggs filled with paint, and balloons filled with feces. During one protest, a man smashed an officer in the head with a hammer.[56]

The mayor's brave words were not backed by actions effective to protect public safety and put an end to the riots. Between May 29 and August 22, the Portland Police Bureau formally declared a riot on eighteen separate occasions, including nine times in August alone.[57] This chaos had disastrous and potentially deadly consequences that spread far beyond the areas directly hit by the rioters. During the overnight hours of August 15–16, for example, more than sixty 911 emergency calls went unanswered because the city's police officers had to direct all of their attention to the riots downtown.[58]

On the night of August 16, a group of black protesters mobbed a pickup truck on a Portland street and dragged the white driver out of the vehicle, pushed him to the ground, and surrounded him as he pleaded for mercy. Before long, one of the crowd members ran toward the unsuspecting victim from behind and kicked him with full force on the side of his face, instantly knocking him out. "What the fuck is you talkin' about, nigger!" the assailant screamed as the victim's head hit the ground and bled profusely while other protesters rifled through the man's truck in search of items they could steal. Meanwhile, other protesters repeatedly taunted the unconscious man. A male shouted at the victim, "Black lives matter, nigger!" And a woman screamed, "Get your bitch ass up!"[59]

During a protest on the night of August 29, a male Antifa member shot and killed a counter-protester, Aaron Danielson, who was wearing a hat with the name of the pro-Trump organization Patriot Prayer. When he first noticed Danielson, the gunman said, "Hey! Hey, we got one right here! We got a Trumper right here!"—and then shot him. Later that night, a female Antifa member using a bullhorn to address a large crowd of Antifa and Black Lives Matter protesters said, to cheers and laughter from the mob, "I just got word that the person who died was a Patriot Prayer Trump person. He was a fucking Nazi! Our community held its own and took out the trash. I am not going to shed any tears over a Nazi. . . . I am not sad that a fucking fascist died tonight. . . . Our community can hold its own without the police. We can take out the trash on our own."[60]

In July, Portland's mayor, who is also the city's police commissioner, joined Black Lives Matter protesters in the streets, where he publicly pledged to support their demands to rein in the police: "We call 911 way too often for a police response, when often times what's needed is an EMT [or] a health professional."[61] But the mayor's effort to appease the mob failed to insulate him from the protesters' ever-smoldering aggression and rage. On the night of August 31, which was Wheeler's birthday, more than two hundred protesters marched on the condominium building where the mayor's $840,000 residential unit was located, demanding his resignation. To the tune of the "Happy Birthday" song, they sang "Happy Tear Gas to You,"—a reference to the Portland Police Bureau's use of irritant gases to disperse protesters. The mob also shattered windows in the building, set fires inside the lobby, looted nearby stores, and set furniture ablaze in the streets. Wheeler was so shaken by the experience that he announced that he would soon be moving to a new residence.[62]

Even under these humiliating circumstances, Wheeler tried to bargain for the good will of his tormenters. On September 10, after more than one hundred consecutive nights of violent protests had reduced his once-beautiful city to a disaster area, the mayor announced he was directing the Portland Police Bureau to stop using tear gas for crowd-control purposes. Such a measure, he said, would help him fulfill his *"obligation to create change"* and achieve *"justice for black people and all people of color."*[63]

New York Chaos

In New York, as in Portland, the mayhem began in earnest on May 29, when more than five hundred protesters demonstrated around the 88th Police Precinct while others attempted to break into the 79th Precinct in Bedford-Stuyvesant, hurling bricks, bottles, and other projectiles at the police.[64] The following day, thousands of people attended various protests around the city. By the end of the day, thirty-three police officers had been injured and forty-seven police vehicles had been damaged or destroyed.[65] On June 1, The Gothamist described the effects of looting in Manhattan's SoHo neighborhood, where the violence had been particularly pronounced:

> Shattered glass, bare mannequins, and flaming dumpsters littered the streets of SoHo in the early morning hours on Monday, as another night of tumultuous protests against police violence ripped through New York City, giving way to widespread looting in one of the city's wealthiest neighborhoods. Bloomingdales,

Chanel, Gucci, Coach, Supreme, and Louis Vuitton were among the retailers picked clean by 3 A.M., their previously boarded-up windows cast aside on the sidewalk. Groups of young people sprinted through the streets carrying sneakers and luxury items, as an army of officers bashed the windows of vehicles believed to be hauling stolen merchandise.[66]

On June 2, The Gothamist ran a similar report describing "groups of looters" who had "surged through much of Manhattan, jumping into and out of smashed storefronts with duffle bags. The atmosphere on the ground was one of disbelief as teenagers found themselves able to fill their bags without opposition." Meanwhile, nearly seven hundred looters and arsonists were arrested in the Bronx, where two police officers were struck and injured by automobiles in hit-and-run incidents.[67]

Between May 29 and June 9, an estimated 450 businesses in New York City were looted or damaged by rioters and arsonists.[68] The costs of the property damages were estimated to be in the "tens of millions" of dollars.[69] By the end of July, at least 303 police vehicles had been destroyed citywide.[70] By the end of September more than 470 officers had been injured.[71]

One of the most remarkable facts about the riots in New York City is that so few of the violent perpetrators faced any consequences for their actions. This was because more than a year earlier, in March 2019, New York Governor Andrew Cuomo, with the enthusiastic approval of New York City Mayor Bill de Blasio, had signed into law a criminal-justice reform measure that allowed most criminal suspects charged with misdemeanors and nonviolent felonies to walk free without having to post bail. Consequently, during the riots of 2020, most of those who participated in property destruction were immune from incarceration.[72] As the *New York Post* explained, "Right now, anyone arrested for looting gets rapidly released, with no need to post bail to avoid jail until trial. . . . [The imposition of bail] requires that the use of a 'dangerous instrument' be part of the alleged crime. And the ruling from the state's top court is clear: Someone has to be on the other side of the window when you throw a brick through it. If no one's there, it's not a weapon, and jail/bail is off the table."[73]

Mayor de Blasio had long praised Black Lives Matter for awakening white Americans to the "implicit bias" that allegedly prevented them from understanding that "young men of color live in fear all of the time."[74] In June, following the example set by D.C. Mayor Muriel Bowser, de Blasio announced that the city would paint the words "Black Lives Matter" onto the pavement of Fifth Avenue directly in front of Trump Tower. "It's an important message to the nation, and, obviously, we want the president to hear it because he has never shown respect for those three words," the mayor said. In a photo op, de Blasio actually helped paint the words on the street, as did his wife and racial demagogue Al Sharpton.[75]

In a July 9 CNN interview, de Blasio said that because "this is a historic moment of change," he would permit Black Lives Matter protesters to continue marching through the streets of the city while all other large events—traditional parades and festivals—would be cancelled at least through September because of the COVID-19 pandemic.[76]

Defund the Police

The anti-police rhetoric of political figures such as Mayors Bill de Blasio, Jenny Durkan, and Ted Wheeler helped fuel the climate of extreme hostility toward law-enforcement officers. Central to creating this toxic environment was Black Lives Matter's call for "a national defunding of police" founded on the premise that "as long as we continue to pump money into our corrupt criminal justice system at the expense of housing, health, and education investments—we [blacks] will never be truly safe."[77] Black Lives Matter co-founder Patrisse Cullors explained that "it's not possible for the entity of law enforcement to be a compassionate, caring governmental agency in black communities."[78]

Democrat leaders across urban America jumped on board the "Defund the Police" bandwagon. On June 26, Minneapolis city council members voted unanimously to "dismantle" the Minneapolis Police Department and replace it with an alternative entity relying heavily on social workers and emergency medical technicians.[79] In late June, New York's Mayor de Blasio reported that his city council had decided to shift more than $1 billion in annual funding out of the New York Police Department.[80] At least eleven more cities voted to defund their police departments to varying degrees. Police budgets were cut by $27 million in Portland, $150 million in Los Angeles, $150 million in Austin, $120 million in San Francisco, and $4 million in Seattle.[81]

Just hours after the Seattle City Council voted on its cuts, a dispirited police chief announced her resignation. Carmen Best was the first African-American police chief in Seattle's history. The budget cut meant she would have to fire a hundred recently hired officers, about 40 percent of whom were non-white. "We have 800,000 calls for service every year," she stated. "If you just lop off, even 100 officers, that's going to be highly detrimental to a department that wasn't staffed enough to deal with the calls we did have."[82]

Crime Wave

The various "Defund the Police" initiatives sent a message to police officers across the United States that they were on their own, that the political leaders under whom they served did not have their backs, and that their careers, pensions, and lives were now in a precarious position. They responded by taking defensive measures, specifically by deciding to be less proactive in apprehending law-breakers.[83] The defunding coupled with police officers' decisions to be less proactive led to sharply increased violent crime rates nation-wide. On August 2, the *Wall Street Journal* reported that among the 50 largest cities in the United States, "homicides were up 24 percent" since the start of the year. "In all," the *Journal* added, "36 of the 50 cities studied saw homicide rise at double-digit rates, representing all regions of the country."[84]

Violence reached particularly disturbing levels in Chicago, which suffered through its bloodiest spring and summer in decades. On May 31, a Sunday, eighteen homicides were committed citywide, shattering Chicago's previous one-day record of thirteen, which had been set twenty-nine years earlier. Over the course of that same weekend, Chicago police responded to at least seventy-three incidents in which ninety-two people were shot, including twenty-seven who died. "I don't even know how to put it into context," said Max Kapustin, the senior research director at the University of Chicago Crime Lab. "It's beyond anything that we've ever seen before."[85] During the month of July, the number of shootings and murders in Chicago were 90 percent and 139 percent higher, respectively, than the corresponding figures for the same period in 2019, making it the city's most violent month in twenty-eight years.[86]

Other cities, including New York, were turned into war zones too. In the first full month of post–George Floyd rallies and riots, the number of daylight shootings—a sign of brazen gang violence—more than tripled across the city.[87] Between June 1 and June 30, there was a 130 percent increase in the number of shooting incidents, a 30 percent spike in murders, a 118 percent rise in burglaries, and a 51 percent increase in auto thefts.[88] June was New York's bloodiest month in a quarter of a century. The NYPD's chief of department, Terence Monahan, blamed the trends largely on the fact that "the animosity towards police has been absolutely unbelievable."[89]

Though a large percentage of the victims of these shootings were black, none were memorialized by Black Lives Matter because, in almost every instance, they were shot by other blacks. Their black lives, quite simply, were irrelevant to Black Lives Matter.

The violence from coast to coast continued at stratospheric levels throughout the rest of the year. In early February 2021, the National Commission on COVID-19 and Criminal Justice issued a report finding that homicide rates in 2020 had exceeded the corresponding 2019 levels in 29 of 34 cities that were studied, and that they had risen by an average of 30 percent in those 34 cities. The 30 percent figure represented the largest single-year percentage change on record and, according to the report, corresponded to an additional 1,268 homicides in the 34 cities (as compared to their 2019 homicide totals).[90]

Civilians were not the only ones to suffer from the heightened violence across America. Police were its targets as well. In just 114 days between May 25 (the date of George Floyd's death) and September 16, two dozen officers nationwide were killed in the line of duty by gunfire or various other forms of assault.[91]

The virulent hate directed at law enforcement—coupled with the fact that numerous Democrat mayors were sympathetic to the attacks on police—caused widespread demoralization in police departments. In New York City, large numbers of officers decided that it was time to leave. Between May 25 and July 3, some 503 NYPD police officers filed for retirement—a 75 percent increase over the 287 who had filed for retirement during the same time period in 2019.[92]

Police in Washington, D.C., were similarly dispirited, as evidenced by a June press release in which the city's Metropolitan Police Union reported that 71 percent of the members it had surveyed were considering leaving the department.[93]

In Minneapolis, where it all began, the Democrat city council voted unanimously on June 12 to approve a measure to disband the city's police department and replace it with what a *Forbes* news report described as "a community-led public safety system."[94] On July 21, the *New York Times* reported that nearly two hundred officers in Minneapolis—roughly one-fifth of the city's police force—had officially filed paperwork to leave their jobs, citing post-traumatic stress.[95]

An Anti-American Meme

One of the hallmarks of Black Lives Matter rioters that emerged clearly during the protests of 2020 was their uncompromising hatred for the country they lived in. In an August protest in Kenosha, chants of "Kill the Police" were accompanied by shouts of "Death to America!"[96] On August 30, hundreds of protesters also chanted "Death to America" as they marched through the streets of Oakland, California, threw projectiles at police officers, lit fires, smashed windows, and vandalized buildings.[97]

July 4th is the nation's holiday, celebrating its birth as a people dedicated to the proposition that all human beings are created equal and have a God-given, unalienable right to liberty. America inherited slavery from the British and abolished it within a little over one generation, at the cost of 350,000 mainly white Union lives—a fact that gets no recognition from Black Lives Matter partisans.

Colin Kaepernick, a former National Football League quarterback, is one of the most prominent supporters of the organization and its cause. Kaepernick was raised by white parents after his black father abandoned him and his white birth mother. On July 4, Kaepernick posted an online video showing images of the Ku Klux Klan, police brutality, slavery, and lynchings. Above the video he had written the following caption: "Black ppl have been dehumanized, brutalized, criminalized + terrorized by America for centuries, & are expected to join your commemoration of 'independence,' while you enslaved our ancestors. We reject your celebration of white supremacy & look forward to liberation for all."[98] Actually, America did not enslave Kaepernick's ancestors. Black African slavers did that and sold them at auctions to British slavers who brought them to America. White Americans, within a short time historically speaking, freed Kaepernick's ancestors.

Kaepernick's historical illiteracy frames the whole Black Lives Matter narrative. It is useful to remind ourselves of the facts. As African American scholar Thomas Sowell explains,

[a] cliche that has come into vogue is that slavery is "America's original sin." . . . Today the moral horror of slavery is so widely condemned that it is hard to realize that there were thousands of years when slavery was practiced around the world by people of virtually every race.

Neither Africans, Asians, Polynesians, nor the indigenous peoples of the Western Hemisphere saw anything wrong with slavery, even after small segments of British and American societies began to condemn slavery as morally wrong in the 18th century.

What was special about America was not that it had slavery, which existed all over the world, but that Americans were among the very few peoples who began to question the morality of holding human beings in bondage. That was not yet a majority view among Americans in the 18th century, but it was not even a serious minority view in non-Western societies at that time.

Then how did slavery end? We know how it ended in the United States—at a cost of one life lost in the Civil War for every six slaves freed. But that is not how it ended elsewhere. What happened in the rest of the world was that all of Western civilization eventually turned against slavery in the 19th century. This meant the end of slavery in European empires around the world, usually over the bitter opposition of non-Western peoples. But the West happened to be militarily dominant at the time.[99]

During the run-up to the July 4th holiday, Black Lives Matter's overt and unapologetic America-hatred came into even sharper focus when scores of statues and monuments in more than thirty different states and the District of Columbia were vandalized and toppled to the ground. The protesters claimed that the monuments were racist and offensive to nonwhite people. Some of the statues were taken down at the order of city officials who were intimidated by raucous protests and threats of violence into removing them from the public square.[100]

On June 1 in Montgomery, Alabama, a statue of Confederate General Robert E. Lee was knocked off its base.[101] That same day in Birmingham, a statue of Charles Linn, a city founder who served in the Confederate navy, was toppled to the ground.[102] On June 10, a statue of Christopher Columbus was decapitated in Boston.[103] The same day, another statue of Columbus was toppled at the state capitol in St. Paul, Minnesota.[104] On June 13, a statue of Confederate President Jefferson Davis was removed from the rotunda of the capitol building in Frankfort, Kentucky, on the order of city authorities.[105]

The targets were by no means limited to Confederates and the discoverer of America. On June 18, a crowd of protesters in Portland set fire to the head of a statue of George Washington before pulling it to the ground with ropes. The statue was spray-painted with the messages "BLM," "Genocidal Colonist," "You're on Native Lands," "Big Floyd" (a reference to the late George Floyd), and "1619" (the year in which allegedly the first African slaves were brought to North America).[106] Those Africans were actually indentured servants, like the majority of the Virginia labor force, which was mainly white.

On June 19, protesters in San Francisco toppled a statue of Francis Scott Key, author of "The Star-Spangled Banner."[107] On June 21, New York Mayor Bill de Blasio announced that the bronze statue of Theodore Roosevelt on horseback, flanked by a Native American and an African, would be removed from the position it had occupied near the entrance to the American Museum of Natural History for eighty years.[108] Roosevelt had invited the former slave Booker T. Washington to dine with him and his family at the White House, in a milestone event in the struggle for equal rights.[109]

On June 22, Black Lives Matter leader Shaun King demanded that religious statues showing a light-skinned Jesus be toppled to the ground because they represented "a form of white supremacy."[110] On June 30, the Boston Art Commission voted to remove from the city's Park Square a replica of Thomas Ball's 1876 "Emancipation Memorial"—a statue depicting President Abraham Lincoln freeing a black slave.[111] The original statue in Washington, D.C., had been donated by liberated black slaves.[112] During the July 4th weekend, a Rochester, New York, statue of the famed abolitionist and former slave Frederick Douglass was ripped from its base and thrown into a gorge, an action that showed that the vandals were motivated by contempt for America rather than any concern for black lives or racial justice.[113]

Capturing the Culture

As the protests and riots gathered steam, a large number of celebrities in the fields of sports, entertainment, and the arts stepped forward to declare their support. Former baseball star Alex Rodriguez and actress Jennifer Lopez joined a rally in Los Angeles at which they carried homemade signs that read, "#EnoughIsEnough" and "Let's Get Loud for Black Lives Matter." On Instagram, Rodriguez lamented "the senseless way George Floyd was killed in Minneapolis and . . . the many brutal, unnecessary, ugly murders that came before him." Other cultural luminaries to declare their solidarity with Black Lives Matter included Beyoncé, Jane Fonda, Madonna, Trevor Noah, Rihanna, Keke Palmer, Jamie Foxx, Adam Lambert, Gigi and Bella Hadid, Ariana Grande, Harry Styles, Blake Lively, Ryan Reynolds, and Drake.[114]

"Even though I will never know the pain and suffering [blacks] have endured, or what it feels like to try to survive in a world plagued by systemic racism," said Kim Kardashian, speaking for many, "I know I can use my own voice to help amplify those voices that have been muffled for too long."[115]

Five of the Black Lives Matter martyrs not only had thousands of people "say their names," but were the subjects of flattering films: Eric Garner, Michael Brown, Freddie Gray, Breonna Taylor, and Sandra Bland.

The extent to which Black Lives Matter had gained the support of America's popular culture was highlighted by the decision of Major League Baseball that its teams would be permitted to stencil "BLM" or "United for Change" on the back of the pitching mounds in each of their respective stadiums. Players would also have the option to wear either of those slogans on T-shirts, wristbands, or patches affixed to their uniforms.[116]

The National Basketball Association announced that it would paint, in huge letters, the words "Black Lives Matter" on all the courts used for upcoming games. Moreover, the league and its players' union agreed on an array of "social justice messages" that the athletes could wear, instead of their names, on the backs of their jerseys. In addition to "Black Lives Matter," the approved slogans included, "I Can't Breathe," "Say Their Names," "Enough," and "How Many More?" The messages included not-so-subtle suggestions that whites are racists: "See Us," "Hear Us," "Respect Us," "Love Us," "Anti-Racist," and "Justice Now." Some urged political activism: "Vote," "Liberation," and "Sí Se Puede" (Spanish for "Yes We Can," a slogan with a long history as a rallying cry for Latino leftists).[117]

The National Football League embraced the Black Lives Matter agenda as well. In a June 2020 statement, NFL Commissioner

Roger Goodell said that "the protests around the country are emblematic of the centuries of silence, inequality, and oppression of Black players, coaches, fans, and staff." The following month, the NFL announced that the song "Lift Every Voice and Sing"—often described as the black national anthem—would be played prior to "The Star-Spangled Banner" before every opening-week game of its upcoming season. The end zones on the field would bear the words "End Racism" and "It Takes All of Us." Players would be permitted, for the first time ever, to place on their helmets political and "social justice" messages—including the names or initials of alleged black victims of racist violence.[118]

It was estimated that during the first six weeks following George Floyd's death between 15 and 26 million people participated in the various demonstrations from coast to coast, prompting the *New York Times* to run this headline on July 3, 2020: "Black Lives Matter May Be the Largest Movement in U.S. History."[119]

PART TWO

BLACK LIVES MARTYRS

If I die in police custody, don't believe the hype.
I was murdered! Protect my family! Indict the system!
Shut that sh*t down!
If I die in police custody, avenge my death!
By any means necessary!
If I die in police custody, burn everything down! No
building is worth more than my life! And that's the only
way motherf***ers like you listen!
If I die in police custody, make sure I'm the last person to
die in police custody. By any means necessary!
If I die in police custody, do not hold a moment of silence
for me! Rise the f*** up!
Because your silence is killing us!

—Black Lives Matter Chant[1]

LIST OF VICTIMS BLACK LIVES MATTER CLAIMS WERE MURDERED OR MAIMED BY POLICE

Trayvon Martin, Sanford, Florida, February 26, 2012

Dontre Hamilton, Milwaukee, Wisconsin, April 30, 2014

Eric Garner, Staten Island, New York, July 17, 2014

Michael Brown, Ferguson, Missouri, August 9, 2014

Ezell Ford, Los Angeles, California, August 11, 2014

Akai Gurley, Brooklyn, New York, November 20, 2014

Tamir Rice, Cleveland, Ohio, November 22, 2014

Tony Robinson, Madison, Wisconsin, March 6, 2015

Meagan Hockaday, Oxnard, California, March 28, 2015

Walter Scott, North Charleston, South Carolina, April 4, 2015

Freddie Gray, Baltimore, Maryland, April 19, 2015

Sandra Bland, Waller County, Texas, July 13, 2015

Alton Sterling, Baton Rouge, Louisiana, July 5, 2016

Philando Castile, Falcon Heights, Minnesota, July 6, 2016

Korryn Gaines, Randallstown, Maryland, August 1, 2016

Terence Crutcher, Tulsa, Oklahoma, September 16, 2016

Keith Lamont Scott, Charlotte, North Carolina, September 20, 2016

Alfred Olango, El Cajon, California, September 27, 2016

Jocques Clemmons, Nashville, Tennessee, February 10, 2017

Ahmaud Arbery, Glynn Country, Georgia, February 23, 2020

Breonna Taylor, Louisville, Kentucky, March 13, 2020

Daniel Prude, Rochester, New York, March 23, 2020

George Floyd, Minneapolis, Minnesota, May 25, 2020

Tony McDade, Tallahassee, Florida, May 27, 2020

Rayshard Brooks, Atlanta, Georgia, June 12, 2020

Jacob Blake, Kenosha, Wisconsin, shot and paralyzed August 23, 2020

THE CAUSE

For the Black Lives Matter campaign to be able to launch its destructive attacks on American cities, raise hundreds of millions of dollars in the process, and gain the support of a major political party for its actions, is a remarkable—even unthinkable—achievement. It was possible only because the campaign was driven by a moral argument so powerful that it touched the hearts of all Americans and intimidated critics from stepping forward to challenge it. That moral argument was framed by a series of capital crimes allegedly committed by a justice system that was "systemically racist," regularly targeting black Americans because of their skin color. The litany of victims from minority communities outraged a majority of Americans who had believed—or wanted to believe—that America had overcome its racial past and had put such legal lynchings behind it.

The overwhelmingly sympathetic response to the slogan "Black Lives Matter" contained an irony, however, that was widely ignored: if Americans of all hues, including white, responded so eagerly and so generously to this cry for social justice, how could the indictment be anywhere close to true?

The indictment is formally stated on the Black Lives Matter web page in these stark and uncompromising words: "Black Lives Matter is an ideological and political intervention in a world where black lives are systematically and intentionally targeted for demise."[1]

"Black Lives Matter" has become a mantra for "social justice" activists as a result of the campaign that Black Lives Matter's cofounders launched in 2013 following the 2012 shooting death of black teenager Trayvon Martin, whose killer was acquitted in a trial that many saw as a miscarriage of justice. During the ensuing seven years of the Black Lives Matter campaign, its accusations have caused a sea change in the attitudes of people one would not have associated with political causes, let alone such inflammatory ones.

In early May 2020, weeks before the death of George Floyd, a black jogger named Ahmaud Arbery was tracked and accosted by a retired police officer and his son who suspected that Arbery was a burglar. In the scuffle that accompanied their attempt to make a "citizen's arrest," Arbery was shot and killed. The perpetrators of this vigilante act were arrested and charged with murder. The extreme reaction to the case was the harbinger of the violent summer ahead. On May 6, black sports icon and centi-millionaire LeBron James tweeted this response to what had happened: "We're literally hunted EVERYDAY/EVERYTIME we step foot outside the comfort of our homes! Can't even go for a damn jog man! Like WTF man are you kidding me?!?!?!?!?!? No man, ARE YOU KIDDING ME!!!!! I'm sorry Ahmaud (Rest In Paradise) and my prayers and blessings sent...."[2]

Five months later, another national sports icon, former National Basketball Association great Bill Russell, published a long essay claiming that "Racial injustice is rampaging throughout every sector of American society. . . . Black kids today don't grow up worried the Klan will kill them in the middle of the night—they worry the police will. . . ." Like James, Russell didn't bother to provide any statistics showing that cops are killing black kids in the middle of the night—or at any hour in the day.

The only facts Russell alleged to support his indictment were these:

> America is not the land of the free when Black people have to worry that they will be murdered in their sleep like Breonna Taylor. America is not the land of the free when Black people have to worry that a police officer will kneel on their necks for eight minutes and 46 seconds [sic] like they did to George Floyd, until the life was choked out of him.[3] America is not the land of the free when Black children can't play with a toy gun without fear of being murdered like Tamir Rice. America is not the land of the free when Black people have to worry about being hunted down and murdered while out on a jog like Ahmaud Arbery. America is not the land of the free when Black people have to worry about being shot in the back in front of their children like Jacob Blake. America is not the land of the free when Black people's murderers always go free.[4]

Russell's last point is particularly odd in light of the fact that Ahmaud Arbery's white killers are in jail, and George Floyd's arresting officers were immediately jailed, while O. J. Simpson, who murdered his white wife and a white stranger, was set free. Moreover, as the following examinations of the Black Lives Matter cases will show, Russell's view of these incidents is far from accurate: Breonna Taylor was not "murdered in her sleep"; George Floyd was not "choked" by the knee on the side of his neck, where there is no windpipe; Tamir Rice's tragic death did not come about because he was playing with anything that looked like a "toy gun"; and Jacob Blake was a sexual predator who chose to fight the armed officers who approached him with an arrest warrant, despite the fact that his children were in the car with him. The officer's bullets hit him in the back because he had turned to lunge for a weapon under the driver's seat of his vehicle.

Coming nearly sixty years after the passage of the Civil Rights Acts, and shortly after eight years of rule by a black president whose electoral victories were secured by white majorities among his supporters, the sweeping indictments of America's attitudes toward its black citizens are hard to square with the reality of twenty-first-century America. In fact, there is not a crime statistic to support the harsh claims of a hunting season on blacks by police. The statistics show that more unarmed whites are killed by police every year than unarmed blacks; in some years, whites account for twice as many victims of police shootings as blacks.[5]

The number of such cases, moreover, is minuscule for blacks as well as whites. Every year, more than 10 million arrests are made by police departments nationally. In 2019, 14 unarmed blacks and 25 unarmed whites were killed by police.[6] Furthermore, it has been known for decades that white police are less likely than their black colleagues to shoot black suspects. As a 2001 Justice Department report stated that "when a white officer kills a felon, that felon is usually a white," and "when a black officer kills a felon, that felon is usually a black."[7] Nor has anything changed in the years since then. In 2017, a study by John R. Lott and Carlisle E. Moody "found that black officers killed unarmed black suspects at a significantly higher rate than white or Hispanic officers."[8] And in 2018, a research team led by Charles Menifield, dean of the School of Public Affairs and Administration at Rutgers University, found that "white police officers actually kill black and other minority suspects at lower rates than we would expect if killings were randomly distributed among officers of all races," while "nonwhite officers kill both black and Latino suspects at significantly higher rates than white officers."[9]

The Black Lives Matter indictment also flies in the face of all the statistics that show that America is a more inclusive, tolerant, and egalitarian society than ever—or than any other society with large ethnic minorities. Never in the history of nations has a previously oppressed minority like black Americans been so integrated into the dominant culture of a nation. This is manifest in the integration of blacks in the sports and entertainment cultures that captivate and inspire America's youth. It can be seen in the sea of commercial advertisements that are eager to showcase integrated families and communities, which would be disastrous for sales if the claims of Black Lives Matter were even remotely true. And of course, America's transracial present is manifest in the election—not once, but twice—of a black president, and in the appointments of black secretaries of state and national security advisers and attorneys general as chief law-enforcement officials. No other nation can make a similar claim about its minority ethnic groups.

How would racist rampages conducted by police officials be possible with a black president, black attorneys general, black mayors, and black police chiefs? Black Lives Matter can't answer these questions and doesn't even recognize that they exist. Black Lives Matter's strategic plan is to replace obvious realities with its litany of racial nightmares: innocent black lives struck down by racist officials who go unpunished because in a white supremacist world, black lives don't matter.

The goal of the Black Lives Matter martyrs list is to put faces on the alleged victims, bring to life the memories of who they were, and generate outrage about the injustices allegedly done to them. The very fact that there is an ocean of such sympathy among Americans is a refutation of the claim that white America is indifferent to black lives. But this is an irony that goes unnoticed.

To generate the sympathy that justifies its rage—and its hate—Black Lives Matter calls on its supporters to "Say Their Names"—to remember the martyrs and secure justice for them. During the riots following George Floyd's death, Oprah Winfrey, a Black Lives Matter supporter, commissioned twenty-six billboards featuring the likeness of Breonna Taylor, a prominent victim of police "murderers" according to the radical script. "Demand that the police involved in killing Breonna Taylor be arrested and charged," said each of the billboards.[10]

Black Lives Matter is still promoting the myth of "Hands Up, Don't Shoot," memorializing Michael Brown's alleged surrender to police, who then allegedly murdered him in cold blood. Black Lives Matter persists in repeating this false version of events despite the fact that an extensive investigation of Michael Brown's death by the Obama Justice Department, an agency headed by Eric Holder, who is black and described himself as

"Obama's wingman," exonerated the officer whom Black Lives Matter calls a murderer, finding that he acted in self-defense.

Black Lives Matter continues to parade the "Hands Up" slogan, despite the fact that five black and two biracial eyewitnesses testified to police, the FBI, and a grand jury that Brown was charging the officer when he was shot.[11] Ignoring these facts, Black Lives Matter still insists that Brown was "murdered"— that he was surrendering with his hands up when he was killed. "Hands Up, Don't Shoot" remains a signature slogan for Black Lives Matter. Despite the fact that it is pure fiction, it adorns T-shirts and other paraphernalia worn by professional athletes and celebrity supporters of the claim that blacks like Michael Brown are being murdered regularly because they are black.

The pages that follow describe the evolution of the Black Lives Matter movement by examining the cases on its martyrs list. These examinations are an attempt to restore the actual circumstances of their deaths, thus performing the traditional but currently neglected work of providing due process to the accused: examining the evidence before drawing the conclusions. These examinations will show that while some of the Black Lives Matter cases reveal tragic errors of judgment, almost all involve resistance by known and armed criminals to warranted arrests. They will show, through examination of the details, that in the vast majority of cases the deceased would still be alive if they had simply obeyed police commands, and that the Black Lives Matter charges are reckless inventions unsupported by the facts.

Obviously, the ramifications of such a conclusion are grave: The worst civil insurrections in American history leading to billions of dollars in damages and scores of lost lives—both innocent and guilty—have been justified by a racial hoax. This hoax, as will become evident, has been perpetrated by anti-American radicals whose motives and goals have nothing to do with black lives' mattering, or with racial equity or social justice.

CHAPTER 1

FACE OF THE MOVEMENT: GEORGE FLOYD

On May 25, 2020, a disturbing video went viral on the Internet. It was so shocking that it made the radical accusations of Black Lives Matter seem persuasive to millions of Americans and allowed BLM to launch the most destructive riots in American history. The video showed a white police officer, Derek Chauvin, pressing his knee against the neck of a black man named George Floyd, who was in a prone position on the ground, and in handcuffs. Officer Chauvin continued to apply the pressure, while Floyd repeatedly pleaded, "I can't breathe," and called for his "mama."[1] The pressure continued for nine minutes and twenty-nine seconds, by which time Floyd had stopped breathing. Floyd had been arrested for passing a phony twenty-dollar bill in a local store.

Black Lives Matter immediately denounced the incident as a racial murder—and praised George Floyd's life as "beautiful," "typical," and targeted for death by a "white supremacist" society because he was black. The officer was described as a "white supremacist" solely because he was white. Permanently displayed on the Black Lives Matter website are these words:

> Rest in Power, Beautiful
> **George Floyd** couldn't breathe. We can't either. We live in fear. Fear of walking outside. Wearing a hoodie. Going for a jog. Sleeping in our own home. Existing.
> Every day, a new hashtag. Every hour, a new injustice. Every second, more pain.
> We don't deserve to live like this—and we continue to fight until white supremacy no longer permeates every corner of this country—until we can live full lives—freely.
> Today, we remember George Floyd. And we remember every other Black life lost to police brutality, racial injustice, and white supremacy. Together, we fight for justice and #SayTheirName. Keep the fight for justice alive. . . . [2] [Emphasis in the original]

Contrary to this Black Lives Matter eulogy, George Floyd's was not a typical black life, and black Americans have no reason to live in "fear of walking outside" lest they meet George Floyd's fate. Police killings of unarmed blacks are exceedingly rare—just fourteen in 2019 compared to twenty-five police killings of unarmed whites.[3]

In the course of George Floyd's forty-six years, he served nine separate jail sentences for various crimes, including a fairly recent five-year sentence for the armed robbery of a young black mother whom he had terrorized by pointing a gun at her abdomen while his five accomplices looted her home. Floyd's rap sheet also featured convictions for such offenses as a firearm robbery, trespassing on private property, and five instances of the theft, possession, or trade of cocaine.[4]

To describe George Floyd as a typical black citizen is to defame the black community, the overwhelming majority of whose members are not drug addicts or drug dealers or armed robbers but law-abiding assets to our nation, to whose well-being they have contributed since its inception. It is also a reprehensible attempt to make them fear for their lives for simply "existing."

Although no one at the time seemed to note the fact or appreciate its implications, the characterization of Floyd's death as a race crime didn't make any sense—and not merely because there was a lack of any evidence that the four officers involved had any racial animus towards him. In advance of any formal investigation, the officers were accused of having participated, to varying degrees, in a murder. The first two officers to arrive at the scene were J. Alexander Kueng, who is black, and Thomas Lane, who is white. It was they who first arrested and handcuffed Floyd.[5] Kueng had recently joined the Minneapolis police force hoping to help reform it and improve its relations with the black community.

Not until nine minutes into the arrest did officers Derek Chauvin, a white man, and Tou Thao, an Asian-American, arrive at the scene.[6] While Chauvin was subsequently the subject of the most serious charges—second-degree murder, third-degree murder, and second-degree manslaughter—both Kueng and Thao were charged, along with Lane, with abetting Chauvin's alleged crimes.[7] How did race factor into Kueng and Thao's behavior? No one thought to inquire.

The officers were charged with murder before prosecutors had received the toxicology report, which showed that when Floyd was arrested he was high on methamphetamines and a dose of fentanyl large enough to be fatal. He was also suffering from severe multifocal arteriosclerosis and hypertensive heart disease, and was positive for SARS-CoV-2, the virus that causes COVID-19.[8] The foregoing facts took on added significance when the autopsy showed that there was no life-threatening damage to his neck. The fact is, Floyd had nearly *four times* the lethal dose of fentanyl in his system. Fentanyl is a drug that suppresses lung function, leading to death if consumed in excessive quantities.[9] According to the Centers for Disease Control, fentanyl is "50 to 100 times more potent than morphine."[10] WebMD explains: "[F]entanyl has rapid and potent effects on the brain and body, and even very small amounts can be extremely dangerous. It only takes a tiny amount of the drug to cause a deadly reaction. . . . Fentanyl can depress breathing and lead to death. The risk of overdose is high."[11]

There were no signs of asphyxiation resulting from the knee Officer Chauvin placed on Floyd's neck, nor would there be, since the knee was not applied to his windpipe. Its purpose was not to shut off Floyd's breathing but to subdue him.[12] As a prosecutor specializing in police brutality cases reported in the American Spectator, "Minnesota police are trained to use a 'neck restraint' technique, which is defined in the official training literature as 'compressing one or both sides of a person's neck with an arm or leg, without applying direct pressure to the trachea or airway (front of the neck).' The video of Chauvin kneeling on the side of Floyd's neck appears to be a textbook application of this officially approved technique."[13] These facts raise the question of whether the police, who already were accused of murder, had even killed Floyd, let alone intended to.

Also missing for the first few months following Floyd's death and the onset of the riots were the body-cam videos of the two officers—one of them Kueng—who assisted in the initial arrest. The videos are crucial to evaluating what subsequently took place. They were deliberately suppressed by Minnesota's attorney general, Keith Ellison—former spokesman for Louis Farrakhan, former DNC chair, and current supporter of Antifa, the vigilante organization that with Black Lives Matter spearheaded so much of the violence that followed. In response to critics who were questioning his decisions, Ellison removed a photo from his website showing him proudly holding up a copy of *Antifa: The Anti-Fascist Handbook*.[14] He also elevated the charges against Chauvin, adding second-degree murder, knowing this would make the prosecution's task harder and also risk igniting a new round of riots if the officers were acquitted.

Nearly three months after Floyd's death, someone leaked the suppressed body cam videos to the U.K.'s *Daily Mail*, which released them to the public. They showed Floyd's resistance to arrest and the officers' efforts to put him in handcuffs and subdue him.[15] At approximately 6′6″ and a muscular 240 pounds, Floyd would have been difficult to control even if he had not been on drugs.[16] The videos showed Floyd to be disoriented, delirious, paranoid and unable to follow a command for more than a few seconds.[17] They showed him panicky and unwilling to be put in the police vehicle, saying that he was "claustrophobic" although he had been arrested while sitting in his own vehicle. They showed him crying "I can't breathe" at least five times while he was still standing, sitting, or kneeling as he refused to cooperate with police—well before he was prone with Chauvin's knee on his neck.

The videos also showed that the officers charged with an alleged racial crime were both polite to Floyd and worried about his condition, asking him if he was on drugs. The videos showed not only that there was no hostility—racial or otherwise—on the part of the arresting officers, but also that they exhibited very obvious concern for the man they were arresting. Approximately one minute after Chauvin began pressing his knee into Floyd's neck, the officers, in response to Floyd's complaints that he couldn't breathe, called an ambulance.[18]

In other words, prior to the infamous video showing him cuffed and prone with Officer Chauvin's knee on his neck, George Floyd was already having difficulty breathing and was likely dying from the lethal levels of fentanyl he had ingested, exacerbated by his serious heart condition. The officers, of course, were unaware of the fentanyl in Floyd's system, his heart disease, or the dangerous impact the drug was having on his respiratory functions. After Chauvin applied his knee to Floyd's neck, Floyd said variations of "I can't breathe," "I cannot breathe," and "Please let me breathe" more than twenty additional times during the next five minutes before passing out.[19]

Officer Chauvin's knee to Floyd's neck, alarming as it appeared, was—as already noted—a standard procedure for Minneapolis police. They had used neck restraint techniques on at least 237 other individuals, rendering 44 of them unconscious, in the previous 5 years in order to prevent them from harming themselves and others.[20] None of them died, which suggests that factors other than Chauvin's knee may have caused Floyd's death.

Although the procedure does not target the subject's airway but is designed to subdue the suspect and in some cases stop blood flow to the brain, rendering the subject unconscious, many police departments regard it as unsafe. Whether it was appropriately applied in this case is a reasonable concern. On the other hand, there is no evidence that the officers intended to kill

George Floyd or to put his life in danger. Moreover, there is no factual basis to indicate there was any racial element involved in his death.

For the skeptical, who think that only blacks are the subject of rough police tactics, there is video evidence readily available on YouTube of unarmed white suspects similarly pleading for their lives, only to die in interactions with police. One video, for instance, shows a young white man named Daniel Shaver being fatally shot while begging for leniency on January 18, 2016, by an Arizona officer concerned that Shaver might have been reaching for a weapon.[21]

Another YouTube video shows a 2016 incident in Dallas with striking similarities to the George Floyd case. In the Dallas incident, a thirty-two-year-old unarmed white man named Tony Timpa—who was high on cocaine and had failed to take his prescription medication for schizophrenia—was handcuffed, forced to the ground in a prone position, and pinned under a police officer's knee for nearly fourteen minutes. Timpa pleaded for mercy more than thirty times before he lost consciousness and died.[22] Moreover, the officers at the scene were highly unsympathetic toward Timpa, laughing and joking even after the man had stopped breathing.[23] Dallas County District Attorney John Creuzot eventually dismissed all criminal charges against the officers in whose custody Timpa had died.[24]

Despite the evidence—crucial parts of which were suppressed for months by Attorney General Ellison—the claims that George Floyd was "murdered," and that his murder was part of a "systemic racism" that targeted blacks for destruction, continued to be a relentless theme of Black Lives Matter spokespeople, the organizations allied with their movement, supportive politicians, and the media. "I Can't Breathe" became the slogan behind which the rioters and looters justified their destructive rampages, despite the evidence that Floyd couldn't breathe because of the lethal dose of fentanyl that he had voluntarily ingested into his system.

White supremacist malice was also the theme of the public memorial held for Floyd, which national celebrities, members of America's corporate elite, and the mothers of three previous Black Lives Matter martyrs—Trayvon Martin, Eric Garner, and Michael Brown—all attended. In keeping with the racial message of the movement, the eulogy for Floyd was delivered by one of the nation's most notorious racial demagogues, Al Sharpton, who used it to indict all white Americans and America itself:

> George Floyd's story has been the story of black folks because ever since 401 years ago, the reason we could never be who we wanted and dreamed of being is you kept your knee on our neck. We were smarter than the underfunded schools you put us in, but you had your knee on our neck. We could run corporations and not hustle in the street, but you had your knee on our neck. We had creative skills, we could do whatever anybody else could do, but we couldn't get your knee off our neck. What happened to Floyd happens every day in this country, in education, in health services, and in every area of American life, it's time for us to stand up in George's name and say "Get your knee off our necks."[25]

A normal human being would have a hard time placing this statement in the year 2020. Today the majority of black Americans are comfortably part of America's middle, upper, and working classes.[26] Black celebrities—sports figures, film stars, singers, and social satirists—occupy an outsized place in America's national culture. They are revered icons of American youth, white as well as black. They are also a powerful constituency in the nation's political institutions, the mayors and district attorneys of major American cities, including Minneapolis.

America's black citizens have more rights, more privileges and more opportunities than blacks anywhere else in the world, including all of black Africa and the black West Indies, where countries like Haiti have been independent and run by blacks for over two hundred years. In the words of Harvard sociologist Orlando Patterson, an award-winning scholar on slavery and race who is himself black, "America, while still flawed in its race relations . . . is now the least racist white-majority society in the world; has a better record of legal protection of minorities than any other society, white or black; [and] offers more opportunities to a greater number of black persons than any other society, including all of Africa."[27]

Sharpton's description of America as a country with its "knee on our neck" fails to acknowledge the 350,000 mainly white lives that were sacrificed to free black Americans from slavery. It also fails to acknowledge the massive affirmative action programs, special race-based scholarship offerings, and diversity seminars designed to give black Americans a leg up in educational and job opportunities and to counter any pejorative attitudes towards them. None of these efforts to support black Americans fits even remotely the caricature of America in Sharpton's racist attack. Yet the Black Lives Matter coalition placed Sharpton at the center of their movement, where he functioned as the mouthpiece for their grievances and goals and their attacks on white Americans. These unfounded slanders inspired the lynch mob mentality that demanded a guilty verdict for the Minneapolis officers in advance of the facts, fueled the riots, and prevailed throughout.

The trial of Derek Chauvin began in a Minneapolis court on March 29, 2021, and was concluded on April 19. During those weeks forty-five witnesses testified, among them forensic scientists, police officers, and George Floyd's girlfriend. Experts provided conflicting testimony on the actual cause of Floyd's death—asphyxiation resulting from Chauvin's knee on his neck or cardiac arrest resulting from Floyd's pre-existing conditions including heart disease and drug abuse. One expert testified that there was no way to determine the specific cause of Floyd's death because there were multiple factors that could have caused him to stop breathing.[28]

Because of the mayhem that preceded the trial—the attacks on American cities, the burnings, lootings, and shootings—it strains credulity to believe that a fair trial was even possible. The jury was not sequestered, so that it was well aware of the clamor demanding the "right verdict" and of the ever-looming threat that there would be hell to pay if any lesser verdict was delivered.[29] There were even specific threats to jurors and witnesses in the case.[30]

Days before the verdict, fifteen-term congresswoman Maxine Waters traveled with a police escort to Minneapolis, where she declared at a rally, "I hope that we are going to get a verdict that will say 'guilty, guilty, guilty.' And if you don't, we cannot go away." When asked what protesters should do in the event of a not-guilty verdict, Waters replied, "We've got to stay on the streets. And we've got to get more active. We've got to get more confrontational."[31] This outburst by an influential public official caused the defense to ask for a mistrial, which was denied, but many legal experts observed that it would be proper grounds for an appeal.[32] Judge Peter Cahill, who presided over the Chauvin trial, told defense attorney Eric Nelson, "I'll give you that Congresswoman Waters may have given you something on appeal that may result in this whole trial being overturned."[33]

The threat of violence was not the only factor pressuring jurors towards a guilty verdict. In an unprecedented move days before the trial, the City of Minneapolis awarded Floyd's family a "wrongful death" settlement of $27 million.[34]

Behind the scenes, the U.S. Justice Department plotted to arrest Chauvin if he were acquitted. According to a report by the *Minneapolis Star Tribune*, "Leading up to Derek Chauvin's murder trial, Justice Department officials had spent months gathering evidence to indict the ex-Minneapolis police officer on federal police brutality charges, but they feared the publicity frenzy could disrupt the state's case. So they came up with a contingency plan: If Chauvin were found not guilty on all counts or the case ended in a mistrial, they would arrest him at the courthouse, according to sources familiar with the planning discussions."[35] In other words, the state had joined the lynch mob: first the verdict; forget the trial. This was what one would normally expect from a police state not a democracy, which operates by due process rather than preemptive convictions and punishments.

The jury began deliberating on April 19, and on April 20, after a mere ten and a half hours of deliberation, they delivered their verdict: guilty, guilty, guilty—on all three counts: second-degree manslaughter, second-degree murder, and third-degree murder.[36] In fact, there was no serious review of the complex, technical, and contested trial evidence. According to the first post-trial press interview with a jury member, the twelve who entered the deliberation room agreed from the outset that Chauvin was guilty on all three counts, and the time was mostly spent convincing one cautious juror who wanted to review the instructions of the judge to make sure their verdict would be legitimate.[37]

The trial revealed one key truth, acknowledged by both sides, though it went almost completely unnoticed. It was a truth that exposed the hoax perpetuated by Black Lives Matter, whose lie became the only acceptable view of these events to the majority of the public and inspired over 600 attacks on 220 American cities. *There was no racial element to the death of George Floyd.* It was a fact obvious from the beginning, since two of the four officers involved were members of racial minorities, including one who was black.

Minnesota Attorney General Keith Ellison was in charge of the prosecution and responsible for the criminal charges. In an interview on CBS's *60 Minutes,* Ellison said there was no evidence George Floyd was a victim of a "hate crime" or racial bias. "I wouldn't call it that because hate crimes are crimes where there's an explicit motive and bias," Ellison said. "We don't have any evidence that Derek Chauvin factored in George Floyd's race as he did what he did."[38] In other words, all the outrage against police racism, and all the mayhem fueled by that outrage, was based on no evidence whatsoever. It was based on a lie.

The reaction of Black Lives Matter to the death of George Floyd mirrors the pattern of its response to all the deaths it has incorporated into its litany of blacks allegedly martyred by the police. With few exceptions, this pattern includes falsifying the lives and actions of the "victims," hiding the specific circumstances of their arrests and deaths, and grossly exaggerating the alleged injustices responsible for their deaths, beginning with the never-documented charge of "systemic racism."

CHAPTER 2

HOW THE MOVEMENT BEGAN

Trayvon Martin

On June 16, 2020, as American cities were being systematically torched and looted by Black Lives Matter vigilantes, an article describing the history of the organization appeared in *Rolling Stone* magazine. It was written with the cooperation of the group's three founders—Alicia Garza, Patrisse Cullors, and Opal Tometi. The article was called "Black Lives Matter from Ferguson to Now" and was authored by Jamil Smith, a sportswriter and supporter of the Black Lives Matter movement.[1]

The seeds of the movement were planted in July 2013, when Alicia Garza read the news announcing the acquittal of Neighborhood Watch volunteer George Zimmerman, who was facing a murder charge for the February 2012 killing of a black teenager named Trayvon Martin in Sanford, Florida. Shocked by the verdict, Garza wrote a Facebook post, which went viral, saying: "Black people. I love you. I love us. Our lives matter. Black Lives Matter." By the next day, Garza had contacted her friends Cullors and Tometi, who were also political activists—"trained Marxists" as Cullors described them—to form what they called the Black Lives Matter Global Network.[2]

"Black Lives Matter," explained Jamil Smith, "was born as an organization with a queer, feminist framework that grasped the importance of intersectionality" (a neo-Marxist theory that posits a hierarchy of alleged "oppressions" that intersect in an individual). He then quoted Garza: "Both Patrisse and I have this experience being queer black women in a movement for black freedom that really isn't shaped in our image. One of the things that actually connected Patrisse and I [sic] very early on is what it meant to try to navigate that space."[3]

The Trayvon Martin case proved to be a watershed moment in the creation of a racial Left ready to support the aggressive tactics of what became the Black Lives Matter movement. The result of the Zimmerman trial was almost certainly a miscarriage of justice. Zimmerman was not a police officer but a Neighborhood Watch volunteer. As such, he was advised by his police dispatcher not to follow Martin and not to leave the vehicle he had been in when he became suspicious of Martin's presence in the neighborhood at night. Zimmerman disregarded the dispatcher, left his vehicle, and accosted the teenager.[4] A fight ensued, which Zimmerman was losing when he pulled out his gun and fired a shot through Trayvon Martin's heart. Whether this is a case of murder is a matter for dispute. But what Zimmerman did was a crime, and at the very least he should have been convicted of manslaughter and given a stiff sentence.

Injustices occur—and occur regularly—in all human institutions and organizations, including organizations that crusade in the name of "social justice" or "law and order." Everything should be done to rectify these injustices and prevent their recurrence. Nonetheless, they are as inevitable as they are regrettable. What made the Martin case transformative was the reaction to it before the verdict was rendered, and indeed before the trial was held.

America's civic order rests on a foundation of "due process"—first the presumption of innocence, then the investigative and trial procedures necessary to collect and evaluate the evidence. These procedures are followed to ensure that the process of justice doesn't lead to injustice. This is why lynchings are so abhorrent. In the name of "justice," lynch mobs dispense with investigations and trials and instead demand a guilty verdict so that they can get on with the executions.

Something like this mentality dominated the reaction to Trayvon Martin's death. The angry responses were triggered when the police released Zimmerman from custody five hours after he was arrested. In a public statement, the police chief said there was no evidence to refute Zimmerman's claim of having acted in self-defense and that under Florida's "Stand Your Ground" statute, the police were prohibited by law from making an arrest. The police chief also said that Zimmerman had a right to use lethal force to defend himself.[5]

These statements were indefensible. A homicide victim and his family have the right to an inquiry into the circumstances of his death—to due process. Was there a racial dimension to the refusal to conduct such an inquiry in the case of Trayvon Martin? There can be little question that there was.

This injustice triggered a massive reaction from Trayvon's defenders on the left. Prior to Zimmerman's indictment for murder on April 11, protests demanding his prosecution were staged at locations all across the United States, with people carrying banners and placards that bore slogans like "Justice for

Trayvon," "We Are All Trayvon Martin," and "Enough Is Enough."[6] Trayvon's parents, Tracy Martin and Sybrina Fulton, initiated a Change.org petition demanding Zimmerman's arrest and conviction. With more than 2.2 million signatures, it became the largest petition in Change.org's history.[7]

Because Martin was wearing a hoodie jacket at the time of his death, hoodies became symbols of protest for people demanding justice in the case. Basketball star LeBron James and all of his Miami Heat teammates posted a photograph of themselves donning hoodies in Martin's honor. In a very different venue, Democrat congressman (and former Black Panther) Bobby Rush wore a hoodie while addressing the House of Representatives on the topic of racial profiling.[8] On March 21, the family of Trayvon Martin joined thousands of demonstrators including Occupy Wall Street activists in a "Million Hoodie March" across New York City to protest the Florida teenager's death.[9] Two days later, students at more than a dozen high schools in Miami-Dade County participated in organized walkouts from their classes.[10]

Florida authorities responded to the protests by arresting Zimmerman and starting the legal process that had been wrongfully delayed. But the protesters went further than demanding due process. Like the lynch mobs they despised, they wanted an immediate verdict. Speaking on April 11, the day of Zimmerman's re-arrest, Al Sharpton said, "Forty-five days ago, Trayvon Martin was murdered. No arrest was made."[11] Jesse Jackson described Martin as "murdered and martyred." He went further, claiming that "blacks are under attack," and that "targeting, arresting, convicting blacks and ultimately killing us, is big business."[12] And the New Black Panther Party offered a $10,000 reward for the "capture" of Zimmerman.[13]

To add credibility to the idea that Trayvon Martin's death was a case of racial lynching, the protesters and their allies in the media even referred to Zimmerman as a "white Hispanic"—to make the facts fit their "white supremacy" narrative.[14] And the president of the United States, Barack Obama, intervened to pour more racial fuel on the fire. Speaking to reporters after federal investigators were deployed to Sanford, Obama said, "When I think about this boy, I think about my own kids, and I think every parent in America should be able to understand why it is absolutely imperative that we investigate every aspect of this. . . . If I had a son, he would look like Trayvon."[15]

The protests and accusations provoked a reaction from defenders of Zimmerman, who felt that the national outrage directed at him looked like its own form of lynching. Former Garland, Texas, NAACP president C. L. Bryant criticized Obama for his statement and dismissed Sharpton and Jackson as "race hustlers" who were "using this child [Trayvon] as the bait to inflame racial passions."[16] Prominent Republican and former U.S. education secretary William Bennett decried the "mob mentality" on display, saying that "the tendency in the first days by some, including Al Sharpton, Jesse Jackson and an angry chorus of followers, was to rush to judgment with little regard for fairness, due process, or respect for the terrible death of a young man."[17] Hoover Institution senior fellow Shelby Steele accused "ambulance-chasing" black leaders who specialize in "the manipulation of white guilt" of promoting blacks' "historical victimization as the central theme of our group identity."[18]

What none of the participants in the acrimonious debate fully realized was this: their opposing hyperventilating views had less to do with the facts of the case—which, in advance of the investigation, were still akin to rumors—than they did with issues much larger than what had taken place between George Zimmerman and Trayvon Martin on that fateful night. These differences could not be resolved in a court of law. The issues that consumed them reflected conflicting views about race relations in America—both past and present—and about the proper concerns of a civil rights movement. If carried far enough, as Black Lives Matter intended, these issues were not only unresolvable legally, they could not be resolved within the framework of America's constitutional order, which is based on compromise and a shared view of the imperfections of the individuals—of every race—who rely on it.

In Jamil Smith's interview of Patrisse Cullors for *Rolling Stone*, the Black Lives Matter co-founder said, "I probably was the one out of the three of us that was like, 'Let's go, let's get big, let's get everybody.' I wasn't necessarily thinking about organizational structure. I was mostly thinking about building a mass movement that people can be a part of and feel an identity around. I was interested in giving folks like black poor people who've been marginalized, brutalized, an opportunity to have more visibility." Then she added this incomprehensible observation: "Before seven years ago [the time of the Trayvon Martin protests] we could barely get the news to talk about police violence, let alone police death."[19]

The statement was incomprehensible because it was so far removed from the reality of American life nearly half a century after the Civil Rights Acts, which were passed by large, mainly white congressional majorities. These acts guaranteed equal treatment under the law to every American regardless of race. Americans—white Americans—were far from being unwilling to talk about police violence involving black citizens. As a direct result of the peaceful protests of Martin Luther King Jr. and his followers, for many decades now white America had been actively concerned about the treatment of black Americans—and actually quick to seize on perceived incidents of injustice, even when the situation hasn't warranted it.

A prime instance was the arrest and beating of Rodney King Jr. in 1991. It was an episode that compelled the attention of the entire nation including President Bush, led to the arrest and incarceration of two of the officers involved, and also precipitated the Los Angeles riots of 1992.

The actual events of that case are instructive. Officers attempted to arrest King for drunk driving and instead were led on a wild and dangerous car chase on the I-210 freeway. When the chase came to an end, King still resisted arrest, refusing to follow the officers' commands. Rodney King was 6'3" and weighed approximately 190 pounds. He was high on PCP (also known as "Angel Dust"), the effects of which include "a sense of super strength and invulnerability, combined with the inability to feel pain and poor judgement."[20] This was evident in a bystander's video of the arrest that showed King being tased twice, with 50,000 volts in each shot. Far from being subdued, he can be seen charging the police with the taser wires attached to him and knocking them over.[21]

This scene had its origin in an earlier decision by the liberal authorities of Los Angeles County to ban "choke holds." Previously, choke holds had provided an efficient if dangerous method of bringing a perpetrator as strong as King to a prone position where he could be handcuffed. Since the tasers had failed and the choke hold was outlawed, the officers were left with one remaining option: to use their batons to club King into submission. Thus, a reform designed to protect perpetrators resisting arrest turned into a prescription for a brutal beating. The video of this beating—with the tasing and charging sequences edited out—was aired on all the TV news shows.

Although they had followed the book laid down by the liberal authorities, the four officers were put on trial for using "excessive force" and committing "assault with a deadly weapon." When all four of them were completely acquitted except for an assault charge against one officer that resulted in a hung jury, the video image of King being beaten into submission sparked a racial rage that led to six days of riots, which ended only with the intervention of the California Army National Guard, the United States Army, and the United States Marine Corps.[22] By the time the destructive energies of the riots were spent, 63 people were dead, more than 2,300 injured, and innumerable neighborhoods in South Central Los Angeles destroyed. Call these the unintended consequences of well-intentioned but ill-thought-out reforms.[23]

Unwilling to let the officers' acquittals stand, the federal government then prosecuted all four officers for alleged violations of King's civil rights, a case of double jeopardy that many regarded as an injustice in itself. The trial resulted in a guilty verdict for two of the four. They were sentenced on April 16, 1993, to serve prison terms. In a separate civil lawsuit in 1994, a jury found the City of Los Angeles liable for King's arrest and awarded him $3.8 million in damages.[24]

In sum, Patrisse Cullors had no idea what she was talking about when she claimed no one cared about injustices to black Americans before the Trayvon Martin shooting. Blacks were not invisible or without support from Americans before she and her fellow Marxists began to promote their racial caricatures of white behavior and to launch an indictment of alleged police malfeasance so extreme as to justify riots and assassinations in the name of "social justice."

Dontre Hamilton

On April 30, 2014, an officer in downtown Milwaukee, Wisconsin, responded to a call from some Starbucks employees reporting a homeless man asleep in a local park. The officer began to pat down the individual, whose name was Dontre Hamilton. Hamilton woke up thinking he was being attacked and began to fight. The officer tried to use his baton to subdue Hamilton, but Hamilton got control of the baton and swung it at the officer, hitting him with great force on the head and the side of the neck. Fearing for his safety, the officer shot Hamilton, who was black, killing him. As a result of the shooting and the public clamor it sparked, the officer was fired from the police force and a decision was made to equip Milwaukee officers with body cameras.[25]

Dontre Hamilton was thirty-one years old and had a history of mental illness, which included treatment for schizophrenia. He also had a prior history of arrests which were "directly connected to mental health issues," according to Milwaukee's police chief. In 2013, for example, Hamilton had attempted suicide by stabbing both sides of his own neck, subsequently telling those who had intervened to interrupt his death wish: "Voices told me to kill myself and you people, too." Hamilton's mother reported that the day before her son died, he had told her that he was "tired and hungry, and that somebody was going to kill him." No one seems to have inquired of his family why a man suffering from these conditions was left alone to sleep on a park bench.[26]

Given these facts, which are readily available on the Internet, it would seem that this was a tragedy with no one really responsible. The officer had no idea that this young man was suffering from severe mental illness. And having been struck in the neck and head with his own baton, the officer would legitimately have feared for his life.

At the time of Hamilton's death, Black Lives Matter was still a fledgling group with no formal organization. But its leaders were not prepared to let the opportunity provided by a white officer's shooting of a black man go to waste. To them it was a clear case of racist oppression—even though there was no evidence to suggest that the officer's patting down of the defendant, or his decision to defend himself, was racially motivated. Black Lives Matter held rallies to protest Hamilton's death and to demand that charges be brought against the officer who had shot him, though given the facts of Hamilton's condition and the absence of any witnesses to what happened, it is difficult to imagine what those charges might be.[27] In attendance at one of the rallies was Hamilton's brother Nate, who made this ignorant racial comment to a reporter covering the event: "I say destroy the whole Constitution, because it never worked to begin with for black people."[28]

Among the speakers at a December 2014 rally organized by Black Lives Matter to protest Hamilton's death was the mayor of Milwaukee, Tom Barrett, who told the protesters, "We need to take the time to get to know each other and to respect each other. That's why I'm here today, because black lives matter." He also said that improving community relations would require effort from both sides.[29]

This even-handed note brought a rebuke from a minister who also spoke at the rally, William Muhammad, who said, "We have to speak straight truth to the mayor, straight truth to the police chief. Those were nice and flowering words, but your actions have not backed what you're saying." The clear implication was that the authorities should have charged the officer with a crime. Another speaker, the Reverend Don Darius Butler, was more direct and expanded the indictment: "We are summoned here because of America's unfinished business with respect to its citizens of African descent."[30] In this remark and other statements of the protesters, the shooting of Dontre Hamilton was fit into a much larger narrative of "white oppression" without any attempt to connect the facts of the case or the actual attitudes and behaviors of the officer and his "victim" to that racial narrative.

It's hard to avoid the conclusion that if there were indeed an injustice in this series of events, it was the decision of the Milwaukee Police Department to fire the officer and end his law-enforcement career in order to appease the protesters.[31]

The family of Dontre Hamilton, who had obviously failed him, filed a civil suit against the City of Milwaukee and was awarded a $2.3 million settlement.[32] The award came after a November 2015 U.S. Justice Department decision stating that there was insufficient evidence to justify the pursuit of a criminal indictment against the officer.[33]

The outrage that Black Lives Matter displayed over the death of Dontre Hamilton provided a stark contrast to the organization's indifference on May 31, 2014—just one month later—when a forty-three-year-old black Georgia police officer named Kevin Jordan was shot and killed while arresting a perpetrator at an all-night eatery where three customers were creating a disturbance. Black Lives Matter had nothing to say about Officer Jordan or the seven children he left behind.[34]

Eric Garner

On July 17, 2014, a black man named Eric Garner died in police custody on Staten Island, New York. Garner was a career criminal who had been arrested thirty-one times in his forty-four years for a variety of petty crimes but also for assaults and grand larceny. His first arrest came when he was ten years old. At the time of his final arrest, Garner was selling loose cigarettes, or "loosies," which were illegal because they evaded the special tax that New York Mayor Bill de Blasio had placed on cigarettes as a measure intended to reduce citizens' smoking.[35]

When four New York Police Department officers attempted to arrest Garner, he refused to cooperate with them, saying that he was simply "minding my business" and was doing nothing wrong.[36] This presented the officers with a dilemma. How to bring down a 6´3˝, 350-pound individual who was resisting arrest so that he could be cuffed? One officer, 29-year-old Daniel Pantaleo, grabbed Garner around the neck, from behind, in what critics would call a "choke hold," and pulled him down. Pantaleo maintained the hold for 15 seconds.[37]

Choke holds—defined by the NYPD as "any pressure to the throat or windpipe which may prevent or hinder breathing or reduce intake of air"—had been illegal in New York since 1993.[38] Pantaleo and his colleagues denied that he had used a choke hold.[39] The autopsy showed that, whether he had or not, the "choke hold" is not what killed Garner. The report showed that there was no damage to Garner's larynx or hyoid bone, the latter of which is almost always fractured in cases of strangulation.[40] The hold was in fact a submission hold, which is permitted by the NYPD. It is designed to deprive the brain of oxygen by stopping blood flow through the carotid artery in order to make the suspect pass out.[41]

During his fateful altercation with the police, Garner complained at least eleven times, "I can't breathe," but all except one of those complaints came *after* Officer Pantaleo had released his hold on Garner.[42] That is, Garner was still alive and conscious *after* having been freed from the alleged "chokehold."[43] He remained on the sidewalk for approximately seven minutes and was then placed in an ambulance where he suffered a cardiac arrest and died on the way to the hospital. His supporters claimed he was not given oxygen by the paramedics at the scene.[44]

Garner died because the physical struggle with Officer Pantaleo triggered a cardiac arrest. The morbidly obese Garner suffered from a number of serious underlying medical conditions of which the officers were unaware: hypertensive cardiovascular disease, heart disease, and severe bronchial asthma. As a result of these conditions, he had a heart that was twice the size of a normal person's.[45] The medical examiner who conducted Garner's autopsy concluded that "a police officer choked him with enough force that it triggered a 'lethal cascade' of events, ending in a fatal asthma attack."[46] Officer Pantaleo, of course, had no idea of Garner's medical condition when Garner decided to resist arrest.

In an article for the American Thinker, a medical doctor provided a detailed analysis of Garner's death, leading to this conclusion: "A normal and healthy male would have been transiently distressed by the actions of the arresting officers. Mr. Garner had no margin of safety, no reserve at all, and was precariously unstable even before he was accosted. The actions of the arresting officers, undoubtedly used many times before without significant ill effect, combined with Garner's pathophysiology to rapidly produce hypoxia, very likely aggravated by carbon dioxide retention and *narcosis*, which suppresses the normal reflex to breathe. This was rapidly followed by cardiac arrhythmia and death."[47]

There is no evidence for Black Lives Matter's contention that racism was the cause of the police officers' actions. It is even contradicted by the fact that the sergeant in charge at the scene of the altercation was an African-American female, who oversaw the whole series of events as they unfolded.[48]

Despite these facts, the public protests led to the firing of Officer Pantaleo, who was also denied his pension.[49] If Eric Garner had been a white career criminal with this medical history resisting arrest, it is difficult to imagine such disciplinary action against the police officer, or the protests that followed Garner's death.

The investigation and the measures taken against Officer Pantaleo were heavily influenced by the public demonstrations and racial accusations that accompanied these events. A coalition of civil rights and "social justice" organizations led the way. Among them was a Chicago-based group calling itself Assata's Daughters after former Black Liberation Army leader and convicted cop-killer Assata Shakur, a fugitive in Communist Cuba. Assata's Daughters was formed in direct response to the fact that Officer Pantaleo had not been criminally indicted.[50]

After a grand jury failed to indict the officer, protesters in New York and San Francisco conducted "die-ins" and chanted "I Can't Breathe" in protest.[51] Thousands gathered in similar demonstrations in Boston, Chicago, Washington, D.C., Baltimore, Minneapolis, Atlanta, Berkeley, and London.[52] In all, dozens of demonstrations in support of Garner were held globally, with hundreds of participants being arrested, mostly for disorderly conduct and blocking the streets, but also for assaulting police officers.[53]

The success of the protests in gaining the support of American elites was reflected in the coverage of the Garner case by the *New*

York Times and other left-wing papers. A *Times* headline stated: "Man's Death after Chokehold Raises Old Issue for the Police."[54] The *New York Daily News* featured a cover with the giant headline "They Killed Him" alongside a photo of "the victim's heartbroken wife." The article quoted Garner's widow claiming "They killed him. . . . They choked him and took him down, and I could hear him screaming that he couldn't breathe."[55]

However, the facts being what they were, the Obama Justice Department decided not to file federal civil rights charges against any of the NYPD officers involved in Garner's death.[56] Nonetheless, the Garner family was able to file a wrongful death suit against the City of New York and win a settlement of $5.9 million.[57]

CHAPTER 3

HOW THE MOVEMENT GREW

Michael Brown

Three weeks after the death of Eric Garner, the police shooting of another black man led to a sea change in the Black Lives Matter movement. The campaigns over the deaths of Trayvon Martin, Dontre Hamilton, and Eric Garner had fanned flames of outrage and inspired the passions of revenge to the point that a new escalation of the war with law enforcement was inevitable. The events that now unfolded in Ferguson, Missouri, prompted Black Lives Matter leaders to make their crusade a full-time effort, and also to formalize their organization and create a movement. Moreover, they were now inspired to harness the heightened passions of their followers to instigate large-scale violence that would set the stage for insurrections to come.

Michael Brown was an eighteen-year-old youth who had just graduated high school and was two days away from starting a training program in heating and air conditioning repair at Vatterott College technical school. At 6′4″ and 292 pounds, Brown was an intimidating physical presence. A sympathetic media softened this obvious fact by referring to him as a "gentle giant."[1] However, the one piece of concrete evidence that exists regarding his character shows him to be a man who was anything but gentle. On that fateful day—August 9, 2014—Brown was caught by security cameras at a local store overpowering an Asian shopkeeper who was half his size, shoving him with great force, and stealing Swisher Sweets cigars off his counter.[2] It was a casual robbery for a small gain—the cigars are used for smoking marijuana—making the violence all the more gratuitous and cruel.[3]

But the passions of the Black Lives Matter movement had so captured a national audience that, in advance of any formal investigation of the facts, as powerful a journalistic institution as the *New York Times* was ready to promote its inflammatory message. In an editorial three days after the shooting, the *Times* editors presented the incident as a textbook expression of raw racism: "The F.B.I. may be able to answer the many questions surrounding the death of Michael Brown, an 18-year-old black student from Ferguson, Mo., who was a few days from heading off to college when he was shot by a police officer on Saturday. The shooting of Mr. Brown, who was unarmed, led to three days of protest, some of it violent, and several tense confrontations between residents of the St. Louis suburban town of 21,000 and the police."[4]

The *Times* editors continued: "But it doesn't take a federal investigation to understand the history of racial segregation, economic inequality and overbearing law enforcement that produced so much of the tension now evident on the streets. St. Louis has long been one of the nation's most segregated metropolitan areas, and there remains a high wall between black residents—who overwhelmingly have lower incomes—and the white power structure that dominates City Councils and police departments like the ones in Ferguson."[5]

The editors went on for several paragraphs, describing the racial inequities of the St. Louis–Ferguson area before conceding that, "The circumstances of Mr. Brown's death are, inevitably, in dispute. Witnesses said he was walking home from a convenience store when stopped by an officer for walking in the middle of the street, and they accused the officer of shooting him multiple times when his hands were raised over his head. The police said Mr. Brown had hit the officer. State and federal investigators are trying to sort out the truth."[6]

This compilation of hearsay and gossip, heavily stacked in favor of the deceased, was not accompanied by any expression of concern about the violence that had erupted in the streets of Ferguson over the previous three days and in advance of any formal inquiry into the facts. Those facts, eventually established by a grand jury and a special investigation by the Obama Justice Department, were these: At approximately noon on August 9, Ferguson policeman Darren Wilson, responding to a call about the strong-arm robbery at a convenience store, met up with Brown and his twenty-two-year-old friend Dorian Johnson as both men were walking in the middle of Canfield Drive, a two-lane street in Ferguson.[7] Wilson instructed them to get onto the sidewalk.[8]

When the pair refused to comply, the officer began to open the door of his car and tried to get out to confront them. But Brown pushed the door shut and then attacked the officer, punching him twice in the face. During the fight, Brown reached through the car window for the officer's service weapon and attempted to wrest it from him.[9] Brown's DNA was subsequently found on Officer Wilson's gun, on the left thigh of

Wilson's pants, and on the inside driver's door handle of Wilson's police SUV, corroborating the officer's testimony regarding the scuffle.[10]

During the fracas, Wilson fired two shots, one of which grazed Brown's hand. Brown at that point retreated and began to flee. The officer exited his squad car and was pursuing Brown on foot. According to more than a half-dozen black and biracial eyewitnesses who testified to police, the FBI, and a grand jury, Brown then turned around and charged the officer who, in response, shot him multiple times in self-defense while backpedaling and ordering Brown to stop. But Brown failed to stop until the fatal bullet was fired.[11]

This was the conclusion of a special inquiry conducted by the Obama Justice Department.[12] The forensic evidence from the autopsy report, which was used to analyze the angles of the shots, supported the same verdict: Michael Brown had his head down and was charging toward Officer Wilson when the final shot struck the top of his head and killed him.[13]

The evidence was conclusive, but not for the Black Lives Matter leaders, who rejected the testimony of the black eyewitnesses, the Obama administration's conclusions, and the forensic evidence. Instead, they clung to the words of Michael Brown's accomplice in the strong-arm robbery, Dorian Johnson, who claimed that Brown had been shot and killed while he was surrendering with his hands up. This was how "Hands Up, Don't Shoot" became the battle cry of Black Lives Matter protesters.[14] It summed up their view of events, which was without a shred of proof: that "Mike Brown was murdered by Ferguson police officer Darren Wilson."[15]

Five years later, one of the three founders of the Black Lives Matter movement, Patrisse Cullors, published a memoir titled

When They Call You a Terrorist. In it, she recalled an incident of police brutality that she had witnessed in her childhood: "I will not think of this particular incident until years and years later, when the reports about Mike Brown start flowing out of Ferguson, Missouri, and he is morphed by police and the press from a beloved 18-year-old boy, a boy who was heading to college and a boy who was unarmed, into something like King Kong, an entity swollen, monster-like, that could only be killed with bullets that were shot into the top of his head. Because this is what that cop did to him. He shot bullets into the top of his head as he knelt on the ground with his hands up."[16]

This delusional racial fantasy, so remote from the facts, remains a principal incitement for the Black Lives Matter movement. The fact that it is believed by so many people—and so many violent people—is a threat to the cohesion of America's communities, and to the people caught in the crosshairs of the hate. The Ferguson officer had done nothing wrong, and he was exonerated by the Democrat authorities in Ferguson, by the grand jury, and by the independent inquiry conducted by the Obama Justice Department. Yet he had to leave the police force, uproot his family, and go into hiding because of the inflammatory lies spread by Black Lives Matter. As in previous cases, the City of Ferguson settled a wrongful death claim by paying Brown's family $1.5 million, despite the culpability of Michael Brown in his own death.[17]

Before any investigation was conducted or any evidence gathered, demonstrators from all over the country began descending on Ferguson. Black Lives Matter leaders decided to join them and use the protests to transform their #BlackLives-Matter hashtag into a movement. During Labor Day weekend of 2014, they organized a number of concurrent "Black Life

Matters Freedom Rides" to Ferguson and aggressively promoted the Black Lives Matter Global Network Foundation as the formal hub of their activities.[18]

The "freedom rides" brought approximately six hundred out-of-state protesters to Ferguson to set the city on fire. In an article for *The Guardian*, Cullors compared their efforts to those of the famous Freedom Riders who had crossed the segregated South during the early 1960s. She called the modern-day rides "a tangible example of self-determination in the face of anti-black violence on the part of Ferguson residents and those of us who traveled from across the country to join them."[19]

Cullors and fellow Black Lives Matter activist Darnell Moore elaborated, on Cullors' blog, on October 30, 2014: "The Black Lives Matter ride was organized in the spirit of the early 1960s interstate Freedom Rides in the racially segregated South, after the visuals of Michael Brown's lifeless and blood-drenched body brought to mind images of lifeless black bodies hanging from lynching trees in the all-too-recent past, after the militarized police forces looked all too similar to the response of police to protestors during the civil rights movement."[20]

Leaving aside the insulting linkage of Michael Brown's fate to the racial lynchings in the South more than half a century before, these "Black Life Matters Freedom Rides" bore no resemblance to the civil rights demonstrations of the 1960s, which led to no looting, arson, or rioting by the participants. This was because their leader, Martin Luther King Jr., was a disciple of Mahatma Gandhi and committed his followers to a strict strategy of non-violence. As Fox TV's anchor Harris Faulkner tersely noted, "Martin Luther King conducted no marches at night"—a stark contrast with the Black Lives Matter riots that typically turned violent after sundown.[21]

The protests of Michael Brown's death started quietly on the evening of August 9, 2014, when Ferguson residents erected a makeshift memorial consisting of flowers, candles, balloons, and teddy bears on the spot where Brown had died.[22] However, the following day a large number of rioters took over the streets, looting businesses, torching vehicles and buildings, and aggressively confronting and attacking police officers who arrived on the scene. There was gunfire from the demonstrators, but no one was shot. By dawn two days later, twenty-eight businesses in Ferguson and the neighboring town of Dellwood had been burglarized, burned, or damaged in some other significant way.[23]

On the night of August 11, a number of protesters in Ferguson threw rocks at police, prompting the officers to respond with tear gas and bean-bag rounds in an effort to disperse the crowds. Among the protesters at the scene was Democrat State Senator Maria Chappelle-Nadal, who attempted to shift responsibility for the violence to the police: "We were tear-gassed. I could not breathe, I could not speak, I could not focus, I could not think because I thought that I was going to die because we were shot at and tear gas was constantly thrown at us and the police officers. I'm the senator for the area, and I felt threatened. Everyone felt threatened."[24]

Serious rioting continued for more than a week. Protesters hurled Molotov cocktails, rocks, and bottles at police officers. President Barack Obama intervened with an incendiary public statement criticizing law-enforcement personnel. "There's . . . no excuse for police to use excessive force against peaceful protests," he said, "to throw protesters in jail for lawfully exercising their First Amendment rights."[25] The First Amendment, however, guarantees the right to "freedom of speech" and "peaceful assembly," not to arson, looting, and violence. Obama's attack on the police was echoed by Missouri Democrat senator Claire McCaskill who claimed, without evidence or logic, that "militarization of the police" had "escalated the protesters' response." Obama's attorney general, Eric Holder, seconded McCaskill's complaint, saying he was concerned about what he described as police use of military-style equipment in putting down the riots.[26] It was a theme among Democrat politicians that would be repeated often as the riots spread.

Far from being characterized by excessive force, the law-enforcement presence was proving insufficient to quell the violence. On August 18, Missouri Governor Jay Nixon broke ranks with his fellow Democrats and issued an executive order calling in the National Guard to "help restore peace and order and to protect the citizens of Ferguson." The following day, forty-seven protesters were arrested, including some from as far away as California and New York. By August 21, order was largely restored in Ferguson, and Governor Nixon withdrew the National Guard from the city.[27] Sporadic protests, some violent, did erupt on a number of occasions during the weeks that followed, however.[28]

One cost of the Ferguson riots was noted in their wake—a nationwide spike in violent crime, as police across the country retreated under the wave of anti-police hostility. In 2015, America's 56 largest cities experienced a 17 percent rise in homicides. Several cities with large black populations saw their 2015 murder totals spike even more dramatically—they went up by 54 percent in D.C., 60 percent in Newark, 72 percent in Milwaukee, 83 percent in Nashville, and 90 percent in Cleveland. St. Louis police chief Sam Dotson, referring to the town where Michael Brown's death took place, attributed the increased criminal violence to "the Ferguson Effect."[29]

Michael Brown's funeral was held on August 25, 2014. The ceremony was attended by such notables as Jesse Jackson, filmmaker Spike Lee, entertainer Sean "P. Diddy" Combs, and some of Martin Luther King Jr.'s children. To drive home the unfounded notion that racism was to blame for Michael Brown's death, the parents of Trayvon Martin and a cousin of Emmett Till—a fourteen-year-old boy infamously murdered by white men in Mississippi fifty-nine years earlier—also attended the service.

The tenor of the proceedings was conveyed by a *Kansas City Star* report that said, "More than 4,500 mourners filled Friendly Temple Missionary Baptist Church in St. Louis for the service, which at times seemed like a cross between a gospel revival and a rock concert. It began with upbeat music punctuated by clapping. Some people danced in place." The eulogy was delivered by the Reverend Charles Ewing, who claimed that the blood of Michael Brown was "crying from the ground, crying for vengeance, crying for justice."[30]

Three months later on November 25, major violence broke out in Ferguson again, after a grand jury decided not to charge Officer Wilson with a crime in the shooting death of Michael Brown. Sixty-one people were arrested in Ferguson that night and into the next morning, in addition to at least another twenty elsewhere in the vicinity. Meanwhile, protests demanding "justice" for Brown and his family erupted in New York, Seattle, Oakland, and other cities.[31]

From August through December, the unrest in Ferguson cost taxpayers at least $26 million in expenses related to the National Guard, the Missouri Highway Patrol, overtime pay for police and other emergency personnel, and the repair of property that was damaged, burned, looted, and vandalized.[32] But this was only the beginning of the costs to Americans generally, since the Ferguson riots provided the template for Black Lives Matter riots to come.

It was the Ferguson riots of 2014—and the massive publicity they generated—that transformed Black Lives Matter from a loosely organized initiative into a highly influential, highly organized insurrection, which large numbers of donors, big and small, were eager to fund. As *USA Today* noted in August 2016, promoting the Brown myth, "Since police officer Darren Wilson fatally shot unarmed teenager Michael Brown . . . in Ferguson, Mo., the words 'Black Lives Matter' have morphed from a public outcry into a national movement."[33]

HOW THE MOVEMENT
BECAME NATIONAL

Ezell Ford

In 2014, Ezell Ford was a twenty-five-year-old black man suffering from depression, bipolar disorder, and schizophrenia.[1] Shortly after 8:00 p.m. on August 11, two Los Angeles police officers spotted Ford in the company of known local gang members.[2] The officers, Sharlton Wampler and Antonio Villegas, were white and Hispanic, respectively. Wampler had previously arrested Ford for marijuana possession. The officers believed Ford was now trying to dispose of illicit drugs. They followed him as he walked to a nearby driveway.[3] According to the officers, when they attempted to arrest Ford, the suspect wrestled with Wampler and took the gun from Wampler's holster while lying on top of him. At that point Wampler shouted, "He's got my gun," prompting Villegas to fire two shots at Ford. At approximately the same moment, Wampler managed to draw his backup gun and used it to shoot Ford once in the back. By the time the scuffle was over, Ford had been mortally wounded.[4] The officers' story was disputed by onlookers, and both Wampler and Villegas were formally investigated.[5]

Black Lives Matter protesters immediately compared this case to the shooting of Michael Brown, which had occurred two days earlier.[6] Based on the evidence, Los Angeles District Attorney Jackie Lacey, a black woman, declined to prosecute the officers, finding that they had "acted lawfully in self-defense and in defense of others when they shot Ezell Ford." Her report explained, "The evidence indicates that Ford was on top of Wampler, struggling to obtain Wampler's primary service weapon and posing an immediate threat to his safety and his partner's safety. In fear for their lives, Villegas and Wampler each responded with deadly force."[7] An autopsy report corroborated the two officers' claim that Ford had fought with Wampler and gained the upper hand just before being shot.[8]

Ford family attorney Steven Lerman framed the events quite differently, claiming that the officers "had nothing better to do" on August 11 than kill Ezell Ford.[9] The family filed a $75 million federal civil rights lawsuit against the city, and received a $1.5 million settlement.[10]

In January 2015, Black Lives Matter demonstrators occupied the sidewalk in front of LAPD headquarters for eighteen days, demanding not only that Police Chief Charlie Beck meet with them, but also that he fire the officers who had killed Ford.[11]

In June 2015, the Los Angeles Police Commission, a police oversight group composed of civilians, ruled that Officer Wampler should neither have drawn his weapon against Ford in the first place nor subsequently shot the suspect when he did. The commission also disapproved of Officer Villegas's initial decision to draw his weapon, but concluded that he was justified in opening fire when Wampler was in danger. Attorney Gary

Fullerton, whose law firm represented the two officers, claimed that in censuring Wampler the commission had "succumbed to the pressure of the mob. . . . It's a shame that police officers can't do their job and protect their lives."[12]

In January 2017, Los Angeles County prosecutors announced that Officers Wampler and Villegas would not face criminal charges in connection with the shooting of Ezell Ford.[13] Nonetheless, Ford remained an important figure in the pantheon of Black Lives Matter martyrs. On August 11, 2019—the fifth anniversary of Ford's death—the Los Angeles chapter of Black Lives Matter issued the following statement: "Today we honor the Spirit of Ezell Ford, who was murdered by LAPD officers. . . . Despite massive protest, which included an 18-day occupation of LAPD headquarters . . . District Attorney Jackie Lacey refused to charge the officers, nor were they fired."[14]

Tamir Rice

A more troubling incident took place on the afternoon of November 22, 2014, when Cleveland police received a call from a man outside of a local recreation center who said, "I'm sitting in the park. . . . There's a guy here with a pistol pointing it at everybody. The guy keeps pulling it in and out of his pants, it's probably fake but you know what, he's scaring the shit out of people."[15] The police dispatcher, Constance Hollinger, did not mention to Timothy Loehmann and Frank Garmback, the two officers who were sent to the scene, the caller's remark indicating that the gun might have been fake.[16]

The suspect in question was a twelve-year-old boy named Tamir Rice, though his 5′7″, 195-pound frame made him look older.[17] The gun was an Airsoft pellet gun which Tamir had borrowed from a friend whose father had purchased it from

Walmart. It was a replica of a Colt M1911 semi-automatic pistol, indistinguishable from the real thing.[18] As Loehmann and Garmback approached Tamir with their police vehicle, they repeatedly shouted, "Show me your hands!" When Tamir didn't respond, they shot him.[19]

When investigators subsequently questioned Officer Loehmann about the incident, he testified,

> I kept my eyes on the suspect the entire time. I was fixed on his waistband and hand area. I was trained to keep my eyes on hands because "hands may kill." The male appeared to be over 18 years old and about 185 pounds. The suspect lifted his shirt and reached down into his waistband. We continued to yell "show me your hands." I was focused on the suspect. Even when he was reaching into his waistband, I didn't fire. I was still yelling the command, "show me your hands." . . . I observed the suspect pulling the gun out of the waistband with his elbow coming up. Officer Garmback and I were still yelling "show me your hands." With his hands pulling the gun out and his elbow coming up, I knew it was a gun and it was coming out. I saw the weapon in hands coming out of his waistband and the threat to my partner and myself was real and active.

Loehmann said he then fired two rounds at Tamir, trying to direct his shot "towards the gun in [the boy's] hand."[20]

Far from reveling in the death of the young man they had shot, the officers struggled to help him. As reported by National Public Radio, "an FBI agent who was on a robbery detail nearby and who is a trained paramedic arrived on the scene to assist and observed that it appeared the officers wanted to help Tamir after the shooting 'but they didn't know what to do.'"[21] Tamir died the next day in a hospital.

Although there was no evidence of racial bias on the part of the officers, Black Lives Matter protested the Tamir Rice shooting as though there was. Members of Black Lives Matter Cincinnati organized a rally on the local courthouse steps, where Black Lives Matter activist Ron Arundell said, "African-Americans are under attack all over the country, especially here in Cincinnati."[22]

Two days after the shooting of Tamir Rice, a grand jury in Ferguson declined to indict the officer who had shot Michael Brown in self-defense. Although it was hard to perceive any relationship between the two cases—Brown was killed resisting arrest for a strong-arm robbery, while Tamir was an innocent child caught up in tragic circumstances—Black Lives Matter didn't distinguish between the two, and they became the focus not only of protests in Cleveland, but of similar demonstrations across the country in the months to come.

On December 5, 2014, Tamir Rice's family filed a wrongful death lawsuit against the City of Cleveland and against Officers Loehmann and Garmback, alleging that they had acted "unreasonably, negligently, [and] recklessly."[23]

In December 2015, a Cleveland grand jury declined to indict the officers, primarily on the grounds that Tamir Rice was drawing what appeared to be an actual firearm from his waist as the police arrived.[24] "Given this perfect storm of human error," said prosecutor Tim McGinty, "mistakes and communications by all involved that day, the evidence did not indicate criminal conduct by police. It is likely that Tamir, whose size made him look much older and who had been warned his pellet gun might get him into trouble that day, either intended to hand it over to the officers or show them it wasn't a real gun. But there was no way for the officers to know that, because they saw the events rapidly unfolding in front of them from a very different perspective."[25]

Black Lives Matter was outraged by the grand jury's decision. In an interview with National Public Radio, Black Lives Matter activist Elle Hearns said, "The reality is, nothing is more unfavorable than having to bury your child, a twelve-year-old child because the police pulled the trigger. . . . Because the police murdered your child. There's nothing more unfavorable or unjust than that."[26]

In April 2016, the Rice family was awarded $6 million in its suits against the officers and the City of Cleveland.[27]

Akai Gurley and Dead Cops

A month after the shooting of Tamir Rice, the anti-police anger stoked by oversimplified or distorted versions of the facts took an ugly turn. On December 13, 2014, three weeks after Rice's death, a protest called the "Millions March" rally was held in New York City. The awkward name was an homage to Louis Farrakhan's "Million Man March" in Washington, D.C., nearly twenty years earlier. Sponsored jointly by Al Sharpton, Black Lives Matter, the Trayvon Martin Organizing Committee, and a group called Turn Up the Anger, the 2014 march featured this chant: "What Do We Want? Dead Cops. When Do We Want It? Now."[28]

Seven days after that march, a gunman named Ismaaiyl Brinsley ambushed and killed two New York Police Department officers, Wenjian Liu and Rafael Ramos. One was a Chinese American and the other a Hispanic American. Brinsley said his action was a protest against the recent deaths of Eric Garner and Michael Brown. Three hours before this double murder, Brinsley had posted the following message on his Instagram page: "I'm Putting Wings on Pigs Today. They Take 1 Of Ours ... Let's Take 2 of Theirs." In a separate post, he wrote, "I [sic] Rather Die a Gangster Then [sic] Go To Sleep A Coward." After killing the two officers, Brinsley committed suicide.[29]

In an effort to counter the bad publicity triggered by the "Millions March" protesters' demand for "Dead Cops ... Now" and the obviously related killings of the police officers only a week later in the same city, Black Lives Matter launched a new campaign designed to show that even Asian American cops were bad and deserving of vigilante justice. On December 27, Black Lives Matter organized a demonstration on behalf of Akai Gurley, a twenty-eight-year-old black man who had been shot by a Chinese-American officer named Peter Liang more than five weeks earlier, on November 20.[30] The targeting of Liang showed just how disconnected from fact, and from any semblance of justice, the Black Lives Matter campaign was.

Here is what transpired between Liang and Gurley, according to the liberal magazine *The Atlantic*: "[On November 20, 2014, Liang] and his partner, another recent graduate [from the police academy], patrolled the eighth floor of the Louis H. Pink Houses in Brooklyn. Liang's defense called the building notorious among officers for crime and said that's why, as he opened the door to the stairwell, Liang drew his gun, his finger off the trigger. In the dark, Liang said a loud noise surprised him. 'It was a quick sound and it just startled me. And the gun just went off after I tensed up.'"[31]

Gurley and his girlfriend, Melissa Butler, had just walked into the stairwell one flight below. The left-handed Liang used his right hand to pull out his flashlight while he unholstered his 9mm Glock pistol with his left hand. He then used his right shoulder to shove open the stairwell door, turned left to face the seventh-floor landing below, and, for safety, placed his finger on the trigger of his gun.[32] Neither Liang nor Gurley was aware of the other's presence in the stairwell at that moment.[33] Then, surprised by the loud noise in the stairwell, Liang accidentally fired one shot in the direction of the seventh floor below. In a tragic twist of fate, the bullet ricocheted off a wall of the stairwell and struck Gurley in the chest.[34]

The Atlantic described what happened next: "After Liang fired, Gurley was left on the ground bleeding from his chest, while Liang and his partner walked back into the hallway to debate who would report the shot. Liang's partner, Shaun Landau, said Liang seemed most concerned about losing his job. (Liang later said he didn't know he'd shot anyone.) When Landau and Liang returned, neither offered to perform CPR." Gurley's girlfriend took instructions from an operator over the phone with the help of a neighbor.[35] "For failing to try to save Gurley's life, Liang was charged with official misconduct. And for shooting Gurley, he was charged with second-degree manslaughter, criminally negligent homicide, second-degree assault, and reckless endangerment."[36]

On February 11, 2016, a jury convicted Liang of manslaughter and official misconduct. He was sentenced to five years' probation and eight hundred hours of community service.[37]

How was this—how were any of these cases—connected to the cause of social justice? How did the demonization of a Chinese-American policeman who fired his weapon inadvertently and without a shred of ill intent, and who was duly convicted and punished for his negligence, make black Americans more protected or respected?

Yet, this combative statement was issued by one of the organizations that had claimed responsibility for the "Dead Cops" chant at the December 13, 2014, "Millions March" rally: "The Trayvon Martin Organizing Committee–NYC commends all demonstrators across the country who refuse to leave their friends in the hands of murderous, abusive police. If this movement has taught us anything, it is that resistance is not only justified, but necessary. We will stand behind our comrades as they face whatever charges the city will throw at them. We know they are the victims here—not the NYPD. We are all victims at the hands of the white supremacist, capitalist state. For the same reason, we are the ones to overturn it."[38]

Tony Robinson

Early in the evening of March 6, 2015, the life of Tony Robinson, a nineteen-year-old biracial man in Madison, Wisconsin, came to an end. Madison police had received reports that Robinson was shouting at bystanders and jumping in front of moving cars on the street. There were also reports that he had just assaulted a man who was walking to a restaurant and that he had attempted to strangle another individual who was fueling his car at a gas station.[39]

When forty-five-year-old white police officer Matt Kenny arrived at the scene, a local bystander informed him that Robinson had just gone into a local apartment house. As Kenny approached that building, he could hear sounds of "a disturbance"—which included a person striking someone or something—coming from the upstairs apartment. The officer ascended the steps to investigate.[40] When Kenny was near the top of the staircase and announced himself as a police officer, Robinson suddenly appeared in the doorway and charged at

Kenny, punching the officer multiple times in the head and causing him to fall to the bottom of the staircase.[41] With Robinson
bearing down on him, Kenny shot Robinson seven times. He
then tried to administer first aid, but to no avail. Robinson died
of his wounds.[42]

An internal police department investigation determined that
when Officer Kenny shot Robinson he had reasonable cause to
believe that he was in imminent danger of death or great bodily
harm, and thus was justified in using deadly force.[43]

An autopsy report revealed that Robinson had ingested
Xanax, psilocybin mushrooms, and marijuana just hours before
the shooting that ended his life.[44] Court documents also showed
that Robinson was on probation after having pleaded guilty to
armed robbery in 2014.[45]

In an online Facebook petition, Black Lives Matter completely misrepresented the circumstances that had led to Robinson's death, saying that "19-year-old Tony Robinson was
murdered by Madison, Wisconsin, police officer Matt Kenny
after Tony and friends called 911 to get him help. Please sign this
petition to demand Justice for Tony Robinson."[46]

During the weekend immediately following Robinson's
death, Madison locals staged "Black Lives Matter" protests. On
March 9, more than a thousand people—including many high
school and university students who walked out of their classes—
held a demonstration at the state capitol building. They chanted
"Hands Up, Don't Shoot," the phrase that activists had used to
falsely frame the death of Michael Brown.[47] In an open letter to
Madison and Dane County officials, local religious leaders
wrote, "Black lives matter. Our history, both nationally and
locally, with respect to our African-American community is
unacceptable. Many of the incidents, shootings, and deaths that

we see reported on the news find their root cause in the intolerable disparity present in our community."[48] On March 14, a crowd of over a thousand people gathered at a Madison high school to demand justice for Robinson.[49]

Protests continued long after his death. On May 13, 2015, for instance, hundreds of people staged walkouts throughout the city of Madison and demanded that Officer Kenny be fired from the police department and charged with murdering Tony Robinson.[50]

In February 2017, Robinson's family was awarded $3.35 million to settle a federal civil rights lawsuit they had filed against the City of Madison over his death. The settlement, paid by the city's insurer, included no admission of wrongdoing.[51]

Black Lives Matter has a long memory for the deaths of black criminals like Tony Robinson. Not so long when it comes to black men like thirty-year-old police officer Robert Wilson, who was murdered when he and his partner interrupted a robbery by two black gunmen at a Philadelphia video-game store on March 5, 2015—just one day before Tony Robinson's death.[52]

Meagan Hockaday

At about 1:00 a.m. on March 28, 2015, the police department of Oxnard, California, sent officers to an apartment where a man had called 911 to request police assistance in a dispute between himself and his live-in girlfriend, twenty-six-year-old Meagan Hockaday, who was black. As Officer Roger Garcia approached the apartment, he heard people screaming inside. Luis Morado, the man who had reported the disturbance, came to meet Garcia at the front door. Morado was shirtless and had visible injuries to his chest.

Twenty seconds later, Hockaday charged the men with a serrated kitchen knife in her right hand. Morado, fearing

Hockaday's advance, ran past Officer Garcia and towards the front door of the residence. Hockaday continued to charge, and Garcia, who later reported that the woman was swinging her right arm in an effort to stab him, shot her three times—once on her elbow, once on her shoulder, and once on the right side of her back. When Sergeant David Walker of the Oxnard Police Department arrived at the scene moments later to back up Officer Garcia, Garcia was kneeling next to Hockaday, saying, "Stay with me."[53]

A lengthy report on the incident by the Ventura County District Attorney's office concluded, "Based on analysis conducted by the Ventura County Sheriff's Office Forensic Sciences Laboratory, Hockaday was no more than 15 inches away from the muzzle of Officer Garcia's gun when Officer Garcia fired the shots. Based on the location of the bullets, Hockaday was swinging the knife with her right arm at the time she was shot [with the bullet that struck the right side of her back]."

The report also noted that: (a) the woman was legally intoxicated at the time of her death, with a blood alcohol content of 0.20 percent; (b) the killing of Hockaday was a "justifiable homicide" because Officer Garcia believed that he was facing "imminent threat of death or bodily injury"; and (c) "Garcia used no more force than was reasonably necessary to defend against the apparent danger posed by Meagan Hockaday."[54]

In a similar vein, District Attorney Greg Totten said, "Any time you have a young woman in the prime of her life who is the mother of three small children shot inside her home, it is a heartbreaking tragedy. But it's equally clear to us that the officer had no choice because he was confronted by this same woman who was about to stab him. It's a very sad case. But our job is to look at the law and the facts, and we have done that and I believe properly concluded that the officer acted in accordance with the law and was justified in his decision."[55]

Black Lives Matter immediately protested Hockaday's shooting as a murder and continued to hold protests long after her death.[56]

Five years after Meagan Hockaday's death, activists were still keeping Hockaday's story alive and capitalizing on the American public's general ignorance of the details of what had taken place, as was evidenced in this description of Black Lives Matter's efforts that appeared in the *Santa Barbara Independent* on June 3, 2020, just over a week after George Floyd's death in Minneapolis:

> Racial injustice and police brutality are issues that affect every community, including Santa Barbara's. A woman who once led the Santa Barbara High School cheerleading squad and graduated from Peabody Charter School was shot and killed by police in Oxnard in 2015. Meagan Hockaday's murder was only one of the tragic stories told on Sunday, May 31, as Simone Akila Ruskamp and Krystle Farmer Sieghart from the Santa Barbara Chapter of Black Lives Matter led a protest against police brutality and racial injustice, drawing a crowd of more than 3,000 supporters to the Santa Barbara Courthouse Sunken Gardens. Speakers shared personal stories, statistics, and information as they tried to compel the Santa Barbara community to begin and continue to take action to address structural racism, including police brutality.[57]

Walter Scott

On the morning of April 4, 2015, Walter Scott, a fifty-year-old unarmed black man, was fatally shot in the back in North

Charleston, South Carolina, by Michael Slager, a white police officer. The incident was immediately fitted into the frame of the Black Lives Matter narrative, triggering protests and political pressures for "justice," which ultimately resulted in a twenty-year murder sentence for the officer.

The pivotal "evidence" affecting public opinion was a bystander's video of the last ten seconds of the incident. The video showed Slager firing eight shots at a fleeing Scott, hitting him five times—three times in the back, once in the upper buttocks, and once on an ear.[58] What the video did not show were the events leading up to the fatal shooting.

Slager had stopped Scott for a broken brake light. As the officer checked Scott's identification, Scott bolted from his parked car and ran.[59] Scott's family later speculated that he had run because he feared that he might be jailed because of child-support payments he had failed to make.[60] It is also possible that he fled because, as a toxicology report would later show, he had cocaine and alcohol in his system at the time.[61]

Slager fired his taser at Scott, but it failed to stop him.[62] When the taser was examined after the incident, the data that the device had recorded showed that it had been fired six times in sixty-seven seconds.[63] Eventually the officer caught up with the fleeing Scott, and the two men wrestled. According to the officer, Scott grabbed the taser and ran away.[64] It was then that Slager fired the fatal shots, which were caught on the bystander's video. A video of Scott bolting from his car and running also existed, but the bystander's video proved decisive. Slager's first trial resulted in a hung jury, but a second was resolved in a plea deal in which Slager agreed to a verdict of second-degree murder and the twenty-year prison sentence.[65]

After Scott's death, Black Lives Matter held rallies with chants of "Hands Up, Don't Shoot"—again, a reference to the false narrative Black Lives Matter had promoted after the death of Michael Brown eight months earlier in Ferguson, Missouri.[66]

Black Lives Matter also demanded that authorities convene a citizen review board to assess Officer Slager's behavior—and promised to hold continued protests until its demands were met.[67]

The Wikipedia account of these events summarizes the massive forces that were brought to bear on Slager to prompt him to agree to a plea deal. It is readily accessible and refutes the Black Lives Matter claim that the "system" is indifferent to black life—so definitively that one can easily wonder if the result was an injustice itself:

> The case was independently investigated by the South Carolina Law Enforcement Division (SLED). The Federal Bureau of Investigation (FBI), the Office of the U.S. Attorney for the District of South Carolina, and the Justice Department's Civil Rights Division conducted their own investigations. In June 2015, a South Carolina grand jury indicted Slager on a charge of murder. He was released on bond in January 2016. In late 2016, a five-week trial ended in a mistrial due to a hung jury. In May 2016, Slager was indicted on federal charges including violation of Scott's civil rights and obstruction of justice. In a May 2017 plea agreement, Slager pleaded guilty to federal charges of civil rights violations, and he was returned to jail pending sentencing. In return for his guilty plea, the state's murder charges were dropped.

In December 2017, Slager was sentenced to 20 years in prison, with the judge determining the under-lying offense was second-degree murder.[68]

In October 2015, in an out-of-court settlement, the City of North Charleston agreed to pay $6.5 million to Scott's family.[69]

Freddie Gray

On the morning of April 12, 2015, in a section of Baltimore infamous for narcotics crimes and violence, a known drug dealer named Freddie Gray inadvertently made eye contact with local police officers and then fled unprovoked, prompting the officers to pursue him.[70] After a brief foot chase, the police caught up with Gray, found a knife in his possession, and made an arrest.[71]

Gray already had a long criminal record consisting of at least eighteen arrests in an eight-year period—mostly for drug-related charges, but also for such offenses as assault, destruction of property, and burglary.[72] In the April 12 incident, he resisted arrest and, after a scuffle with the officers, was placed, alone, in the back of a police van at 8:42 a.m. Just four minutes later, at 8:46 a.m., the van stopped because Gray was becoming "irate," according to police, who placed leg shackles on him at that point.[73]

Thirteen minutes after that, at 8:59 a.m., as the van headed toward Central Booking, the driver, a black policeman named Caesar Goodson, asked another officer to "check on" Gray. When the officers checked on Gray again at 9:24 a.m., they called a medic to report that he was in "serious medical distress," because, accord-ing to Deputy Police Commissioner Jerry Rodriguez, "he could not talk and he could not breathe." Paramedics responded and spent

21 minutes treating Gray. They then, at about 10:00 a.m., delivered him to the Maryland Shock Trauma Center.[74]

Gray soon fell into a coma and eventually died on April 19, seven days after his arrest, from what were described as injuries to his spinal cord. Murder charges were filed against six Baltimore police officers—three of whom were black—who were involved in Gray's arrest.[75] Prosecutors alleged that by failing to strap Gray into the van with a seat belt, the officers had violated a recently enacted rule and created a situation where Gray might have been vulnerable to a serious injury such as the one he suffered.[76]

Gray's arrest and death set off more than a week of Black Lives Matter protests and riots. On one night, just hours after Gray's April 27 funeral, which was attended by thousands of people, rioters burned 144 vehicles and 15 buildings, and injured at least 20 police officers.[77] The violence escalated to such a point that on the tenth day of the riots Maryland Governor Larry Hogan called in the National Guard and 5,000 state police to restore order.[78]

During the final weekend of April 2015, Baltimore's black mayor, Stephanie Rawlings-Blake, said, "I've made it very clear that I work with the police and instructed them to do everything that they could to make sure that the protesters were able to exercise their right to free speech. It's a very delicate balancing act, because, while we tried to make sure that they were protected from the cars and the other things that were going on, *we also gave those who wished to destroy, space to do that as well*" [emphasis added].[79]

Similar protest-riots were instigated by Black Lives Matter in other cities, including Minneapolis, where the demonstrators chanted, "No Justice, No Peace, Prosecute the Police."[80] The officers who had arrested Freddie Gray were indeed prosecuted, but a black judge found them innocent of the charges. All six were acquitted.[81]

Following those acquittals, Mayor Rawlings-Blake announced that the city had agreed to pay Freddie Gray's family a $6.4 million settlement without conceding that any injustice had been done.[82]

Four years later, Black Lives Matter co-founder Patrisse Cullors shared her memory of these events with the readers of her memoir: "I will think of [the killing of Michael Brown] again when I watch bike-riding Freddie Gray, just 25, snatched up and thrown into the back of a police van like he was a bag of trash being tossed aside. Freddie Gray, taken for a Baltimore 'rough ride' vicious enough for the cops in the case to be charged with depraved heart murder. Those actual words. Cops who would be, like most law enforcement accused of shooting Black people, acquitted. Even with the presence of video."[83]

It took a single tweet by black talk-show host and bestselling author Larry Elder to sum up the absurdity of Black Lives Matter's claim that the death of Freddie Gray was the result of a racist attack on a black American, killed because he was black and because black lives didn't matter. Elder's tweet also exposed the utter disregard the Black Lives Matter leaders had for the most basic facts, despite the destructive consequences—racial and otherwise—of their false claims:

(FREDDIE GRAY DIED 2015)
President of the United States: black
U.S. Attorney General: black
Baltimore Mayor: black
City Council: mostly black
Police Department Head: black

Assistant Police Department Head: black
State Attorney: black
3 of 6 cops charged with murdering Freddie Gray: black
Judge who 2 times ruled the officers not guilty: black[84]

Alton Sterling

Alton Sterling was a thirty-seven-year-old black man who was fatally shot at close range at about 12:35 a.m. on July 5, 2016, during a scuffle with two white Louisiana policemen, Howie Lake II and Blane Salamoni. The officers were responding to a report that a black man in a red shirt (Sterling) was selling CDs outside a convenience store and that he had used a gun to threaten a homeless man at that location.[85] Sterling had a long criminal record that included violent crimes, and he had served a five-year sentence for resisting arrest in a 2009 incident during which an illegal gun fell out of his waistband.[86] He was also a registered sex offender.[87]

When Lake and Salamoni tried to arrest Sterling on July 5, he refused to comply with their commands.[88] During the subsequent scuffle, the officers tased Sterling twice and then wrestled him to the ground, pinning him except for his arms, which remained free.[89] A video of the arrest showed one of the officers yelling, "Going for his pocket! He's got a gun! Gun!"[90] Body-cam footage from one of the officers also showed that officer warning Sterling that he would be shot if he moved.[91] The video then showed Sterling reaching for his right side, and then one of the officers firing three shots, followed by another three, and then Sterling's body sprawled out on the ground. The officers retrieved a loaded, illegal .38-caliber revolver from Sterling's front pants pocket.[92]

According to the coroner's toxicology report, various quantities of alcohol, caffeine, cocaine, opiates, THC (which is the active ingredient in marijuana), and amphetamines including methamphetamine were found in Sterling's body.[93]

A Department of Justice investigation of the matter concluded that "the evidence is insufficient to prove beyond a reasonable doubt that Officers Salamoni and Lake willfully violated Sterling's civil rights." The investigation concluded, "Given the totality of the circumstances—that the officers had been fighting with Sterling and had attempted less-than-lethal methods of control; that they knew Sterling had a weapon; that Sterling had reportedly brandished a gun at another person; and that Sterling was much larger and stronger than either officer—the Department cannot prove either that the shots were unconstitutional or that they were willful. Moreover, two different, independent experts opined that this shooting was not unreasonable given the circumstances."[94]

But the Black Lives Matter propaganda claiming that there was an open hunting season on blacks had already created a national—and even international—response team, which is the only way to describe those who led the protests following the death of Alton Sterling.

On the night of July 5, more than a hundred demonstrators in Baton Rouge shouted, "No Justice, No Peace," set off fireworks, and blocked an intersection to protest Sterling's death.[95]

On July 9, another Sterling protest in Baton Rouge involving the New Black Panther Party turned violent, with one police officer getting several teeth knocked out. All told, police arrested 102 people and confiscated 8 firearms (3 rifles, 3 shotguns, and 2 pistols) from the protesters.[96]

In a July 2016 opinion piece published in the *Globe and Mail*, Professor Peniel E. Joseph, founding director of the Center for the Study of Race and Democracy at Tufts University, said that "the deaths of Alton Sterling and Philando Castile [a black man killed by police the day after Sterling's death] evoke the past spectacle of lynching," the "grotesque" practice that "normalized horrific brutality against black bodies in one era, just as the videotaped killings of black people do in our own."[97]

In early July, three young black males stole several guns as well as ammunition from a home and a pawn shop in Baton Rouge, with the intent of using the stolen items to shoot local police officers at protests for Alton Sterling.[98]

On July 13, local organizing groups and the American Civil Liberties Union's Louisiana branch filed a lawsuit against the Baton Rouge Police Department for violating the First Amendment rights of demonstrators. The plaintiffs claimed they had been protesting peacefully against Sterling's death.[99]

On July 17, a black gunman named Gavin Long murdered three police officers and wounded several others in Baton Rouge before he was killed by a SWAT team. "There is no doubt whatsoever that these officers were intentionally targeted and assassinated," Colonel Michael Edmonson, superintendent of the Louisiana State Police, said at a news conference. "It was a calculated act."[100]

Two years after Sterling's death, Black Lives Matter co-founder and serial liar Patrisse Cullors issued a statement saying, "We continue to mourn the brutal murder of Alton Sterling."[101]

Philando Castile

Philando Castile was a young black man killed by a police officer in Falcon Heights, Minnesota, following a routine traffic stop for a broken tail light. His killing took place on July 6, 2016, the day after the death of Alton Sterling. Jeronimo Yanez, the officer who shot Castile, was Hispanic and clearly—but inexcusably—panicked. Castile informed the officer that he was carrying a firearm, which indicated that he was not intending to use it on the officer and did not present a danger to him. But when Castile reached for his ID, the officer panicked and fired seven quick shots, ending the young man's life.

At his trial, Officer Yanez cried on the witness stand, claimed that Castile did reach for his gun, and recalled his own state of mind. "I told him, 'Don't pull it out," he said, referring to the gun. But then "I was able to see the top of the slide and the back of the tab of the firearm . . . that's when I engaged with Mr. Castile and shot him."[102] Yanez continued, "My family popped into my head. My wife. My baby girl. I did not want to shoot Mr. Castile at all. Those were not my intentions. . . . I was scared to death. I thought I was going to die."[103]

The trial jury, which included two black members, voted to acquit the officer. They apparently had trouble understanding the charge, which was "culpable negligence." Castile's death was a tragedy that never should have happened. But there was no evidence of malice on the part of the officer who killed Castile. The officer was fired from the police force, and the Castile family received a $3 million settlement, although that could hardly compensate them for their loss.

The criminal justice system had failed, but it was hard to see what could be done to remedy the failure, which was the result of human error rather than racial malice—as the protests that followed contended. The slogan of the Black Lives Matter protests was "Philando can be any of us."[104] This was false and incendiary.

Meanwhile, the war that Black Lives Matter had declared on law enforcement, and specifically the calls for "dead cops," could lead a police officer to think, "That dead cop could be me." Fear is always present when an officer attempts to make an arrest. Thanks to Black Lives Matter, the fear is there the minute an officer puts on his uniform. It was made clear just how realistic that fear was when, two days after Alton Sterling's death and one day after Philando Castile's, a Black Lives Matter demonstration in Dallas ended with a massacre.

CHAPTER 5

FIVE DEAD COPS IN DALLAS

O n July 7, 2016, Black Lives Matter held a march in Dallas to protest the deaths of Alton Sterling and Philando Castile, which had taken place during the preceding two days. The contrast between the two men could not have been starker. Sterling was a violent criminal who had robbed people at gunpoint only days before, was high on drugs, and was carrying a weapon he took pains to conceal. He resisted arrest and was reaching for his gun despite warnings from the officers that he would be shot if he did so. Philando Castile was a law-abiding citizen who informed the officer that he was carrying a firearm and was the victim of a panicked, unjustifiable (but not malicious) police shooting.

The inability of Black Lives Matter to distinguish between two such different cases, or to hold individuals accountable for their acts if they are black, is indefensible—and racist—and shows that justice is the last thing its leaders have in mind. In case after case, their failure to hold black criminals accountable for their actions is coupled with their reckless insistence that any cop involved in a shooting incident with a black adversary is a "murderer," regardless of circumstances or intentions.

This pattern has justified both BLM's indictment of the entire criminal justice system as "systemically racist," and their incitement to black Americans to regard police as their enemies and even to kill them. This accurately reflects the way the criminal element in the black community sees things, but not how the vast majority of law-abiding black citizens view them. When Black Lives Matter launched a campaign to "defund the police" and "dismantle" police departments, a Gallup Poll showed that 81 percent of black America opposed them.[1]

The Dallas protest of the deaths of Sterling and Castile, one of several similar protests in various parts of the country, involved approximately eight hundred demonstrators. The Dallas demonstrators shouted, "Enough is enough!" and held signs bearing slogans such as: "If all lives matter, why are black ones taken so easily?" Their march was overseen by a hundred Dallas police officers and was ostensibly peaceful. At the same time, according to Dallas Police Chief David Brown, about twenty to thirty open-carry gun-rights activists joined the protest march, some wearing gas masks, bulletproof vests, and fatigues.[2] Everyone had the sense that war could break out at any moment. That included one particular individual lurking in the shadows, who had his own idea of what "Black Lives Matter" and resisting "systemic racism" entailed.

Micah Xavier Johnson was an Army Reserve veteran of the Afghan War who had associations with black extremist organizations like the New Black Panthers, the Nation of Islam, and the Black Riders Liberation Army, who were part of the movement that Black Lives Matter had unleashed. During negotiations with Dallas Police Chief David Brown, Johnson, according to Brown, "stated he wanted to kill white people, especially white officers." In a matter of minutes, Johnson killed five officers and wounded seven others. Two civilians were also wounded.[3]

The officers killed were:

- Senior Corporal Lorne Ahrens, age forty-eight, who had been with the Dallas Police Department for fourteen years, in addition to eleven years' service in California;
- Officer Michael Krol, forty, who had been with the department for nine years, in addition to four years' service in Michigan;
- Sergeant Michael Smith, fifty-five, a former Army Ranger who had been with the department for twenty-seven years;
- Officer Patricio "Patrick" Zamarripa, thirty-two, a former Navy sailor and Iraq War veteran who had been with the department for six years; and
- Officer Brent Thompson, forty-three, a former enlisted Marine who had been with the Dallas Area Rapid Transit (DART) department for nine years and was the first DART officer to be killed in the line of duty since the department's inception in 1989.

This was the deadliest single incident for law-enforcement officers in the United States since the September 11, 2001, terrorist attacks.[4]

In the firefight that ensued, Johnson was hit but was able to make his way to the campus of El Centro College, where he shot and wounded two campus police officers and then found a secure spot from which he fired intermittently at police. A stand-off ensued and negotiations were attempted. Johnson said that he would only talk to black officers. Police Chief David Brown, who is black, then attempted to negotiate Johnson's surrender. Johnson told Brown that he had acted alone. According to Brown, Johnson appeared delusional: "We had negotiated with him for about two hours, and he just basically lied to us, playing games, laughing at us, singing, asking how many did he get and that he wanted to kill some more."[5]

Brown saw no possibility of persuading Johnson to surrender, and Johnson remained armed and dangerous. To end the threat, Brown ordered his officers to use a bomb disposal remote-control robot armed with C-4 explosive, maneuver it against a brick wall, and then detonate it so the wall fragments would kill the shooter swiftly. The plan worked perfectly. The device exploded as intended, instantly killing Johnson.[6]

Black Lives Matter co-founder Patrisse Cullors wasted no time casting Johnson as yet another victim of America's systemic racism against blacks. Ignoring the fact that Johnson was a homicidal maniac, and that the police chief who made the decision to kill him was black, Cullors described the episode this way: "In the early morning hours of July 8, 2016, [Micah Johnson] became the first individual ever to be blown up by local law enforcement. They used a military-grade bomb against Micah Johnson and programmed a robot to deliver it to him. No jury, no trial. No patience like the patience shown the [white] killer who gunned down nine worshippers in Charleston, or moviegoers in Aurora, Colorado."[7]

Despite Black Lives Matter's years of incitements to violence against police, its racist attitudes, and its disregard for the facts, President Obama had invited its leaders to the White House a number of times. When the Black Lives Matter leaders arrived at the White House on one of those occasions, in February 2016, Obama put his arms around them figuratively and said: "They are much better organizers than I was when I was their age, and I am confident that they are going to take America to new heights."[8]

Several months before that, in August 2015, the Democratic National Committee had passed a resolution endorsing the Black Lives Matter movement and its false narrative: "[T]he DNC joins with Americans across the country in affirming 'Black lives matter' and the 'Say her name' efforts to make visible the pain of our fellow and sister Americans as they condemn extrajudicial killings of unarmed African American men, women and children." The Democrats' resolution went on to: (1) claim that the American Dream "is a nightmare for too many young people stripped of their dignity under the vestiges of slavery, Jim Crow, and White Supremacy"; (2) demand the "demilitarization of police, [an end to] racial profiling, criminal justice reform, and investments in young people, families, and communities"; and (3) assert that "without systemic reform this state of [black] unrest jeopardizes the well-being of our democracy and our nation."[9]

In September 2015, Black Lives Matter activists Brittany Packnett, DeRay McKesson, and Johnetta Elzie were invited to the White House to meet again with President Obama, as well as with senior advisor Valerie Jarrett and other administration officials. For Packnett, it was the seventh visit to the Obama White House. Afterward, Packnett told reporters that the president personally supported the Black Lives Matter movement. "He offered us a lot of encouragement with his background as a community organizer, and told us that even incremental changes were progress," she stated. "He didn't want us to get discouraged. He said, 'Keep speaking truth to power.'"[10] Evidently it was the police forces in Dallas, Chicago, Baltimore, and other cities, headed by blacks and under siege from the Left, that constituted the "power" needing to be confronted.

Obama used the occasion of the July 12, 2016, funeral for the slain Dallas policemen to lecture the surviving officers rather than the rioters, schooling them and their grieving family members about the alleged racism of America's police departments: "We also know that centuries of racial discrimination, of slavery, and subjugation, and Jim Crow; they didn't simply vanish with the law against segregation . . . we know that bias remains."[11]

Exactly whose bias? White Americans played a large and historic role in the civil rights struggles that ended segregation, and overwhelmingly white majorities passed the Civil Rights Acts. There is no evidence that the shooter, Micah Johnson, was harassed by white people or suffered at their hands. But there *was* evidence that he was influenced by the slanderous campaigns of Black Lives Matter and similar organizations at war with the police. He was deeply affected by the false, racist narratives promulgated by these organizations and their allies in the press about the police shootings that had occurred over the previous two years.[12]

Underlying the conflict between Black Lives Matter and law enforcement were fundamentally opposed views of human behavior. Law enforcement's mission was to hold individuals accountable for their choices and actions. Black Lives Matter had the opposite point of view, at least as far as blacks were concerned. Someone else was always responsible for whatever happened to them.

Thus, in her memoir *When They Call You a Terrorist*, Patrisse Cullors refuses to hold any of the individuals in her own life responsible for their actions—her mother, who had her first child when she was fifteen and worked three jobs that kept her from home from 6:00 in the morning until 10:00 at night; the man Cullors thought was her father who abandoned the family when she was six years old; her biological father who was a drug dealer and addict. Instead, she regards all the difficult circumstances of her life as the results of structural white racist oppression: "I try continually to talk to my [drug addict] father about structural realities, policies and decisions as being even more decisive in the outcomes of his life than any choice he personally made. I talk about the politics of personal responsibility, how it's mostly a lie meant to keep us from challenging real-world legislative decisions that chart people's paths, that undo people's lives."[13]

It's not hard to see how this rejection of personal accountability could lead to the conclusion that "systemic racism" is the cause of all the miseries and tragedies that afflict black people in trouble with the law, even if the racism is invisible. As Cullors also wrote in her memoir, "It was easy to understand that [the politics of personal responsibility was a lie] when race was a blatant factor, a friend says to me in a political discussion one afternoon. Jim Crow left no questions or confusion. But now that race isn't written into the law, she says, look for the codes. Look for the coded language everywhere, she says. They rewrote the laws, but they didn't rewrite white supremacy. They kept that shit intact, she says."[14]

"Look for the coded language everywhere": these are the words of paranoid delusion. If in fact white supremacy, even after being outlawed, remains a palpable factor in institutions and behaviors, then the "rewritten" civil rights laws provide remedies to punish the perpetrators. Racial discrimination, like murder, is illegal, and there are penalties for practicing it. There are thousands of black judges, prosecutors, lawyers, and officers of the law. Where are the legal cases exposing and punishing the implementers of these supposed "codes"? There are none, because these "codes" and "systemic racism" are political myths invented by the Left to use as weapons against their political opponents.

CHAPTER 6

THE TARGET IS THE LAW

Sandra Bland

S andra Bland was a twenty-eight-year-old Texas school teacher and Black Lives Matter activist who became involved in an acrimonious argument and scuffle with an officer following a traffic stop in Prairie View, Texas, on July 10, 2015. Her erratic behavior and refusal to comply with police orders led to her being arrested and charged with assaulting an officer. Three days later she was found hanged in her jail cell. The hanging was ruled a suicide after security surveillance videos failed to show anyone entering her jail cell in the time frame surrounding her death. A toxicology report found "a remarkably high concentration" of THC (the active ingredient in marijuana) in her system for someone who had been incarcerated for three days. A toxicologist for the county medical examiner's office concluded that Bland "either had access to the drug in jail or she was a consistent user of the drug and her body had accumulated THC to the point that it was slowly releasing it over time."[1]

In March 2015—four months before her death—Bland had posted a video to her Facebook page in which she said she was suffering from "a little bit of depression as well as PTSD" (Post-Traumatic Stress Disorder). Following Bland's death, county officials produced jail intake forms that indicated Bland had previously attempted suicide.[2] One stated that Bland had taken pills in 2015 after having a miscarriage. Another form said that she had attempted suicide even earlier, in 2014. Her family adamantly denied she was suicidal.[3]

It is probable that the drug in Bland's system contributed to the altercation with the officer, who was later reprimanded and then fired for not following protocols when making the arrest. Within three days after Bland's death, some two hundred thousand Internet users had tweeted her name.[4] By July 29, 2015, there had been at least a dozen protest demonstrations across the U.S., including a July 17 event where 150 protesters gathered outside the jail chanting, "No Justice, No Peace."[5] The Democrat Party invited Bland's mother to speak at the 2016 Democrat convention, suggesting that an injustice had been done—though no evidence of foul play was ever produced.[6]

According to the *New York Times*, "The case [of Sandra Bland] was considered a turning point in the Black Lives Matter movement, intensifying outrage over incidents of mistreatment of black people by white officers."[7] The Prairie View City Council voted to change the name of the street on which Bland had been arrested to the Sandra Bland Parkway.[8] HBO made a documentary treating her as a victim of racism titled *Say Her Name: The Life and Death of Sandra Bland*.[9] The Los Angeles Sparks, a professional women's basketball team, viewed the film and, to honor Bland, devoted all their games in the week of August 2–9, 2020, to her memory. Their official website explained, "Bland's story lives on as the Black Lives Matter movement continues to combat racial violence and police brutality."[10]

In September 2017, the Texas Senate passed S.B. 1849, the Sandra Bland Act, which mandated policy changes with regard to suspects with substance abuse or mental health issues.[11] This law requires "de-escalation training" for police officers and "mandates [that] county jails divert people with mental health and substance abuse issues toward treatment, makes it easier for defendants to receive a personal bond if they have a mental illness or intellectual disability, and requires that independent law enforcement agencies investigate jail deaths." [12]

All fine and good, but how do the police whose lives have been demonized by Black Lives Matter and their supporters get their reputations back—and a modicum of justice for themselves?

Although Bland killed herself, a "wrongful death" suit against Waller County, Texas, resulted in a $1.9 million settlement for the Bland family.[13]

Korryn Gaines

Korryn Gaines was a twenty-three-year-old black woman who lived in Randallstown, Maryland. On August 1, 2016, three officers attempted to serve her with a warrant related to a March 10 incident in which she had been stopped for driving without a license plate. Although her five-year-old son was in the car with her, Gaines refused to cooperate or give police her driver's license. She told them that if they put their hands on her, they would have to "murder me" and "carry [me] out in a body bag."[14] She also called the officers "pigs" and urged her child to bite them.[15]

Gaines subsequently failed to show up for her court date related to the March 10 incident.[16] Anticipating that police would eventually come to re-arrest her, she posted on Instagram a picture of herself loading a shotgun, along with a caption thanking her father for teaching her "how to protect myself" and "who to protect myself from."[17] The officers did indeed go to Gaines's house, on August 1, to serve her with a warrant, as well as to serve a separate warrant for her fiancé, who was wanted for assault. Gaines refused to open the door for the police. One of the officers then borrowed a key from the apartment rental office of the complex where Gaines lived and unlocked the door, but found it to be chain-locked as well. At that point, the officer kicked in the door and entered the apartment, only to find Gaines pointing a shotgun at him. As in the car stand-off of March 10, her five-year-old son was with her.[18]

The officer retreated from the apartment, and thus began a standoff that lasted more than five hours. Gaines was livestreaming on Facebook during the standoff, and the people following along were encouraging her to defy the police with all necessary violence. Law enforcement worked with Facebook to get Gaines's account shut down while they tried to negotiate with her.[19] At one point several hours into the standoff, Gaines told the officers: "If you don't leave, I'm going to kill you."[20]

It is difficult for an outsider to understand what was in this woman's mind. Eventually one of the officers saw Gaines raising her shotgun to a shooting position. He fired one round in her direction. Gaines fired back two rounds. Officers then responded with three shots, hitting Gaines and killing her. Her five-year-old was wounded in the arm, though it was unclear whether he was struck by a bullet from an officer's or his mother's gun.[21]

In 2018, an all-female jury decided that the fatal shot was a violation of Gaines' civil rights and awarded the Gaines family $38 million in damages.[22] The verdict was overturned in February

2019 when a judge ruled the officers had acted "in an objectively reasonable" way.[23] The case became a focus of Black Lives Matter protests in Baltimore, New York, Portland, Phoenix, and numerous other cities across the country.[24]

Terence Crutcher

Shortly after 7:30 on the evening of September 16, 2016, Tulsa police received a 911 call reporting an abandoned SUV with open doors and engine running. The vehicle had been left on the double yellow lines in the middle of a street, where it was blocking traffic. The caller said the driver who had abandoned the vehicle seemed to be impaired and was claiming that the car was going to blow up. Police came to the scene and observed Terence Crutcher walking towards his vehicle. He had his hands up as he was approaching the SUV while several officers walked toward him. One officer said Crutcher was sweating heavily and smelled of PCP chemicals. PCP is a drug commonly called "Angel Dust" and is known for its mind-altering effects.[25] At a certain point, however, Crutcher placed his hands on the vehicle and then moved to reach into the vehicle despite being told to stop. One officer tased Crutcher, and another, a female, shot him.[26]

Crutcher died later that evening in a local hospital.[27] No weapon was recovered from the scene of the shooting, either on Crutcher's person or in his vehicle.[28] Autopsy results released by the Oklahoma State Medical Examiner indicated that at the time of the shooting Crutcher had "acute phencyclidine (PCP) intoxication."[29] The report further indicated that Crutcher had tested positive for tenocyclidine (TCP), a psychostimulant and hallucinogen that is even more potent than PCP.[30]

The district attorney charged the female officer who shot Crutcher with manslaughter, but a jury acquitted her because

Crutcher, despite being ordered to stop, had reached into his car, provoking the fatal shot.[31]

Black Lives Matter protested Crutcher's death and held a "die-in" in his memory. The event was organized by the Revolutionary Baddies, a student organization at the University of Oklahoma led by black women and created to protest not only Crutcher's death, but all police violence. They chanted, "No Justice, No Peace, No Racist Police"—although there was no indication that race had played any part in the incident, whose main contributing factor was drugs.[32]

On September 16, 2020—the fourth anniversary of Crutcher's death—religious leaders from Tulsa's churches and temples gathered outside a midtown Unitarian Church to commemorate Crutcher and to endorse the message that "Black Lives Matter." Rabbi Dan Kaiman of Congregation B'Nai Emunah said, "We . . . see a need, the need, right now to hold up this phrase, 'Black Lives Matter,' and to reclaim it for our lives, for all our lives, here in Tulsa. We do not view this phrase, 'Black Lives Matter,' as political speech but as a declaration of something that should be obvious but is not."[33]

Keith Lamont Scott

On September 20, 2016, two plainclothes officers in Charlotte, North Carolina, were sitting in an unmarked police vehicle in the parking lot of the apartment complex where a forty-three-year-old African American named Keith Lamont Scott resided. The officers were preparing to serve an arrest warrant on Scott, who had a long record of criminal violence, including felony assault with a deadly weapon with intent to kill and aggravated assault with a deadly weapon in a case where Scott had fired two gunshots at police officers.[34]

Eventually, Scott pulled up beside the officers in a white SUV and proceeded to roll a marijuana blunt. The officers then saw Scott holding a gun as he exited the vehicle. The *Washington Post* describes what happened next: "Due to the combination of illegal drugs and the gun Mr. Scott had in his possession, [the] officers decided to take enforcement action for public safety concerns. [They] departed the immediate area to outfit themselves with marked duty vests and equipment that would clearly identify them as police officers. Upon returning, the officers again witnessed Mr. Scott [in his vehicle] in possession of a gun. The officers immediately identified themselves as police officers and gave clear, loud, and repeated verbal commands to drop the gun. Mr. Scott refused to follow the officers' repeated verbal commands."[35]

A third uniformed officer soon arrived to assist those already at the scene, and he used his baton to smash the front passenger window of Scott's car in an effort to make an arrest. But Scott exited the vehicle with his firearm and ignored the officers' repeated, loud verbal demands that he drop the weapon. One of the officers, an African American named Brentley Vinson, perceived Scott's actions as an imminent physical threat to himself and his fellow officers and shot and killed him.[36]

Scott's relatives said he didn't have a gun, but according to the district attorney, "all the credible evidence" led to the conclusion that Scott was armed. He said Scott's DNA was on the grip of a gun found at the scene. After a two-month investigation, the DA determined that Vinson's action had been justified.[37]

In short, Scott was killed resisting arrest by a black police officer. Nonetheless, protesters took to the streets of Charlotte. In one of the protests, a civilian was shot and at least four police officers were injured. The governor of North Carolina, Pat

McCrory, declared a state of emergency and said he would deploy the state National Guard and Highway Patrol to Charlotte.[38]

The protesters were demanding that Brentley Vinson, a black police officer, be prosecuted because "Black Lives Matter." Apparently not law-abiding black lives.

Alfred Olango

Alfred Olango was a thirty-eight-year-old black man who had come to the U.S. as a teenage refugee from Uganda in 1991. Over the years, he had committed such offenses as: taking a person's car without consent, burglarizing a home, selling crack cocaine, driving with a fraudulent license plate, possessing 185 grams of marijuana, illegally carrying a loaded 9mm semi-automatic pistol in his car, and driving under the influence.[39]

On September 27, 2016, the day of Olango's death in El Cajon, California, his sister noticed that he was behaving strangely. She called the police three times, asking urgently for some intervention that might help her brother. When two uniformed police officers, Josh McDaniel and Richard Gonsalves, subsequently approached Olango, he retreated into a corner formed by a fence and an unoccupied parked truck. There he paced back and forth, refusing to comply with instructions to remove one of his hands from his pocket. He then withdrew his hand and rapidly drew an object—which was later discovered to be a vape pen—and extended it in two hands towards the police in a shooting stance. This caused the officers, who thought the object was a gun, to simultaneously taser and shoot him.[40] The fatal gunshot was fired by Officer Gonsalves. Olango was rushed to a local hospital, where he died.

Although mental illness rather than race was the central fact of this tragic incident, and the officer who shot Olango was

Hispanic, the Black Lives Matter protesters who gathered to chant "No Justice, No Peace" found a way to put race at the center. "You don't shoot someone who is having a mental breakdown," said one protester. "Dylann Roof was given a bulletproof vest after he shot nine black people in a church, but this man gets shot for what? For having a mental crisis?"[41]

Dylann Roof—a young white supremacist who had perpetrated a mass shooting at a church with a black congregation in Charleston, South Carolina, fifteen months earlier—was definitely a mental case, but he surrendered quietly. That, not the fact that he was white, was the reason he was not shot by police.

In January of 2017, San Diego County District Attorney Bonnie Dumanis ruled that the shooting of Olango was legally justified. "The law recognizes police officers are often forced to make split-second decisions in circumstances that are tense, uncertain, and rapidly evolving," she said during a news conference at the downtown Hall of Justice.[42] In a similar vein, former Florida police chief Chuck Drago commented, "An officer doesn't have enough time to wait to determine if that's a gun in his hand. If a person is pointing something at an officer, and he believes it's a gun, and it is a gun, and that officer doesn't have his gun out, that officer will lose that gunfight."[43]

In July 2019, a jury in a civil trial unanimously found that El Cajon police officer Richard Gonsalves was not negligent when he shot and killed Olango.[44]

The killing of Alfred Olango sparked weeks of Black Lives Matter protests on the streets of El Cajon, where demonstrators blocked traffic, vandalized automobiles, threw projectiles at police officers, and shouted the slogans "Black Lives Matter" and "No Justice, No Peace, No Racist Police!"[45]

As all these cases show, the rationales for Black Lives Matter—systemic racism and police brutality—have nothing to do with the actual cases they are protesting. The real target of the Black Lives Matter insurrectionists is law enforcement itself.

Jocques Clemmons

Jocques Clemmons, thirty-one, was fatally shot in Nashville, Tennessee, on February 10, 2017, after a traffic stop. When Clemmons exited his vehicle, he began a confrontation with the police officer, Joshua Lippert. During their altercation, Clemmons's 357 Magnum fell to the ground. When Clemmons picked up the weapon, the officer shot him, once in the abdomen, once in the hip, and twice in the back as Clemmons tried to flee.[46]

Investigations by the Davidson County District Attorney, the Tennessee Bureau of Investigation, and the Nashville Police Department exonerated the officer, and no charges were filed against him, but Black Lives Matter and a local group calling itself the Justice for Jocques Coalition protested. Donning black outfits and carrying a symbolic coffin, they demonstrated in the predominantly white neighborhood of Hillsboro Village. The protesters also displayed signs accusing Mayor Megan Barry of having influenced the district attorney's decision not to prosecute Officer Lippert, and they deposited the coffin outside her house.[47]

The Justice for Jocques Coalition claimed that the failure to indict Officer Lippert was evidence of racism in the Metropolitan Nashville Police Department.[48] NAACP Nashville chapter president Ludye Wallace said it was a "sad day for Nashville," adding, "It's more likely you going to get sent to jail for kicking a dog than shooting a black man down in his back while he's running."[49] Another organization, Gideon's Army, claimed that Officer Lippert had long been more inclined to stop black drivers than white drivers. The Nashville chapter of Black Lives Matter demanded Lippert's dismissal, stating, "Today Nashville, the liberal stronghold of Tennessee, joins the other numerous localities that fail to find fault or even recognize criminality in police officers when their violence and brutality takes the lives of black people."[50]

As in so many of these cases, the fact that Clemmons was armed, resisting arrest, and refusing to comply with the commands of an officer of the law, was deemed irrelevant by the protesters, who only seemed able to see things in black and white.

CHAPTER 7

THE SUMMER OF
GEORGE FLOYD

Ahmaud Arbery

On February 23, 2020, Ahmaud Marquez Arbery, a twenty-five-year-old black man, was killed near the city of Brunswick in Glynn County, Georgia. Arbery had been pursued by three white residents who were armed and suspected him of being a burglar running from the scene of a crime. Most news reports stated that Arbery was merely out for an afternoon jog when he was accosted by the white men. One of those men, Travis McMichael, attempted to perform a "citizen's arrest" of Arbery, who resisted and was fatally shot in the scuffle.[1]

Like the killing of Trayvon Martin, this was not a case of police misconduct, although McMichael's father, a retired police officer, seems to have directed the pursuit and arrest attempt. As in the killing of Trayvon Martin, this was a case of unauthorized vigilantes taking the law—or what they thought was the law—into their own hands. They were criminally charged by the authorities, and deservedly so. Each of the three was indicted on nine counts: malice murder, four counts of felony murder, two counts of aggravated assault, false imprisonment, and criminal attempt to commit false imprisonment.[2]

Even so, there is no evidence to suggest that the three white men were motivated by racial animus. The case was far more complex than most news reports and the charge of "malice murder" indicated. In April 2021—more than a year after Arbery's death—newly released court documents based on police reports, videos, and eyewitness accounts indicated that he had a history of running away from various locations after committing criminal trespass, or theft, or both. "In 2019 and 2020," said one such document, "local convenience store witness interviews reveal [that] Mr. Arbery became known as 'The Jogger' for his repeated conduct and behavior of running up, stretching in front, and then entering several convenience stores where he would grab items and run out before he got caught." Another court document stated, "In 2020, witness cell phone video reveals Mr. Arbery was confronted at a convenience store by employees about his theft conduct and behavior. Mr. Arbery, concerned about his thefts, chose to fight a man who worked on location at the adjacent truck stop who tried to confront him about it."[3]

Ironically, the Arbery case shows why law enforcement by professional police forces that impose guidelines on their officers and provide them with training designed to minimize the risks to subjects' life and limb is important. Far from serving the black community, the "defund the police" and "abolish the police" agenda of Black Lives Matter would increase exponentially the incidence of lawless vigilantism—and the vulnerability of law-abiding black citizens.

Daniel Prude

On March 22, 2020, Daniel Prude, a forty-one-year-old African American from Chicago, traveled to Rochester, New York, to visit his older brother, Joe. After he arrived at his destination, Daniel began to display a variety of bizarre behaviors—for example, jumping headfirst down a flight of stairs and running naked through the streets of Rochester. This was the result of his having ingested the hallucinogen phencyclidine (PCP). Alarmed by these actions, his brother called for emergency medical services, and they transported Daniel Prude to Strong Memorial Hospital.

The hospital released Prude that same night, but within a few hours he was again behaving erratically, fleeing his brother's house at approximately 3:00 a.m., and running into the street, where he shed most of his clothes despite the cold, snowy weather. The brother called emergency services once again.[4] A truck driver also called 911 to report that the naked Prude was attempting to break into a car and claiming that he was infected with the coronavirus.[5]

When the Rochester police arrived at the scene, Prude was walking, naked and bleeding, down Jefferson Avenue in southwest Rochester.[6] One of the officers pointed a taser at Prude and instructed him to get on the ground and place his hands behind his back. After the sixth time the officer issued that instruction, Prude complied.[7] But within a few minutes, he became agitated and began spitting at the officers. At that point one officer placed a spit hood over Prude's head, and Prude yelled, "Give me that gun, give me that gun!"[8]

During this effort to restrain Prude, the officers held him facedown on the pavement for two minutes and fifteen seconds, repeatedly telling him to "stop spitting" and "calm down."[9] He stopped breathing and was given CPR on the scene, then hospitalized and placed on life support.[10] Seven days later, after being taken off life support, he died. The Monroe County medical examiner determined that Prude's death had been caused by "complications from asphyxia in the setting of physical restraint."[11] The autopsy report showed that factors contributing to his death were "excited delirium" and "acute intoxication" by the PCP.[12] According to the spokesman for the coroner's office, Prude also "had a history of a brain injury previous to this incident that was giving him some lack of oxygen and blood flow to his brain."[13] Medical officials further noted that Prude had a clinical history of agitation, combative behavior, suicidal ideation, auditory hallucinations, and paranoia.[14]

Given the facts in this case, the attempt by Black Lives Matter and its supporters to lay blame for the death of Prude at the feet of the Rochester police and call it the result of police racism, is a travesty all too familiar from other Black Lives Matter indictments. The immediate results of the campaign to weaponize the death of Daniel Prude were four days of violent riots and arsons in Rochester by angry mobs who had to be contained by tear gas and pepper pellets.[15] Black Lives Matter played a prominent role in these disturbances.[16]

In the face of these attacks, Rochester's mayor, Lovely Warren, who is black, distanced herself from her police force, claiming that its chief, an African American named La'Ron Singletary, had not informed her fully of the circumstances of the Prude incident. She also made the following concession to the anti-police mob: "We had a human being in need of help, in need of compassion. In that moment, we had an opportunity to protect him, to keep him warm, to bring him to safety, to begin the process of healing him and lifting him up. We have to own the fact that in the moment we did not do that."[17] To foster this compassion, she promised far-reaching police reforms.

The mayor's failure to support her police force led directly to the resignation of Chief Singletary and his entire command staff. The chief, who had served on the force for twenty years, wrote in his resignation letter of September 8, 2020, "As a man of integrity, I will not sit idly by while outside entities attempt to destroy my character. The events over the past week are an attempt to destroy my character and integrity."[18] Six days later, Mayor Warren formally fired Chief Singletary. A month after that, the mayor was indicted for "felony campaign finance fraud."[19]

In addition to depriving Rochester of its chief law-enforcement officer, who was black, the Daniel Prude episode led to widespread property damage, various injuries and arrests, a dramatic weakening of public support for Rochester's "thin blue line," and thus a weakening of protection for Rochester's citizens, both black and white.

Breonna Taylor

Breonna Taylor was a twenty-six-year-old emergency-room medical technician.[20] Her death on March 13, 2020, at the hands of Louisville, Kentucky, police officers became a marquee case for the Black Lives Matter movement. One of the most celebrated figures in American life, Oprah Winfrey, took up Breonna's cause and commissioned twenty-six giant billboards across Louisville, each one representing a year of the young woman's short life. The billboards featured Taylor's image and the words: "Demand that the police involved in killing Breonna Taylor be arrested and charged."[21] A website called UntilFreedom.com, describing itself as "an intersectional social justice organization rooted in the leadership of diverse people of color to address systemic and racial injustice," joined Oprah in carrying out the initiative.[22]

In addition to the billboards, Oprah put Taylor's photo on the cover of her bestselling monthly magazine *O*, which had featured only Oprah herself on the cover of every previous issue since its inception twenty years before.[23] For this special issue, Oprah wrote a moving editorial tribute to Breonna, which contained this account of the incident that ended her life: "We know how Breonna died. March 13. Louisville police storming into her apartment in the middle of the night. No uniforms. No 'This is the police!' Terrifying Breonna and her boyfriend, Kenneth Walker."[24]

Well, not exactly. Along with other sources available, the CNN account to which Oprah provided a link tells a more complicated story.[25] The raid on Taylor's apartment was one of five taking place that night, all on locations that were suspected distribution centers for a crack cocaine and fentanyl dealer named Jamarcus Glover.[26] Glover had been Taylor's boyfriend two years before, and Taylor had kept in touch with him and been involved in his criminal activities. According to the *New York Times*, after they first became a couple in 2016, Taylor agreed to rent a car for Glover and ended up being interviewed in a murder investigation when a man—the brother of one of Glover's co-conspirators—was found shot to death behind the steering wheel of the car, eight bullet wounds in his body. Drugs were also found.[27]

Drawing on the *Times* investigation, former federal prosecutor Andrew C. McCarthy summarized the continuing relationship between Glover and Taylor: "In the years that followed, Glover was repeatedly arrested on drug charges, and Taylor arranged bail for him and one of his confederates on at least two occasions. Weeks before the fateful March 2020 raid, when Glover was in custody after yet another arrest, they were recorded exchanging intimacies on the phone. After that, police surveillance established that Glover continued to make regular trips to Taylor's apartment, and Taylor herself was seen outside a house that investigators say was part of the drug trafficking operations."[28] Moreover, Glover had called Taylor from jail dozens of times since their breakup.[29]

Taylor's car was seen in the vicinity of a "trap house" associated with Glover several times and was photographed in front of that location in mid-February 2020. Trap houses are used for storing drugs. Police also had evidence that Glover used Taylor's address to receive parcels sent by mail. He was seen leaving her apartment carrying a package directly to a trap house in mid-January.[30]

All these facts led police investigators to think Taylor's apartment might have been part of Glover's drug network.[31] As it turned out, there were no drugs in Taylor's home at the time of her death, but this knowledge came tragically too late.

In the hours after he was arrested in a separate raid on March 13, Jamarcus Glover made repeated phone calls from the jail in which he was being held. In those calls, which were recorded by police, he informed a man that he had exchanged text messages with the now deceased Breonna Taylor the day before about items that he had arranged to have shipped to her apartment.[32] Glover also told the man that Taylor had been "hanging onto my money," while he tried to come up with enough cash to post bond.[33] Glover actually detailed the amounts of money involved, saying: "Tell Cuz, Bre [Breonna] got down like $15 (grand), she had the $8 (grand) I gave her the other day, and she picked up another $6 (grand)." And when he spoke to the mother of his child in a police-recorded phone call that same day, Glover said, "This is what you got to understand, don't take it wrong, but Bre been handling all my money, she been handling my money. . . . She been handling sh*t for me and Cuz, it ain't just me."[34]

Breonna Taylor's life ended in violence and blood. At 12:30 on the morning of March 13, three officers appeared with a "no-knock" warrant at the door of Taylor's apartment.[35] Their supervisors had told them to knock anyway and announce that they were police, and they later claimed to have done so, although Taylor's new boyfriend, Kenneth Walker, who was also in the apartment, claims not to have heard them.[36] Whatever the case, the officers, having elicited no response to their verbal announcements, used a battering ram to break down the door.[37]

Roused either by the officers' voices or by the sound of the breaking door, Taylor and Walker got out of bed and went to the entrance hall. Walker was carrying a weapon that was legally registered.[38] He fired at the intruders in the darkness, hitting Sergeant Jonathan Mattingly in the leg.[39] This triggered a hail of bullets from the officers, six of which hit Taylor and killed her.[40] Contrary to the Black Lives Matter accusations, social media posts, and media reports claiming that Taylor had been shot "in her sleep," she actually died on the floor of her hallway, where she had followed Walker.[41]

If this was a racial killing, why not shoot the boyfriend, who was armed and also black, instead of the unarmed woman? It is more likely that the boyfriend jumped out of the line of fire after pulling the trigger, but Breonna did not.

Contrary to the cries of the lynch mob seeking to destroy the lives of police officers doing their job, Taylor was not killed because she was black. Nor was she innocent in the creation of the situation that led to her death. The police were at her house because she was an accomplice to a known drug dealer. One can understand how the heart can lead perfectly decent people to be drawn into indecent situations, but Breonna Taylor had serious warnings—the dead body in the car she had rented for her boyfriend should have been sufficient—that she should cut off contact with a dangerous criminal.

Anyone looking at this incident with hindsight can identify multiple parts of the search plan and pre-raid investigation that might have been faulty and could have been modified to prevent the tragedy that occurred. What is difficult for an impartial observer to see is how any of the officers, obviously fearful for their lives and acting in the dark, could be held criminally accountable for the death of Breonna Taylor.

Amidst the public uproar over the incident, in June of 2020 the Louisville city council passed "Breonna's Law," legislation that banned no-knock warrants and required officers serving search warrants to wear body cameras.[42]

Many entertainers, celebrities, athletes, and political figures became outspoken champions of the effort to win "justice" for Breonna Taylor and her family. During a post-game interview on June 23, 2020, NBA basketball star LeBron James demanded that the police officers involved in Taylor's death be arrested.[43] In the Women's National Basketball Association, numerous players dedicated their season to Taylor and wore her name on the backs of their jerseys.[44] On June 5, Democrat Senator Cory Booker tweeted that Taylor's "life was tragically taken by police and we will not stop marching for justice until it's served for her and her family."[45] That same day, Senator Kamala Harris lamented that Taylor's life had been "horrifically" snuffed out, and she urged Americans to "keep up the calls for justice."[46]

Thanks to Black Lives Matter's successful propaganda campaign and the efforts of celebrities like Oprah Winfrey, despite the fact that Breonna Taylor was a criminal accomplice to a major drug dealer and was killed while resisting arrest, her family received a $12 million settlement from the City of Louisville on September 15, 2020.[47]

Tony McDade

Tony McDade was a thirty-eight-year-old black transgender man who lived in Tallahassee, Florida.[48] He had a serious criminal record involving armed robbery and battery, and he was in a relationship with a white neighbor named Jennifer Jackson, the mother of a twenty-one-year-old black youth named Malik Jackson.[49] McDade pistol-whipped Jennifer Jackson in her home on May 25, 2020, and then returned to her home the next day to verbally abuse her.[50] While McDade was in Jackson's house, he texted the following message to an acquaintance: "I'm sitting in the kitchen looking at this motherfucker wanting to off her for playing [with] my mind. The bitch and her fam have to pay in blood."[51]

After admonishing McDade for his volcanic behavior, Jennifer Jackson's son, Malik, went outside to his SUV in hopes that McDade's temper might slowly burn out. But McDade followed him, circling the vehicle with a gun and knife while he cursed at Jackson and threatened to kill him. In response, Malik Jackson told McDade: "I don't fight women—go home—and I don't play with guns and knives." When, shortly thereafter, other members of Jackson's family tried to intervene, McDade challenged them to a fight. A violent street brawl ensued, in which several people beat McDade badly.[52]

Two days later, early on May 27, McDade went live on Facebook to recount the altercation and to vow revenge. "It took five of you to kick and punch and have me on the ground in a fetal position," he said in the video. "And I came out looking the same way I was before I went in that fetal position. But y'all know what, y'all ain't gone look the same when them bullets touch your dome. And I'm posting this live. Warning comes before destruction. And I'm telling you five m—f— that you're going to die."[53]

In the same video, McDade also said, "Just know before I kill myself through a shootout, because that's what's going to happen, because I'm gonna pull it out and you know these officers nowadays they see a gun they just gonna shoot. So that's what I'm pushing for, because I don't want to be here on earth dealing with the government."[54]

McDade stabbed twenty-one-year-old Malik Jackson to death that same day.[55] When police approached McDade as a suspect in the killing, he was armed with a gun. In the confrontation that ensued, McDade pointed his weapon at an officer, and the officer shot and killed him.[56] This occurred just two days after the death of George Floyd in Minneapolis.

Intersectionality theory, which Black Lives Matter leaders claim to be guided by, views black transgendered people as "oppressed" on multiple levels. This made Tony McDade a special cause for BLM activists—more important than the black youth he had murdered. A week of Black Lives Matter protests followed McDade's death, featuring signs like "Protect Black Trans People." It was more evidence of the ideological deceits of Black Lives Matter leaders and their followers.

On June 20, 2020, hundreds of demonstrators gathered at Public Square Park in Nashville to commemorate McDade's death and support "Black *Trans* Lives Matter."[57] "Justice for Tony McDade," a Change.org petition directed at BLM activists, describes McDade as "a transgender black man who got killed by police in Tallahassee." As of March 2021, it had gathered nearly 1.7 million signatures.[58]

Rayshard Brooks

Rayshard Brooks was a twenty-seven-year-old black man who was fatally shot by a police officer in Atlanta, Georgia, on June 12, 2020. Shortly after 10:40 p.m., Officers Garrett Rolfe and Devin Brosnan responded to a complaint that Brooks was asleep in a car which was blocking a Wendy's restaurant drive-through lane.[59] A sobriety test found him to have alcohol levels above the legal limit.[60] At the time of this incident, Brooks had recently been released from jail and was on probation for four crimes, including cruelty to his own children. If charged with a DUI, he would have faced the prospect of going back to jail.[61] Notably, Brooks had a long history of criminal violence starting when he was fourteen, including such offenses as obstruction of an officer, false imprisonment, cruelty to children, felony cruelty, possession of a weapon, receiving stolen property, theft, false imprisonment, and various forms of battery.[62]

When the officers initially approached him, Brooks engaged in a civil conversation at first. But when they tried to arrest him, Brooks instigated a violent fight, during which he wrestled Brosnan's taser gun away from him, fought his way free, punched one of the officers, fired the stolen taser, and then began to flee on foot. At that moment Officer Rolfe fired his taser at Brooks, but it failed to bring Brooks down.[63] Rolfe then proceeded to chase Brooks, who at one point hurriedly turned and fired the stolen taser in the officer's general direction. The officer drew his handgun and shot Brooks twice in the back as he turned to run.[64] Brooks was then rushed to a nearby hospital, where he died after undergoing surgery.[65]

Thousands of people took to the streets to demand that Officer Rolfe be criminally charged. Riots ensued, and arsonists set fire to the Wendy's where Brooks had been blocking the drive-through lane.[66] Rioting continued intermittently for weeks, at one point resulting in the death of an eight-year-old black girl, who was shot by protesters during one of their demonstrations.[67]

Under this type of extreme public pressure, the police chief of Atlanta resigned, Officer Rolfe was fired, and on June 17 a politically motivated prosecutor arraigned Rolfe for murder.[68] The prosecutor, Fulton County District Attorney Paul Howard, announced eleven charges against Rolfe: felony murder, five counts of aggravated assault, four police oath violations, and damage to property.[69] Howard explained that Brooks, who had been "peacefully sleeping in his car," had been generally "cooperative" and "never presented himself as a threat" during the first forty-one-plus minutes of his interaction with the officers.[70] At the time, District Attorney Howard was already under investigation for having used a nonprofit to funnel nearly $200,000 of city funds into his personal bank account.[71]

Leading Democrats were quick to cast blame on the police. Former Georgia Democrat gubernatorial candidate Stacey Abrams complained that "a man was murdered because he was asleep in a drive-through, and we know that this is not an isolated occurrence."[72] "The decision to shoot him in the back," added Abrams, "was one made out of maybe impatience or frustration or panic, but it was not one that justifies deadly force. It was murder."[73]

In a similar vein, Atlanta Mayor Keisha Lance Bottoms said, "I do not believe that this was a justified use of deadly force and have called for the immediate termination of the officer."[74]

On June 15, thousands of people took to the streets for a Black Lives Matter rally in Atlanta to protest Brooks's death.[75]

Beginning the day after charges against Rolfe were announced, Atlanta police officers called in sick for their shifts, staging a "blue flu" protest.[76] In the four days from June 17 to June 20, 2020, about one hundred seventy officers called in sick, and officers in three of the city's six police zones did not respond to calls.[77] On the evening of June 19, every police officer failed to report for duty in Zone Five, leaving only the three supervisors on active duty.[78] Atlanta's acting police chief, Rodney Bryant, said that the department had "to shift resources to insure proper coverage" because of police absenteeism.[79] Total arrests citywide dropped by 71 percent during the sickout.[80] Mayor Bottoms said the sickout was a reaction to two weeks of strife during which eight Atlanta Police Department officers were criminally charged in two separate incidents, sinking morale in the department "ten-fold."[81]

Jacob Blake

In the late afternoon of August 23, 2020, police officers in Kenosha, Wisconsin, responded to a 911 call from a woman claiming that her ex-boyfriend, Jacob Blake, a twenty-nine-year-old father of six, had violated a restraining order by coming to her home, taking her car keys, and refusing to give them back.[82] The restraining order was related to a previous incident in which Blake was alleged to have committed felony sexual assault against her. In that incident, she claimed, Blake had entered her apartment at about 6:00 a.m., walked into her bedroom while she was sleeping with one of her small children in the bed, and told her, "I want my shit." The woman testified that Blake had used his finger to sexually assault her, sniffing it afterward and saying, "Smells like you've been with other men."[83] There was a warrant out for Blake's arrest related to this incident.

Such behavior was in keeping with Blake's volatile personality and volcanic temperament. The woman alleged, for instance, that Blake sexually assaulted her approximately twice a year, generally after drinking heavily.[84] In September 2015, Blake had been charged with resisting an officer and multiple gun-related offenses after allegedly pulling a handgun in a Racine bar, then leaving and being arrested during a combative traffic stop.[85]

When the Kenosha police went to look for Blake on August 23, 2020, they were aware of the sexual assault charge and the outstanding warrant for his arrest.[86] Upon arriving at the scene, they found Blake in his car with three of his young sons in the back seat.[87] Instead of submitting to the arrest, Blake engaged in a violent fight with the officers, two of whom tased him unsuccessfully.[88] Unable to restrain Blake, the officers then drew their firearms and ordered him to stop. Disregarding their commands, Blake walked purposefully around the vehicle, opened the driver's-side door, and lunged downward. Fearing that Blake might be reaching for a weapon—a knife was later found on the floor of the car—one officer shouted, "Drop the knife! Drop the knife!"[89]

When Blake failed to comply, the officer fired seven shots at him, hitting him four times in the back. Blake was rushed to a Milwaukee hospital, but his wounds left him paralyzed from the waist down.[90]

From his hospital bed, the delinquent Jacob Blake pleaded not guilty to the sexual assault charges against him. Blake was represented by attorney Benjamin Crump, who had also represented the families of Trayvon Martin, Michael Brown, George Floyd, and other members of the Black Lives Matter martyrs list.[91] Crump called for the arrest of the officer who shot Blake, and for the firing of the others who were involved.

The damage that ensued because of Black Lives Matter protests over Blake's arrest dwarfed everything involved in his criminal acts.[92] In riots that lasted a week, the small city of Kenosha suffered millions of dollars in damages from wanton acts of violence, which included arsonists' deliberately burning a number of businesses, a local courthouse, and a parking lot full of automobiles. During the riots, lawlessness prevailed as the streets were patrolled by armed protesters and counter-protesters. Two people were killed in gun incidents.[93] In one horrific attack, a Wisconsin police officer was knocked out by a brick thrown at his head, prompting the angry mob to cheer, "He just got bricked! He just got bricked. . . . Fuck the police!"[94] Kenosha County declared a "state of emergency" while the Democrat mayor and governor remained reluctant to authorize a sufficient law-enforcement presence to discourage the rioters. One hundred twenty-five Wisconsin National Guardsmen were eventually deployed.[95] The violence only stopped completely when President Trump sent in federal agents to restore peace.[96]

Wisconsin Governor Tony Evers's support for the rioters played a significant role in enabling the violence. Evers issued a statement denouncing the excessive use of force by police and invoking the names on the Black Lives Matter martyrs list. Evers said, "While we do not have all of the details yet, what we know for certain is that [Jacob Blake] is not the first black man or person to have been shot or injured or mercilessly killed at the hands of individuals in law enforcement in our state or our country."[97] Evers called Wisconsin state lawmakers to a special session in order to pass legislation addressing police brutality.

Multiple professional sports teams went on strike to support the protests, refusing to play their scheduled games. The NBA's Milwaukee Bucks boycotted their August 26 first-round playoff game against the Orlando Magic. That same day, the National Basketball Association and the National Basketball Players Association announced that all games for the day would be postponed. This led to other boycotts from other American sports leagues, including the Women's National Basketball Association, Major League Baseball, the National Hockey League, and Major League Soccer.[98]

In September, presidential candidate Joe Biden traveled to Kenosha to give moral support to Blake and his family. "What I came away with," Biden said of the Blake family, "was the overwhelming sense of resilience and optimism that they have about the kind of response they're getting."[99]

CHAPTER 8

THE EVIDENCE ON POLICE SHOOTINGS, RACE, AND CRIME

L ooking at the lists of the individuals that Black Lives Matter supporters claim were victims of wanton "police brutality" and "systemic racism," one fact stands out. With the exception of Trayvon Martin and Ahmaud Arbery, who were not killed by police officers, and Tamir Rice, Philando Castile, and Akai Gurley, who were victims of tragic circumstances, the twenty-one other "victims" were either criminals resisting arrest or so high on illegal substances as to be unconscious of the fact that resisting arrest was a crime. In other words, the racial charges at the heart of Black Lives Matter's indictment of America have no basis in fact, and its leaders are the cynical perpetrators of deadly lies.

The actual facts in these cases bring to mind comedian Chris Rock's classic video, "How Not to Get Your Ass Kicked by the Police."[1] The video's advice: *"Obey the law."* Every one of the celebrated victims of alleged police malice—Eric Garner, Michael Brown, George Floyd—would be alive today (or, in

Jacob Blake's case, whole today)—if he had obeyed the law and followed the commands of the arresting officers.

Here's another thought: As is clear from the preceding profiles, not one cop accused by Black Lives Matter can reasonably be described as having committed a cold-blooded murder, that is, a premeditated killing without extenuating circumstances. Nor can they be described as white racists determined to kill innocent blacks. By contrast, every cop killed by an individual inspired by Black Lives Matter's reckless claims—the five Dallas officers, the three in Louisiana, the two executed in their squad car in New York—was murdered in cold blood, and murdered because he was a cop and not black.

The casualties of the scorched-earth war unleashed by Black Lives Matter dwarf the total casualties of all the alleged racial injustices the organization has protested. The atrocities instigated and inspired by BLM encompass scores of innocent wounded and dead, both black and white. The crippling of police departments has led to out-of-control rates of murder and violent crime that affect, ironically and first of all, America's most vulnerable black communities. Livelihoods lost, community centers destroyed, and massive flight of tax-paying citizens make the prospect of recovery a distant one—particularly if the Democrat Party continues its support for criminality and destruction. Surveying these disasters, one could reasonably conclude that, thanks to Black Lives Matter campaigns to abolish police departments, advances in both race relations and protections for urban black communities have been set back fifty years.

Black Critics of Black Lives Matter

James Craig was Detroit's chief of police from 2013 to 2021. Detroit is 79 percent black, making it the American city with the highest concentration of black citizens. Craig himself is black. During the riots that erupted across the country Detroit remained calm. This was due to Craig's determination to stop lawlessness and prevent violence from being visited on the residents of his city.[2] Craig's resistance was made possible because, in contrast to the way things played out in other Democrat cities, such as Minneapolis, Portland, Kenosha, Seattle, and New York, Craig's defense of law and order was backed by his Democrat mayor.

Craig and his officers were confronted by a Black Lives Matter organization called "Detroit Will Breathe." Their message to these protesters was conveyed in a statement by Deputy Police Chief Todd Bettison, who is black: "To 'Detroit Will Breathe': You're not welcome. Go."[3] The message was delivered to a crowd of rioters who were occupying a downtown stretch of Detroit's Woodward Avenue around midnight. The police on the scene ordered them to disperse or face arrest.

As the *Detroit Free Press* reported, "[T]he protesters instead stood their ground and hurled insults at police. Police Chief James Craig said officers waited more than an hour and issued at least eight warnings before advancing on the gathering and making arrests. 'We have been very patient,' he said. The police then proceeded to make forty-four arrests and disperse the crowd."[4]

Police Chief Craig told reporters, "I've had a chance over the last several weeks to see many Detroiters. They are sick and tired of the disruption in their neighborhoods—our neighborhoods. Defunding the police is not something they want here in Detroit. In fact, what I'm constantly told is, 'Chief you need to hire more police officers. And we want you to have the equipment necessary to effectively do your job.'"[5]

By all indications, that is what black communities across America want. They are the principal victims of black criminals, and, unlike the celebrity millionaires and billionaires who promote and fund Black Lives Matter, they live in the eye of the urban storm created by baseless attacks on their law-enforcement protectors.

But what of the claims of systemic racism in the criminal justice system and an open hunting season on black Americans? Examination of the facts of the cases making up the Black Lives Matter martyrs list shows just how far from reality BLM's claims are. The national crime statistics that Black Lives Matter won't talk about further confirm that the idea of a police war on blacks is a malicious racial fiction.

The Statistics on Crimes and Race

According to Black Lives Matter propaganda, black Americans live under a "white supremacist system" in which they are routinely targeted for "extrajudicial killings . . . by police and vigilantes."[6] This is how Black Lives Matter defines itself on its website: "Black Lives Matter is an ideological and political intervention in a world where Black lives are systematically and intentionally targeted for demise."[7]

There is no evidence to support this claim. None. A 2001 Bureau of Justice Statistics report, for instance, examined incidents where police used deadly force to kill criminal suspects in 1998. It found that blacks were actually *under*represented in such killings—that is, African Americans were 40 percent of all persons arrested for violent crimes, but just 35 percent of felons killed by police.[8] If an individual is a violent criminal, one would expect that individual to be more likely to be involved in armed encounters with the law and perhaps to be killed in the process. That is particularly true if the individual resists arrest.

A decade later, a 2011 Bureau of Justice Statistics study showed that of all suspects killed by police from 2003 to 2009, 41.7 percent were white and 31.7 percent were black. During this period blacks accounted for 38.5 percent of all arrests for violent crimes—that is, the type of crime most likely to trigger potentially deadly confrontation with police.[9] These numbers do not in any way suggest a lack of restraint by police in their dealings with black suspects. On the contrary, they strongly suggest *exactly the opposite.*

Recently, the evidence that police do not shoot and kill African Americans in disproportionately high numbers has only grown stronger. In 2017, blacks were arrested for 37.5 percent of all violent felonies, but were just 24.7 percent of people killed by police. The corresponding figures in 2018 were 37.4 percent and 26.4 percent. And in 2019, the numbers were 36.4 percent and 29.3 percent.[10]

If we look at the raw numbers of fatal shootings by police in recent years, we find that more whites than blacks are killed by police every single year, without exception. In some years, whites account for twice as many victims of police shootings as blacks.[11] In 2017, for example, 457 whites and 223 blacks were killed by police officers in the line of duty. In 2018, the corresponding figures were 399 whites and 209 blacks. In 2019, the totals were 370 whites and 235 blacks. And in 2020, the numbers were 432 whites and 226 blacks.[12] While blacks make up only about 13 percent of the U.S. population, they commit nearly 40 percent of all violent crimes and more than half of all murders, statistics which would predict a significantly higher rate of police shootings of blacks than we actually see.[13]

The central accusations made by Black Lives Matter radicals and widely accepted by a credulous public are that the police killings of blacks are racially motivated and that unarmed blacks are 4 times as likely as whites to be killed by cops.[14] These accusations are false. In 2019, police in the line of duty shot and killed just 14 unarmed blacks and 25 unarmed whites. This figure for unarmed black shooting victims was 63 percent lower than the corresponding figure from 2015, the year in which the *Washington Post* initially began tabulating such statistics.[15] And, as noted earlier, John R. Lott and Carlisle E. Moody found in 2017 that "black officers killed unarmed black suspects at a significantly higher rate than white or Hispanic officers."[16]

The aforementioned 2001 Bureau of Justice Statistics report found that in nearly two-thirds of all justifiable homicides by police during 1976–98, the officer's race and the suspect's race *were the same*. When a black officer killed a suspect, that suspect was black 81 percent of the time. When a white officer killed a suspect, that suspect was white 63 percent of the time. The rate at which black officers killed black felons was more than double the rate at which white officers killed black felons.[17] In short, the notion that white police officers are somehow predisposed to indulge their alleged racism in the form of gunslinging against black targets has been a demonstrable lie for decades.

Thus it was no surprise in 2018 when a research team led by Charles Menifield, Dean of the School of Public Affairs and Administration at Rutgers University, found that "white police officers actually kill black and other minority suspects at lower rates than we would expect if killings were randomly distributed among officers of all races," while "nonwhite officers kill both black and Latino suspects at significantly higher rates than white officers."[18]

Roland Fryer is an African American economist at Harvard. In a 2018 study titled "An Empirical Analysis of Racial Differences in Police Use of Force," Fryer concluded that Houston police officers were nearly 24 percent less likely to shoot black suspects than white suspects. In studies of three Texas cities, six Florida counties, and the city of Los Angeles, Fryer found that: (a) officers were 46.6 percent less likely to discharge their weapon without first being attacked if the suspect was black than if the suspect was white; (b) black and white individuals shot by police were equally likely to have been armed at the time of the shootings; (c) white officers were no more likely to shoot unarmed blacks than unarmed whites; (d) black officers were more likely to shoot unarmed whites than unarmed blacks; and (e) black officers were more likely than white officers to shoot unarmed whites.[19]

A 2019 study published in *Proceedings of the National Academy of Sciences* shows that white officers are no more likely than black or Hispanic officers to shoot black civilians. "In fact," writes Manhattan Institute scholar Heather Mac Donald, the study found that "if there is a bias in police shootings after crime rates are taken into account, it is against white civilians." The authors compiled a database of 917 officer-involved fatal shootings in 2015 and found that 55 percent of the victims were white, 27 percent were black, and 19 percent were Hispanic.[20]

In Mac Donald's words, "The per capita rate of officers being feloniously killed is 45 times higher than the rate at which unarmed black males are killed by cops. And an officer's chance of getting killed by a *black* assailant is 18.5 times higher than the chance of an unarmed black getting killed by a cop" [emphasis in the original].[21] Naturally, this makes officers jittery when they face armed individuals who are black, and that fear can lead to fateful misjudgments in their reactions.

What's true for cops is true for the population at large: There is no racist "open season" on blacks. Quite the reverse. In 2012 and 2013, blacks in the U.S. committed an annual average of

560,600 violent crimes (excluding homicide) against whites, while whites committed a yearly average of 99,403 violent crimes against blacks. In other words, blacks were the attackers in about 85 percent of violent crimes between blacks and whites, while whites were the attackers in 15 percent.[22]

If we factor into the equation the relative sizes of America's white and black populations, we find that, statistically, any given black person in 2012–13 was about 27 times more likely to attack a white person than any given white person was likely to attack a black person.[23] In more recent years, the disproportionate prevalence of black-on-white crime has only gotten worse. According to the Bureau of Justice Statistics, in 2018 there were 593,598 interracial violent victimizations (excluding homicide) between blacks and whites in the United States. Blacks committed 537,204 of those interracial felonies, or 90.4 percent, while whites committed 56,394 of them, or about 9.5 percent.[24]

The facts show that blacks are far more likely to commit racist crimes against whites than vice versa. According to Heather Mac Donald, based on Justice Department data, in 2018 blacks were overrepresented among the perpetrators of offenses classified as "hate crimes" by 50 percent—while whites were underrepresented by 24 percent.[25]

The deliberate misrepresentations of police attitudes and actions spread by the leaders of Black Lives Matter are on dramatic display in Black Lives Matter promoter Jamil Smith's seminal *Rolling Stone* history of the organization, written with the cooperation of BLM's three co-founders. In his article, Smith comments on the CBS documentary series *Cops*, which the network terminated during the George Floyd protests of 2020. The show filmed officers in all parts of the country on their routine runs dealing with domestic disputes, traffic stops, robberies, drug cases, and the like. The series showcased the positive side of police work—naturally, as that would have been a condition of its arrangements with the various police departments. If there were instances of actual police brutality, one would not expect them to be shown. As a result, watching the show, one could not help being impressed by the self-discipline and restraint of the officers dealing with human beings often at their worst. Yet this is how Smith described the cancellation of the series: "Paramount is canceling the squalid *Cops,* squashing television's cockroach after more than three decades of glorifying police brutality and dehumanizing victims of it."[26]

But then, lying about police conduct is the very lifeblood of Black Lives Matter.

PART THREE

BLACK LIVES MATTER, INC.

CHAPTER 9

WHAT KIND OF MOVEMENT IS THIS?

If Black Lives Matter were a civil rights organization, one would reasonably expect its patron figure to be Martin Luther King Jr., and its aspiration to be King's vision of a race-free America where individuals are judged on their merits and not by their skin color. Instead, the revered figure and inspirational icon for Black Lives Matter activists is a designated terrorist and convicted cop killer: Assata Shakur.

In the 1970s Shakur was a member of the Black Liberation Army, a group that robbed banks and murdered police officers to achieve a Marxist revolution.[1] Shakur is still wanted for the 1973 murder of Werner Foerster, a New Jersey state trooper who stopped her for a broken tail light on her car, whereupon she pulled out a gun and shot him. The thirty-four-year-old officer and Vietnam vet was lying wounded on the pavement pleading for his life when Shakur walked over and finished him off, execution-style. Foerster left behind a wife and two young children. Shakur was convicted of the murder but escaped from prison in 1979 with the help of left-wing terrorists, including Susan Rosenberg. With the help of Rosenberg and others, Shakur fled to Communist Cuba, where she has lived as a fugitive for nearly forty years.[2] After being pardoned by Bill Clinton, Rosenberg went on to become board vice chair of Thousand Currents, the left-wing nonprofit organization that served as Black Lives Matter's fiscal sponsor from 2016 to 2020.[3]

The dedication page of Patrisse Cullors's memoir, *When They Call You a Terrorist*, contains these lines written by Shakur, which allude to the most famous incitement from Marx's *Communist Manifesto*:

> It is our duty to fight for our freedom.
> It is our duty to win.
> We must love each other and support each other.
> We have nothing to lose but our chains.

These four sentences are chanted in unison at every meeting and rally of Black Lives Matter, accompanied by a tribute to the revolutionary mother.[4]

After fleeing the United States, Shakur was given sanctuary courtesy of Cuba's sadistic dictator Fidel Castro, who is also a Black Lives Matter icon. When Castro died in 2016, the leaders of Black Lives Matter released a statement titled, "Lessons from Fidel: Black Lives Matter and the Transition of *El Comandante*."[5] The opening paragraph reads: "We are feeling many things as we awaken to a world without Fidel Castro. There is an overwhelming sense of loss, complicated by fear and anxiety. Although no leader is without their flaws, we must push back against the rhetoric of the right and come to the defense of El Comandante. And there are lessons that we must revisit and heed as we pick up the mantle in changing our world, as we aspire to build a world rooted in a vision of freedom and the peace that only comes with justice. It is the lessons that we take from Fidel."

The statement continues: "As a Black network committed to transformation, we are particularly grateful to Fidel for holding Mama Assata Shakur, who continues to inspire us. We are thankful that he provided a home for Brother Michael Finney, Ralph Goodwin, and Charles Hill [fugitive cop killers and airplane hijackers], asylum to Brother Huey P. Newton [former Black Panther Minister of Defense, drug addict, rapist, and killer], and sanctuary for so many other Black revolutionaries who were being persecuted by the American government during the Black Power era."

The statement closes with this pledge: "As Fidel ascends to the realm of the ancestors, we summon his guidance, strength, and power as we recommit ourselves to the struggle for universal freedom. Fidel Vive!"

Black Lives Matter, Black Racists, and Anti-Semites

If Black Lives Matter were a civil rights organization, one might reasonably expect its leaders to condemn or at least distance themselves from well-known race haters like Louis Farrakhan and Al Sharpton. But Black Lives Matter leaders embrace both of those demagogues. Black Lives Matter joined Farrakhan's "Justice or Else" march in Washington on October 10, 2015, and chose Sharpton to give the eulogy at George Floyd's memorial service, where he accused white America of having pressed its knee on black America's neck for 401 years.[6]

In March 2018, Republican Congressman Todd Rokita introduced a resolution calling on the House of Representatives to condemn Farrakhan for a recent speech in which he had ranted, "White folks are going down. And Satan is going down. And Farrakhan, by God's grace, has pulled the cover off of that Satanic Jew and I'm here to say your time is up, your world is through." A demonstration was organized to oppose the congressional resolution condemning Farrakhan. Black Lives Matter was part of the protests, along with the New Black Panther Party and Al Sharpton's National Action Network.[7]

If Black Lives Matter were a civil rights organization, one would expect it to respect all ethnic groups, particularly Jews, who have made major contributions to the movement for civil rights and are the targets of far more "hate crimes" than any other religious group.[8] But over the Shavuot festival on May 30, 2020, the Los Angeles chapter of Black Lives Matter carried out a violent pogrom in Fairfax, a Los Angeles community largely populated by orthodox Jews. The activists not only vandalized five synagogues and three Jewish schools but also looted most of the Jewish businesses along the main avenue, while chanting "Fuck the police and kill the Jews."[9]

Melina Abdullah, the leader of Black Lives Matter in Los Angeles, helped organize the pogrom. She explained the attack on the Jews this way: "We've been very deliberate in saying that the violence and pain and hurt that's experienced on a daily basis by black folks at the hands of a repressive system should also be visited upon, to a degree, those who think that they can just retreat to white affluence."[10]

In August 2015, Black Lives Matter co-founder Patrisse Cullors was one of more than a thousand black activists to sign a statement proclaiming "solidarity with the Palestinian struggle and commitment to the liberation of Palestine's land and people."[11] Among the prominent signatories of the petition were communist apparatchik and Lenin Peace Prize winner Angela Davis, radical Hamas supporter Cornel West, and convicted cop-killer Mumia Abu-Jamal.

For the record, the Palestinian "struggle" is a seventy-year genocidal aggression against Israel by Islamic terrorists whose stated goal is the obliteration of the Jewish state and the ethnic cleansing of its Jews. The statement signed by Cullors repeated the lies of Hamas and the terrorist Palestine Liberation Organization: that Israel "occupies" a country called "Palestine" and is guilty of colonialism. Since the Jews have lived continuously in the West Bank for three thousand years and there has never been a Palestinian state, the claim is absurd on its face. Since Israel's nearly two million Arab citizens have the same civil rights as Jews, and more rights than the Arabs of any Arab state, the accusation that Israel is an "apartheid" state is equally mendacious and malicious. The statement Cullors signed also "wholeheartedly endors[ed]" the Boycott, Divestment, and Sanctions (BDS) movement, a Hamas-inspired campaign to strangle the Jewish nation. The BDS movement has been denounced as anti-Semitic by Democrats such as Hillary Clinton, as well as by the Trump administration.[12]

At a July 1, 2020, demonstration in Washington, D.C.—an event that was billed as a rally supporting the Palestinian Authority's "Day of Rage" against Israel—protesters repeatedly claimed that the Palestinian movement is "intrinsically tied to Black Lives Matter." Chants alternated between "Black Lives Matter!" and "Palestinian Lives Matter!" Another popular chant was "Israel, we know you, you murder children, too."[13]

That same day, at a separate Black Lives Matter rally in Brooklyn involving several hundred people, its organizer, Nerdeen Kiswani, said, "The land that Israel exists on is still stolen.

The 1948 lands are still stolen—Jaffa, Haifa, Tel Aviv . . . was stolen." This is just more malevolent slander. Israel was created under the United Nations' auspices on land that had previously been part of the Turkish empire for four hundred years. The Turks are neither Arab nor Palestinian. In case the genocidal intentions of the Black Lives Matter demonstrators were missed, Kiswani said, "We don't want to go just back to our homes in Gaza and the West Bank. We want all of it. We don't want a fake Palestinian state that they give us while Israel still exists."[14]

Black Lives Matter's Assault on the Nuclear Family

In a document titled "What We Believe," Black Lives Matter laid out a number of major principles for which it stands. Among the more noteworthy was this: "We disrupt the Western-prescribed nuclear family structure requirement by supporting each other as extended families and 'villages' that collectively care for one another, especially our children, to the degree that mothers, parents, and children are comfortable."[15]

This is a profoundly significant facet of the Black Lives Matter agenda because by rejecting the nuclear family it rejects the single value that, if it were to be embraced, would offer black Americans the tools they most need in order to carve out for themselves a prosperous and fulfilling life. At present, the traditional two-parent family is a statistical rarity in the black community. Roughly 70 percent of black babies today are born to unmarried mothers in fatherless homes.[16] This fact has a host of catastrophic implications for those youngsters.

For example, father-absent families—black and white alike—generally occupy the bottom rung of our society's economic ladder.[17] Unwed mothers, regardless of their race, are much more likely to live in poverty than the average American.[18] As Heritage

Foundation research fellow Robert Rector has explained: "Out-of-wedlock childbearing and single parenthood are the principal causes of child poverty and welfare dependence in the U.S. . . . Children born out-of-wedlock to never-married women are poor 50 percent of the time. By contrast children born within a marriage which remains intact are poor 7 percent of the time. Thus, the absence of marriage increases the frequency of child poverty 700 percent."[19]

Children in single-parent households are raised not only with economic but also social and psychological disadvantages. For instance, they are much more likely than children from intact families to be abused or neglected, to struggle academically, to drop out of school, to have behavioral problems, to experience emotional disorders, to have a weak sense of right and wrong, and to be unable to delay gratification of their violent or sexual impulses. Conversely, they are much likelier to be sexually active as teens, to conceive children out-of-wedlock when they are teens or young adults, and to be on welfare when they reach adulthood.[20]

In addition, growing up without a father is a far better forecaster of a boy's future criminality than either race or poverty.[21] Regardless of race, a large percentage of all rapists, adolescent murderers, young people in state reform institutions, and long-term adult prison inmates were raised in fatherless homes.[22] As Rector notes, "Illegitimacy is a major factor in America's crime problem. Lack of married parents, rather than race or poverty, is the principal factor in the crime rate."[23]

And yet, in spite of all this, Black Lives Matter holds the nuclear family in contempt. Why? Because Marxist ideology demands it. As California State University professor Richard Weikart has explained, Marx and Engels "usually wrote about the destruction, dissolution, and abolition of the family" as a natural outgrowth of "the abolition of private property and the introduction of socialism."[24] The goal is to replace all voluntary associations and non-governmental authorities with an all-powerful state.

In late September 2020, in a propaganda effort to defuse the growing criticism it had been receiving for its hostility to the nuclear family—Black Lives Matter quietly, and without explanation, removed from its website all references to its anti-family creed.[25]

Black Lives Matter: A Revolutionary Insurrection

Abolishing the nuclear family and supporting Islamic imperialism are not civil rights causes, and Black Lives Matter is not a civil rights organization. It is a revolutionary criminal movement whose goals are openly Marxist and communist. "We are trained Marxists," Patrisse Cullors has proudly proclaimed, "We actually do have an ideological frame. Myself and Alicia [Garza], in particular, are trained organizers; we are trained Marxists. We are super-versed on, sort of, ideological theories. And I think what we really try to do is build a movement that could be utilized by many, many black folks."[26] Similarly, Alicia Garza describes herself as a "queer social justice activist and Marxist."[27] The fact that Marx was a well-known racist and anti-Semite who once called the socialist Ferdinand LaSalle a "Jewish nigger" seems not to have registered on either woman's radar.[28]

With approximately forty chapters of its own in the U.S. and abroad, Black Lives Matter is also the face of a coalition of radical groups that include the violent militia Antifa and numerous fronts for the Freedom Road Socialist Organization.[29] Freedom Road is a Marxist-Leninist coalition whose name is taken from the title of a famous novel by the American communist author Howard Fast. Other revolutionary groups in the coalition include the Advancement Project, the Movement Strategy Center, the Black Left Unity Network, Black Workers for Justice, the Grassroots Global Justice Alliance, Causa Justa/Just Cause, Hands Up United, Intelligent Mischief, the Organization for Black Struggle, the Revolutionary Student Coordinating Committee, Showing Up for Racial Justice, Strategic Concepts in Organizing and Policy Education, and the Labor/Community Strategy Center.

The Labor/Community Strategy Center is headed by former Weather Underground terrorist Eric Mann. Mann was Patrisse Cullors's ideological mentor.[30]

Indoctrinating American Schoolchildren

Despite its embrace of black racists like Sharpton and Farrakhan, its support for Islamic terrorists abroad and violent anarchists at home, its criminal attacks on police, and its lack of respect for anyone who doesn't agree with its extremist agenda, Black Lives Matter has been able to engage in a successful campaign, courtesy of the left-wing teachers' unions, to indoctrinate K–12 schoolchildren to advance its revolutionary goals.

In October 2016, teachers in Seattle organized a "Black Lives Matter at School Day." When the National Education Association subsequently adopted a resolution endorsing that program, "Black Lives Matter at School Day" was expanded into a "Black Lives Matter at School National Week of Action." That "Week of Action" was scheduled to be held annually in early February as part of Black History Month activities. In 2018, school districts in more than twenty major cities incorporated "Black Lives Matter at School Week" into their curricula.[31]

A key resource for these indoctrination sessions is a textbook titled *Teaching for Black Lives,* which opens with this sentence: "Black students' minds and bodies are under attack." It features stories on subjects such as "the continuing police murders of black people," whose "lives are meaningless to the American Empire." Its essays include "Rethinking Islamophobia: Combating Bigotry by Raising the Voices of Black Muslims"; "Plotting Inequalities, Building Resistance"; and "Racial Justice Is Not a Choice: White Supremacy, High-Stakes Testing, and the Punishment of Black and Brown Students."[32]

Even very young schoolchildren are targeted with Black Lives Matter gender propaganda in classrooms. An early childhood teacher's guide emphasizes the importance of using "age-appropriate language" to help youngsters understand various concepts that are central to Black Lives Matter's philosophy. For example, teachers are urged to cultivate "transgender affirming" students by telling them, "Everybody has the right to choose their own gender by listening to their own heart and mind. Everyone gets to choose if they are a girl or a boy or both or neither or something else, and no one else gets to choose for them." And to promote what the guide calls "the disruption of Western nuclear family dynamics and a return to the 'collective village' that takes care of each other," teachers are instructed to say, "There are lots of different kinds of families; what makes a family is that it's people who take care of each other; those people might be related, or maybe they choose to be family together and to take care of each other. Sometimes, when it's lots of families together, it can be called a village."[33]

By 2020, "Black Lives Matter at School Week" was being observed by thousands of educators in public school districts across the United States.[34]

Black Lives Matter's Corporate Funders

Despite its anti-capitalist, anti-family, anti-wealth, anti-Semitic, anti-white and anti-American agenda, Black Lives Matter has received hundreds of millions of dollars from Democrat donors like George Soros, from America's biggest businesses including Amazon, Gatorade, Microsoft, Nabisco, and Dropbox, from its wealthiest philanthropies such as the Ford and Kellogg Foundations, and from high-profile billionaires and centi-millionaires like Michael Jordan and LeBron James.[35]

From 2016 to 2020, Black Lives Matter was a fiscally sponsored project of Thousand Currents, a California-based left-wing 501(c)(3) nonprofit organization. As Robert Stilson of the Capital Research Center explains, a "fiscal sponsorship" arrangement means that an organization, like Black Lives Matter, "does not have its own IRS tax-exempt status but is operating as a 'project' of an organization that does." In 2018 and 2019, respectively, Thousand Currents funneled $2,622,017 and $3,354,654 in donor-restricted assets to Black Lives Matter.[36]

The convicted terrorist Susan Rosenberg has served as a vice chair of the seven-member board of Thousand Currents. In the 1970s and '80s Rosenberg was a member of the May 19th Communist Organization, which murdered a Brink's guard and two police officers during a 1981 armored-car robbery in Rockland County, New York. One of the policemen, Waverly Brown, was the first black ever hired by the police force in the town of Nyack. The killings left nine young children without fathers. Rosenberg was also wanted in connection with the 1979 prison escape of Assata Shakur. When Rosenberg was arrested in 1984, she was in possession of 740 pounds of dynamite (the May 19th group had previously bombed the U.S. Capitol and other sites).[37] Convicted at trial, she was sentenced to fifty-eight years in prison for her crimes but served only sixteen because she was pardoned by President Clinton in 2001. On receiving her sentence, a defiant Rosenberg urged her comrades to join her in "rededicat[ing] ourselves to our revolutionary principles, to our commitment to continue to fight for the defeat of U.S. imperialism."[38]

Thousand Currents is only one avenue by which donors have been able to support Black Lives Matter and its agenda. Since July 2020, BLM's new fiscal sponsor has been the Tides Center, a longtime funder of far-left causes and organizations.[39] Moreover, when people click the "Donate" button on the Black Lives Matter website, they are redirected to a subdomain called Act-Blue Charities. ActBlue describes itself as "a powerful online fundraising platform for Democratic candidates up and down the ballot, progressive organizations, and nonprofits." As the site further explains, ActBlue "is available to Democratic candidates and committees, progressive organizations, and nonprofits that share our values for no cost besides a 3.95 percent processing fee on donations." As of May 21, 2020, ActBlue had already given $119 million to the presidential campaign of Democrat Joe Biden—plus another $187 million to the Bernie Sanders presidential campaign and $93 million to the Elizabeth Warren Presidential Exploratory Committee.[40]

Black Lives Matter is already such a powerful force in the Democrat Party that Democrat governors and mayors across the country stood back and encouraged the 2020 Black Lives Matter riots—the largest and most destructive civil disorders in U.S. history—refusing to deploy the necessary law enforcement to end the violence and rejecting all federal offers of help until it was too late. At least twenty-five people, mostly black, lost their lives during the insurrections.[41]

Perpetuating Destructive Myths

Each year, Democrat leaders observe the anniversary of Michael Brown's death by repeating the falsehoods that led to the 2014 race riots in Ferguson, Missouri. On August 9, 2020, presidential candidate Joe Biden tweeted, "It's been six years since Michael Brown's life was taken in Ferguson—reigniting a movement. We must continue the work of tackling systemic racism and reforming policing."[42]

The year before, Biden's soon-to-be Vice President, Kamala Harris, said, "Michael Brown's murder forever changed Ferguson and America. His tragic death sparked a desperately needed conversation and a nationwide movement. We must fight for stronger accountability and racial equity in our justice system."[43] Thirty-five minutes later, Senator Elizabeth Warren tweeted, "5 years ago Michael Brown was murdered by a white police officer in Ferguson, Missouri. Michael was unarmed yet he was shot 6 times. I stand with activists and organizers who continue the fight for justice for Michael. We must confront systemic racism and police violence head on."[44]

All three made these statements knowing that the Obama-Biden Justice Department had conducted a thorough investigation of the shooting of Michael Brown, had refuted these claims, and had found his killing justified. Five black and two biracial eyewitnesses had testified to police, the FBI, and a grand jury that the much larger Brown was charging the officer despite being shot multiple times and ordered to stop.[45] That three Democrat leaders would knowingly lie about this shooting with the intention of attacking police and supporting a violent criminal movement that played fast and loose with the truth, should be deeply disturbing to every American, black and white.

Black Lives Matter is supported by the largest and most powerful coalition in American political history. What has made it so powerful is its central idea, which is embraced by the Democrat Party, the partisan media, and America's academic and cultural elites: *White America enslaved black America four hundred years ago and has kept its knee firmly on black people's necks ever since.* These are transparent but frequently repeated racial lies. America is not four hundred years old; it was black Africans who enslaved blacks and sold them to Europeans at slave auctions; white America abolished slavery at the cost of 350,000 mainly white lives and created the most equal and inclusive society on the face of the earth. Yet this sinister and powerful anti-American, anti-white meme of the Left has now become a currency of America's public culture and is spread by America's major educational and cultural institutions and its corporate elites.

Apple, for example, one of the world's largest companies, has announced a program "to challenge systemic racism," which it calls, "Taking Action on Racial Equity and Justice."[46] The program defines racism in these words: "Racism is the marginalization or oppression of people of color based on a socially constructed racial hierarchy that privileges white people."[47]

In other words, racism is specific to white people who oppress "people of color"—90 percent of the world's population. Blacks can't be racist. The fact that America's black communities are the most prosperous, free, and empowered black communities in the world—thanks in large part to its white majority—is invisible to the Apple creed. The fact that the Chinese have enslaved 2 million Uighur Muslims and are busily harvesting their body parts is also off Apple's radar screen, since the business Apple does with China's genocidal regime is too lucrative to pass up. Apple is not about to give up the billions of dollars it makes off the slave labor that China's racist regime provides to make its products. The fact remains that the largest racist organization in America is a black church called the Nation of Islam, whose leader preaches that whites are morally and mentally inferior to black people and need to be exterminated.[48] But this is also off the radar for Apple's social justice executives and the "woke" chorus generally.

Democrats who support and enable Black Lives Matter revolutionaries are constantly warning about "existential threats" to America such as "climate change." But the movement that has coalesced behind the meme that America is a white supremacist nation conducting a genocidal war against blacks and all "people of color" is a far more palpable existential menace.

Black Lives Matter is run by violent Marxists and anti-white racists whose mentality is that of a lynch mob with no regard for facts or the law. Their goals are the abolition of police, the dissolution of the family, and the dismantling of America's constitutional order. Their oft proclaimed concern for justice is non-existent. The resources this organization has already accumulated and the political power it has amassed are disturbing, but there is some hope in the fact that these assets were achieved by a fraudulent public-relations campaign, which cannot be sustained once the facts are known. To the vast majority of white Americans, black lives do matter. To the vast majority of black Americans, as national polls attest, the lives of America's law-enforcement officers matter, too.[49]

Do Black People Matter to Black Lives Matter?

Americans, black and white, are already asking, "Are black lives really a concern to the leaders and activists of Black Lives

Matter?" The decimation of urban police forces as a result of Black Lives Matter attacks has led to dramatic spikes in murders and other violent crimes committed against black citizens. A 2021 study of crime rates in 34 American cities concluded, "Homicide rates were higher during every month of 2020 relative to rates from the previous year." The report summarizing the findings of this study described the 30 percent surge as "a large and troubling increase that has no modern precedent."[50] In cities like Chicago and Atlanta, the surge was well over 50 percent.[51] As Manhattan Institute scholar Heather Mac Donald wrote in January 2021, "The year 2020 likely saw the largest percentage increase in homicides in American history. Murder was up nearly 37 percent in a sample of 57 large and medium-size cities. Based on preliminary estimates, at least 2,000 more Americans, most of them black, were killed in 2020 than in 2019. . . . The local murder increases in 2020 were startling: 95 percent in Milwaukee, 78 percent in Louisville, Ky., 74 percent in Seattle, 72 percent in Minneapolis, 62 percent in New Orleans, and 58 percent in Atlanta."[52]

The blood of every victim of this surge in homicides can be attributed to the mendacious claims of Black Lives Matter, the incitements to violence by its activists, and the baseless attacks on police that accompanied them.

So far, the seven-thousand-plus annual murders of blacks by other blacks haven't attracted the slightest attention or concern from Black Lives Matter leaders and activists. So far, there have been no Black Lives Matter community projects to benefit disadvantaged black communities. Where are the hundreds of millions of dollars Black Lives Matter has collected being spent? There is no Black Lives Matter campaign to provide scholarships for inner-city black children so their parents can get them out of failed public schools, which year-in and year-out fail to provide them with the skills they need in order to survive and flourish. In what way, then, do black lives actually matter to these "anti-racist" social justice warriors? In fact, they don't. What matters to them is the anti-American revolution they are advancing and the fantasy world they think they will achieve by destroying the most equitable, inclusive, tolerant, and free society that has ever existed.

CHAPTER 10

WHOSE FUTURE?

During the 2016 presidential campaign, candidate Donald Trump made a direct appeal to black America: "Look how much African American communities have suffered under Democratic control," he began. "To those I say the following: 'What do you have to lose by trying something new like Trump? . . . You're living in poverty. Your schools are no good. You have no jobs. Fifty-eight percent of your youth is unemployed. What the hell do you have to lose?" Democrats responded by stigmatizing him as a "white supremacist" and "racist."[1]

Eight months after Trump's election, the *Los Angeles Times* interviewed Black Lives Matter co-founder Patrisse Cullors. The interviewer asked her if Black Lives Matter would be open to a conversation with the new president. Cullors responded, "We wouldn't as a movement take a seat at the table with Trump, because we wouldn't have done that with Hitler. Trump is literally the epitome of evil, all the evils of this country—be it racism, capitalism, sexism, homophobia."[2]

On November 3, 2020, Joe Biden defeated Trump, having run arguably the most dishonest election campaign on record. Trump had kept the promises he had made four years earlier to win public support. In 2020, Biden made promises he did not keep. Aside from maliciously blaming Trump for the coronavirus pandemic, Biden's campaign featured three major themes: that he was a moderate, that he was a healer, and that he would be the president of all Americans—those who voted for him and those who did not.[3] Within hours of entering the Oval Office, Biden exposed these promises as brazen deceptions. In his first week as president, despite having won both houses of Congress, Biden issued nearly forty executive actions—a practice that during the campaign he had told ABC newsman George Stephanopoulos was a hallmark of dictators (like Donald Trump).[4] The sole unifying theme of Biden's executive orders was the undoing of measures that Donald Trump had put in place and thus poking sticks in the eyes of the 74 million Americans who had voted for Trump, regardless of the consequences.

Black Lives Matter's Agenda, and Biden's

Four days after Biden's election, Patrisse Cullors sent a letter bearing a request to the new president and vice president in the name of Black Lives Matter. In the letter she claimed, "Black people won this election. Alongside Black-led organizations around the nation, Black Lives Matter invested heavily in this election. 'Vote and Organize' became our motto, and our electoral justice efforts reached more than 60 million voters. We want something for our vote. We want to be heard and our agenda to be prioritized."[5]

Cullors then described that agenda:

Black people can neither afford to live through the vitriol of a Trump-like Presidency, nor through the indifference of a Democrat-controlled government that refuses to wrestle with its most egregious and damnable shame. President-Elect Biden and Vice-President-Elect Harris: both of you discussed addressing *systemic racism* as central to your election campaigns. The best way to ensure that you remedy past missteps and work towards a more just future for Black people—and by extension all people—is to take your direction from Black grassroots organizers that have been engaged in this work for decades, with a legacy that spans back to the first arrival of enslaved Africans [emphasis in the original].[6]

Biden's response was direct and affirmative. On the very day he took possession of the presidency—January 20, 2021—Biden issued Executive Order 13985, which he introduced with these words: ". . . a historic movement for justice has highlighted the unbearable human costs of systemic racism." Then he announced, "It is therefore the policy of my Administration that the Federal Government should pursue a comprehensive approach to advancing equity for all, including people of color and others who have been historically underserved, marginalized, and adversely affected by persistent poverty and inequality."[7]

President Biden's embrace of a violent Marxist organization openly at war with America, went virtually unnoticed. The same was true of the malicious assumptions of the order and the claim he made days later when he said: "The fact is that systemic racism touches every facet of American life."[8]

Far from being a "fact," Biden's assertion was a monstrous lie. It was tantamount to the claim that America was a "white supremacist" country, and that black Americans—who have held the highest offices in the land, are a dominant force in America's popular culture, and are the main recipients of government racial privileges—are "marginalized" and "underserved." The federal government has provided nearly $30 *trillion* in welfare payments and other poverty handouts in the last fifty-odd years, of which all poor blacks have been legitimate recipients, along with members of other racial groups.[9]

Moreover, only 20 percent of black Americans live below the poverty line.[10] Given the fact that 80 percent of black Americans are productive citizens who are not poor, the claim that "systemic racism" or "marginalization" by race, or being "underserved"— rather than individual choices and failures—is to blame for black poverty is a politically useful and socially pernicious myth. The handouts and other government programs that the Democrats support in the name of fighting racial inequality only forge dependency and provide disincentives that discourage people from taking responsibility for their condition and from making the adjustments and commitments necessary for success.

For the political Left, which seeks to erase individuals and their responsibilities in favor of their racial, gender, and ethnic identities and victim entitlements, "systemic racism" is an indispensable slander against a nation that has actually outlawed racial and gender discrimination and provided generous subsidies to those who have fallen behind. The false charge of "systemic racism" is a convenient cover for the Left's inability to identify actual racists directly responsible for inequalities in American life. It is unable to do so because America's culture is so egalitarian and *anti*-racist that the numbers of actual racists (outside the Left itself) are so few, and their impact so inconsequential, that they don't amount to a national problem.

Undaunted by this reality, the Left invokes "systemic racism" to describe every statistical disparity in social and economic outcomes. When Americans are viewed as individuals responsible for their decisions it is apparent that disparities in income, education, and even susceptibility to diseases flow principally from poor choices made by individuals who fail to take advantage of the opportunities available to them in a country where discrimination by race or gender is illegal. If America were a white supremacist nation where systemic racism in fact touched every facet of the nation's life, the majority of black Americans would not be prospering, as they currently are, in the working, middle, and upper classes.[11]

In a white supremacist society, whites would be the richest racial group. But they are not. Asian Americans from the Indian subcontinent are "people of color" and experience prejudice at the hands of individual bigots. But they are also the richest ethno-racial group in America, with median household incomes of $120,000 per year, twice the national average. More pointedly, this is $44,000 more than white households' median income.[12] For Asian American households as a whole—including Japanese, Pacific Islanders, and others, the median annual income is $98,174—far higher than the $76,057 median for white households.[13] How is this possible if America is a white supremacist nation and systemic racism causes adverse consequences for "people of color"? It is not possible, and the president's claim that income disparities are caused by racial injustice is a lie.

Even if he is not familiar with these facts, a fair-minded observer can see that the president's statement that "systemic racism touches every facet of American life" is a lie because the Civil Rights Act of 1964 outlawed systemic racism more than fifty years ago. According to the description by the U.S. Department of Labor, "The Civil Rights Act of 1964 prohibits discrimination on the basis of race, color, religion, sex, or national origin. Provisions of this civil rights act forbade discrimination on the basis of sex as well as race in hiring, promoting, and firing. The Act prohibited discrimination in public accommodations and federally funded programs. It also strengthened the enforcement of voting rights and the desegregation of schools."[14]

Assume, for the sake of argument, that all whites are racists (something too many Democrats—following their leaders—actually seem to believe). There are still tens of thousands of black attorneys, prosecutors, attorneys general, judges, Department of Justice officials, police chiefs, mayors, city council members, and other public office holders in a position to remedy this evil—if it existed. If there were in fact "systemic racism," if racism actually "touched every facet of American life," there would be thousands, even tens of thousands of lawsuits to end racist practices and compensate the victims. Because systemic racism is illegal. But there is no such blizzard of legal actions because systemic racism is a political myth invented by the Left to advance its destructive agenda.

The significance of the president's response to Black Lives Matter and his executive order alleging "systemic racism" is this: the racial hoax that incited the summer of violence and destruction in two hundred twenty American cities is now the official policy of the United States. The purpose of the hoax and of the violence is to justify a wholesale assault on the Constitution's most basic principles, starting with the rights to be judged on one's individual merits and to freedom of speech. The so-called "anti-racists" of Black Lives Matter are adamant that free speech and other civil rights cannot be granted to racists—in other words, to anyone who opposes them—and that racial attributes are defining features of individual character.

Irregularities and Illegalities

The Democrats' assault on freedom of speech was on full display in their post-election vendetta to impeach and permanently bar from political office the forty-fifth president of the United State—*after* he had left the White House. These efforts focused on Trump's determination to question the result of the 2020 presidential election.

The 2020 presidential campaign had begun in earnest in July, when six hundred Democrat lawyers and ten thousand Democrat "volunteers" were dispatched across the country on a mission to change the rules by which votes would be counted.[15] Their specific goal was to loosen legal strictures and restraints that had been designed to prevent voter fraud. The Democrat election team attacked these strictures as "voter suppression" measures even though minorities—and blacks in particular— were already voting in record numbers.

The principal "reform" the Democrats advocated was the massive use of unsolicited mail-in ballots, which were known to be particularly susceptible to fraud. That same July, President Trump warned that the mail-in ballots—almost 66 million of them—would lead to "the most corrupt election in U.S. history," a charge he repeated many times in the ensuing months.[16]

In fact, a 2005 bipartisan election commission co-chaired by Jimmy Carter had already identified mail-in ballots as the most easily susceptible to fraud.[17] It came as no surprise, therefore, when the 2020 election saw the most massive election irregularities and illegalities in a presidential election ever. The Democrats' response to the president's desperate efforts to investigate the election procedures was to claim there was "no evidence" of irregularities and illegalities, which was false, and then to say that the courts had examined and dismissed Trump's claims, which was also false—in most cases they had simply refused to hear the evidence.[18] Even worse, the Democrats and their network allies warned that anyone questioning the election result was undermining the public's faith in the integrity of the voting process, an act which they said was tantamount to treason. The result of these Democrat attacks was that by January 6, when Congress was scheduled to certify the electors, there had been no serious examination of the integrity of the process.

There were roughly 159 million total votes cast in the 2020 presidential election. Biden's margin of victory was 43,000—or 0.027 percent of the total—spread across three battleground states: Arizona, Georgia, and Wisconsin.[19] If the results in those states were flipped, both candidates would have received 269 Electoral College votes and the decision would have been thrown into the House of Representatives, where Republicans controlled a majority of the states. The result would have been a second term for Trump. In other words, Biden's margin was so razor thin—less than three one hundredths of one percent of the vote—that there was obviously a credible basis for concern. But when Trump and his allies raised concerns, they were dismissed as "conspiracy theorists," "crackpots," "insurrectionists" and "traitors"—a threat to American democracy itself.[20]

To counter the Left's claim that Trump's team had produced no evidence, the White House issued a thirty-six-page report written by author and economist Peter Navarro presenting the facts that Trump's lawyers had been able to collect in the short time available and without the cooperation of state legislatures and the courts. The report, titled "Immaculate Deception," was, like every other Trump claim, summarily dismissed or simply ignored by the Democrats and their kept media, while feckless Republican state legislatures sat on their hands.[21]

"Evidence used to conduct this assessment," Navarro explained, "includes more than 50 lawsuits and judicial rulings, thousands of affidavits and declarations, testimony in a variety of state venues, published analyses by think tanks and legal centers, videos and photos, public comments, and extensive press coverage."[22] The report's summary noted that in 5 of the 6 main battleground states Biden's margins of victory were a total of 158,114 votes, while legally questionable votes in those same states exceeded 1.4 million—more than enough to change the outcome of the election.[23]

Trump was particularly isolated since the Republican-controlled legislatures of five of the six battleground states agreed to go along with obvious illegalities, as did leading Republican figures like Senate Majority Leader Mitch McConnell. Refusing to remain silent in the face of a stolen election, Trump decided on a last-ditch effort to pressure Republican members of the House to challenge the certifications of electors who were prepared to validate the flawed votes in their states. To exert this pressure he announced a "Stop the Steal" rally for January 6, the day the certification was to take place. The site of the rally was the Ellipse, a large park about a mile from the Capitol in Washington, D.C.

Over a hundred thousand Trump supporters showed up to hear his speech. In it he listed in detail the illegalities, irregularities, and fraudulent practices of the election process. But his main ire was reserved for "weak" Republican elected officials who gave in to political pressures and were willing to go along with so great a crime as the theft of a presidential election. He told his followers that if the Congressional Republicans failed to "Stop the Steal" by decertifying the electors who were there because of fraud, they should return home and primary the weak Republicans in the 2022 elections.[24]

In an article on Trump's speech, *Claremont Review* editor Charles Kessler correctly reported the thrust of his remarks:

> If Trump's speech has a political target, it's the "weak Republicans" who acquiesce in election fraud and will not fight in the trenches alongside him—the "Liz Cheneys of the world," as he calls them. . . . "We've got to get rid of them," he says. He specifies how that should be done: "we have to 'primary' the hell out of the ones that don't fight. You primary them." Later he adds, "in a year from now, you're going to start working on Congress and we've got to get rid of the weak congresspeople, the ones that aren't any good." A year from now means as the 2022 election cycle gears up. His incitement, so to speak, is to oppose the weak Republicans by challenging them in the normal process of American primary elections.[25]

This totally innocuous proposal, well within the boundaries of the democratic process, was immediately characterized by Democrats as "an incitement to violent insurrection" and treason, providing the basis for a new impeachment trial. Trump's actual instructions to the crowd that came to hear him were, "I know that everyone here will soon be marching over to the Capitol Building to *peacefully* and *patriotically* make your voices heard" [emphasis added].[26]

Before Trump had finished speaking, a small segment of the crowd he had assembled—likely hundreds, rather than thousands, judging from the 510 arrests—had already made their way to the Capitol, a mile away, where they broke into the basically unguarded building and proceeded to stage a mini-riot in the chambers and threaten some legislators.[27] Four people died in the melee inside the Capitol—all of them Trump supporters. One died of a heart attack, another of a stroke, and a third from an indeterminate "medical emergency."[28] The fourth victim was a female Air Force veteran, Ashli Babbitt, who was shot by a trigger-happy Capitol policeman even though she was unarmed and was not attacking him.[29] The officer who killed Babbitt was neither investigated nor punished for what was clearly a case of manslaughter—possibly murder.[30]

Democrats who had been in an uproar all summer whenever an armed black felon resisting arrest was shot by police were silent over this miscarriage of justice. Worse, House Speaker Nancy Pelosi, who was responsible for the Capitol Police, concealed the identity of the killer of Ashli Babbitt, whose fatal shot at an unarmed and non-threatening woman was captured on video. The Hispanic journalist who took the video was subsequently arrested and jailed for being present at the event, even though he was there as a reporter. While he had posted his video to the internet, the Democrats refused to release fourteen thousand hours of video from security cameras in the Capitol, perhaps because the footage would have illustrated how mild the January 6 episode was when compared to the hundreds of Democrat-approved riots that preceded it.[31] Perhaps because it would have led to the indictment of the anonymous Capitol Police officer who killed Ashli Babbitt, and whom the Biden Justice Department announced would not be charged.

A fifth casualty, Capitol Police Officer Brian Sicknick, was at first alleged—on the basis of a fallacious *New York Times* story that was repeated by news outlets nationwide—to have died as a result of a blow to the head with a fire extinguisher. He was given the extraordinary honor of lying in state in the Capitol rotunda in a ceremony attended by Speaker Pelosi and other leading Democrats, who praised him as a heroic officer who had given his life defending the Capitol against the insurrectionists.

The Democrats' House impeachment managers cited the claim about the fire extinguisher in their trial brief when they exhorted the Senate to convict Trump of having incited the insurrection. But the allegation that Sicknick had been struck by a fire extinguisher proved to be false. The day after the Capitol melee he died of natural causes, suffering two strokes on January 7. Moreover, he was an ardent supporter of Donald Trump.[32]

The Democrats' *Reichstag* Fire

Nancy Pelosi and the Democrats were perfectly comfortable with three months of violent riots attacking federal courthouses and police stations, killing scores of people, and causing billions in property damage. They even raised bail money for the rioters so they could riot again. They called all the federal agents Trump sent to stop the rioting "storm troopers." Nonetheless, in the January 6 Capitol protest and Trump's "Stop the Steal" rally, they saw a golden opportunity to criminalize their opponents and launch a nationwide witch hunt to silence dissenters. Immediately, they began distorting Trump's speech, in which the president urged his followers to primary weak Republicans and told them to protest "peacefully and patriotically." Inventing words he had never uttered, the Democrats called his speech a summons to "armed insurrection" and grounds for impeachment—in other words treason. Democrats compared the Capitol protest, which burned no buildings and killed no one, to the 9/11 attacks, Pearl Harbor, and even the Holocaust.[33]

A more appropriate comparison would have been to the 1933 Reichstag Fire. Four weeks after Hitler was elected chancellor in a democratic election, a Dutch Communist set fire to the Reichstag, which was the Capitol of the Weimar Republic. The Nazis seized on the incident to pass the Reichstag Fire Decree designed to suppress their political opponents and create the legal foundations of the Third Reich.[34] Democrats who had resisted calls for National Guard deployments when Washington was burning at the hands of Black Lives Matter rioters months before now deployed twenty-six thousand troops to Washington, D.C., at a cost of $500 million without any evidence of a threat, imminent or otherwise.

As political commentator Daniel Greenfield observed, these thousands of troops occupying Washington at the behest of the Democrats were

> authorized to use deadly force as they were forbidden to do either at the border or during the Black Lives Matter assault on the White House. While walls, razor wire, and military encampments rise outside the halls of government, inside them the Democrats have unleashed a true coup. Protesters have 'stormed' Congress before, from both the left and the right, which cannot be called overthrowing the government. But Democrats began their own overthrow by launching an unconstitutional post-office impeachment of President Trump for speaking at a peaceful protest and pushing to remove Senate members who objected to the stolen election. . . .

The fascist theater of the military occupation is a pretext for a political occupation with Democrats inciting political purges in legislatures, both state and national, of any Republicans who criticized the stolen election and called for accountability on behalf of the voters. A purge is also underway of the military and law enforcement to root out "extremists" from the same forces that the Democrats have deployed to intimidate Americans and suppress political dissent.[35]

In the House of Representatives, newly elected "Squad" member Cori Bush joined Black Lives Matter in calling for the expulsion of more than one hundred Republican members who had questioned the election results.[36] In typical Black Lives Matter manner, Congresswoman Bush called the Republicans and the protesters "white supremacists" because they were largely white and disagreed with her. In a tweet she explained the objective of the Black Lives Matter campaign: "Expel the Republican members of Congress who incited the white supremacist attempted coup."[37] Meanwhile, Black Lives Matter warned on its website on February 1, "There are *still* people in Congress who played a role in the violent insurrection a few weeks ago. It is not enough to denounce the white supremacy behind the attack. We must remove its endorsers from Congress—Ted Cruz, Josh Hawley, Lauren Boebert, Marjorie Taylor Greene, and the over 100 Republicans who voted against certifying the Electoral College."[38]

Inciting Insurrection

The fake foundation of the Democrats' attacks, which were aimed at criminalizing and suppressing their legitimate opposition, was exposed in their accusation that Trump had incited a "violent insurrection" that was comparable to 9/11 and therefore treasonous in intent. This was the thrust, for example, of the preposterous statement made by Congressman Eric Swalwell, one of the House members chosen by Speaker Pelosi to prosecute Trump in the Democrats' post-presidency impeachment attempt. Swalwell's political career had been funded and orchestrated by a Chinese spy who began bundling money for him when he was still an obscure city council member.[39] Like the Capitol Police officer who shot Ashli Babbitt, Swalwell was protected by Speaker Pelosi. When Swalwell was only in his second year in Congress, Pelosi made him the ranking member of the House Intelligence Committee, whose authority he used to falsely claim multiple times that he had evidence that Trump had colluded with the Russians and was therefore a traitor. Swalwell never produced any evidence for his claim, but also never stopped repeating his slanders.

Here is Swalwell's attack on Trump a week after the January 6 event, as reported by RealClearPolitics:

> During an interview Tuesday with PBS *NewsHour*, Democratic Rep. Eric Swalwell said that President Trump is responsible for the riot last week on Capitol Hill in the same way that Osama bin Laden was responsible for 9/11. "Osama Bin Laden did not enter U.S. soil on September 11, but it was widely acknowledged that he was responsible for inspiring the attack on our country and the president, with his words, using the word fight. That is hate speech that inspired and radicalized people to storm the Capitol," [Swalwell] said. "I'm comparing the words of an individual

who would incite and radicalize somebody as Osama
Bin Laden did to what President Trump did. You don't
actually have to commit the violence yourself but if
you call others to violence that itself is a crime."[40]

Not a single instance of Trump's issuing a call to violence on
January 6 was produced by Swalwell or any other Democrat.
And not a critical comment on Swalwell's slanderous remarks
issued from his patroness's office.

Swalwell's malicious fantasy was such a brazen distortion of
what Trump actually said in his speech, and so false about what
in fact took place, that it explains why the eighteen hours of
televised impeachment time the House managers were given to
make their case was a showcase of lies, misrepresentations,
doctored videos, gross omissions, and tortured connections. The
actual text of Trump's speech refuted the claim that it was an
"incitement to violence" let alone to "insurrection."

Since violent attacks on cities and government buildings—
protected and even funded by the Democrats themselves—had
been normalized all summer as legitimate "protests," the potential for violence did of course exist. After all, rioting was now a
widely accepted form of "protest," and why would fringe elements on the political right think they should be denied the
license? To discourage such fringe elements, Trump himself had
offered to deploy ten thousand troops to be present on January
6 in order to quell any violence that might occur.[41] Trump even
ordered the secretary of defense to prepare the ten thousand
troops for this duty.[42] Not exactly the actions of an inciter of
violence, let alone an "insurrectionist," but pretty normal for a
"law and order" president like Trump, who had made similar
offers during the summer of Black Lives Matter riots. Like those

offers, Trump's January 6 proposal was rejected by the Democrats who controlled the city.[43]

Finally, an interrogation of three of the arrested riot leaders from the pro-Trump organization "Oath Keepers" revealed that their plans for the riot were already in place in November, two months before Trump's remarks at the Ellipse.[44]

Nonetheless, the sole article of impeachment filed by Pelosi accused Trump of "Incitement to Insurrection." Lacking any credible evidence to sustain this inflammatory libel, the Democrat prosecutors resorted to a dangerous, open-ended attack on the First Amendment. To make their case they played videos of Trump speeches warning in July and subsequent months of the threat of election fraud because of the reckless use of unrequested mail-in ballots, and also his speeches during the post-election period questioning the results as fraudulent. In the House managers' presentation, this exercise of Trump's First Amendment right was an "incitement to insurrection." Jamie Raskin, the lead prosecutor for the House managers, described Trump's claim that the election was stolen as "the big lie that was responsible for inflaming and inciting the mob in the first place."[45] The phrase "the big lie"—which was featured in Adolf Hitler's *Mein Kampf* as a political weapon—became a mantra for Democrats seeking to make any questioning of the election result tantamount to an attack on democracy and an existential threat to the nation. If any Republican suggested that the 2020 election result might be "problematic," Democrats dismissed him as repeating "the big lie" and thus endangering the nation.

An obvious problem with Raskin's accusation—aside from the fact that it would outlaw constitutionally protected speech—was that the Democrats had formally challenged the election results after all three Republican presidential victories since

2000. In 2017 Raskin himself had personally gone to the well of the House along with other Democrat members, including Jim McGovern, Maxine Waters, Sheila Jackson Lee, Pramila Jayapal, and Barbara Lee, to challenge the certification of Trump electors and claim election fraud.[46]

As with all the hypocrisies that peppered their impeachment arguments, the House managers attempted to deny any similarities between their election challenges and Trump's. But there was no difference except in the scale of the alleged fraud and in the political environment that had dramatically changed when hundreds of violent insurrectionary riots went mainly unpunished and—worse—were openly supported by Democrat mayors and congressional leaders like Nancy Pelosi and Kamala Harris.

This was in fact the Democrats' most glaring hypocrisy: their inability to recognize their own responsibility for the attack on the Capitol. When Islamist activist and Black Lives Matter supporter Linda Sarsour led a mob into the Senate Judiciary Committee hearings in 2018 with the intent of disrupting the procedure and stopping the confirmation of Justice Brett Kavanaugh, Democrats had reacted by calling it "democracy in action."[47] When future Black Lives Matter activist Susan Rosenberg was sentenced to fifty-eight years in prison for setting a bomb inside the Capitol, Bill Clinton pardoned her after she had served just sixteen years behind bars.[48] And after Black Lives Matter had incited more than six hundred violent riots in two hundred twenty American cities, President Joe Biden made Black Lives Matter's racist demand that he attack America as "systemically racist" his first order of business.

Nor was this the end of the matter. On the contrary, it was a harbinger of things to come. On February 6, 2021—the one-month anniversary of Trump's "Stop the Steal" speech—Black

Lives Matter and Antifa radicals staged a march in Washington, D.C., with chants of "Whose Streets? Our Streets," "F—k the Police," and "Burn It Down."[49] While draconian investigations and charges were being launched against the pro-Trump Capitol rioters, and six thousand National Guard troops were still deployed around the Capitol to confront an imaginary threat, the BLM-Antifa outburst took place without outrage or condemnation from the House managers or the new occupant of the White House. Nor was there any attempt to hold the leaders of Black Lives Matter and Antifa to account. "Burn it down" was considered a normal protest in the same manner as the Black Lives Matter insurrections that had torn up two hundred twenty cities in the summer of the presidential election.

Worse still, Nancy Pelosi led the Democrats on a campaign to demonize Republicans as "enemies of the state" and "domestic terrorists" in those exact words.[50] Witch hunts were launched to ferret out "extremists" in the Capitol Police, the Department of Homeland Security, and other government agencies in advance of any serious investigation into the motives of the protesters, who—unlike the summer's left-wing rioters—set no fires and killed no one. On February 3, Biden's new secretary of defense, Lloyd Austin, ordered a Department of Defense stand-down to purge "domestic terrorists" and "extremists" from the ranks.[51]

If anyone doubted that this was an effort to weed out Republicans, Black Lives Matter opponents, and Trump supporters— "enemies of the state" in Nancy Pelosi's preposterous phrase—the firing of Matthew Lohmeier, a commander in the newly created Space Force, served to put such doubts to rest. As the *Washington Times* reported on May 16, 2021, "Lt. Gen. Stephen Whiting, who heads Space Operations Command, effectively fired Lt. Col. Lohmeier on Friday, citing a loss of confidence in his ability to carry out his command of a Space Force unit that detects ballistic missile launches."[52]

What caused General Whiting to lose confidence in Lieutenant Colonel Lohmeier's ability to carry out his command of a unit that detects ballistic missile launches? The lieutenant colonel had self-published a book, *Irresistible Revolution*, decrying the inclusion of neo-Marxist anti-American ideology in military training courses. Lohmeier regarded the racial attacks and anti-America attitudes embedded in these doctrines as "divisive" and a threat to unit cohesiveness and military morale. The new training curriculum included the pernicious racism of Critical Race Theory and the fraudulent 1619 Project, which claims that racism is America's national essence and replaces the 1776 American Founding and its declaration of equality and liberty for all with a date marking the shipment of twenty African slaves, to the Virginia colony in 1619.[53] Not only was Virginia an *English* colony on that date—America's actual founding occurred 168 years in the future—but slavery was outlawed in the Virginia colony at the time. The twenty Africans were not slaves but indentured servants like the majority of the white labor force. The fraudulent 1619 Project uses these core lies to paint present-day America as a repellent, racist oppressor of the richest, freest, most privileged black population anywhere in the world, including all of black Africa and the West Indies. Lieutenant Colonel Lohmeier's offense was to ask how we can depend on our troops to defend our country if our military teaches them that America has been a vile, oppressive, racist nation since its inception.

The doctrines that Lieutenant Colonel Lohmeier objected to—the fraudulent attempt to make America a nation conceived in slavery and racism and the claim that white people are racist by virtue of their skin color because it makes them part of a system of white supremacy—are the central doctrines promoted by the Black Lives Matter Marxists and other leftists who are self-declared allies of America's terrorist enemies Al-Qaeda, ISIS, Hezbollah, and Hamas. The Black Lives Matter creed inspires its followers to burn American cities and declare war on America's law enforcement officers. How, then, can our young military recruits be motivated to defend our country if the military itself views America as a racist nightmare rather than a force for equality and freedom? The answer is obvious, but worries only patriots who love their country, not the anti-American ideologues of the Left, and apparently not the White House, the secretary of defense, or the military brass either.

In a podcast interview that precipitated his firing, Lieutenant Colonel Lohmeier argued that the leftist ideas and practices embraced by the Biden White House, academia, the media, and now the U.S. military are proving to be a divisive force in the ranks and that the Department of Defense should take steps to return to a more "politically nonpartisan" course. Since "nonpartisan" precludes a left-wing orthodoxy, such a view qualifies as "extreme" in the eyes of Democrats and needs to be purged.[54]

Disturbing as General Whiting's action may be, it reflects the new orthodoxy that is being imposed by the Biden administration. Biden's Department of Education has proposed a rule that would be the first step toward making Critical Race Theory and 1619 Project slanders the core curriculum of K–12 education in the United States. As if that were not enough, the proposed rule also approvingly cites the "scholarship" of Ibram X. Kendi, whose "anti-racism" program essentially defines racism as any viewpoint on racial issues that is not endorsed by Kendi and the political Left.[55]

If there has been a coup in Washington, it took place on January 20, 2021, when Biden issued the first of his executive orders, targeting America as a "systemically racist" society and proclaiming "equity"—the redistribution of wealth and privilege according to race—as America's new guiding principle and moral compass. This unconstitutional policy violates the Civil Rights Act and renders Martin Luther King Jr.'s profoundly American vision of a "color blind" society—where individuals are judged according to their merits and not their skin color— just another expression of American racism. The orthodoxy of our new Democrat rulers is as anti-American a vision as can be. It is the fruit of the Black Lives Matter insurrectionists and their racist ideology. It will require a new Supreme Court that is an appendage of a Democrat Congress to install it. But make no mistake, Democrat leaders Pelosi and Schumer and the shadow government behind the feeble Joe Biden have the will and the ruthlessness to achieve it.

Having turned the incident of January 6 at the Capitol into their own version of the Reichstag Fire, the Democrats are determined to achieve their totalitarian vision of a one-party state. Their determination is reflected in their attempt to seduce Republicans into cooperating in their own Nuremberg Trial to indict them as criminals. This is the so-called "January 6 Commission," explicitly modeled on the 9/11 Commission, which was formed to investigate the worst terrorist attack on American soil in our history. As proposed by the Democrats, the Commission's purpose would be to validate the malicious claims that January 6 was comparable to the Civil War, Pearl Harbor, and 9/11 as an existential threat to the nation. Fortunately, most House Republicans refused to provide bipartisan support for this witch hunt—hopefully because they have finally grasped the sinister design of the Democrats' agenda.

This design was unmasked by Fox commentator Tucker Carlson on May 20, 2021: "The bill [to create the commission] that the House passed yesterday was taken directly from the law that established the 9/11 Commission, almost twenty years ago. That legislation instructed Congress to, quote: 'Investigate and report to the President and Congress on its findings, conclusions, and recommendations for corrective measures that can be taken to prevent acts of terrorism. . . .'"

Carlson went on to observe that "[t]he new legislation that will create a January 6th Commission demands the very same. Congress must . . . 'Investigate and report to the President and Congress on its findings, conclusions, and recommendations for corrective measures that could be taken to prevent future acts of targeted violence and domestic terrorism.'"

The "virtually identical language," Carlson pointed out, is "not accidental. This is the new war on terror. But this war isn't aimed at Al-Qaeda or ISIS or any foreign power. This war is aimed at you and anyone else who stands in the way of the Democratic Party's agenda."[56]

In sum, the Pelosi response to January 6, 2021, was a dramatic escalation of the efforts by Democrats and the racist Left to put in place the elements of an American fascism suppressing the diversity of opinion that has been the lifeblood of our country for nearly 250 years. America has proven itself a resilient republic in the past; hopefully enough Americans will wake up to this threat before it is too late.

NOTES

PART ONE: An American Catastrophe

A Summer of Insurrections

1. Eric Levenson, "Former Officer Knelt on George Floyd for 9 Minutes and 29 Seconds—Not the Infamous 8:46," CNN, March 30, 2021, https://www.cnn.com/2021/03/29/us/george-floyd-timing-929-846/index.html.
2. Joy Pullmann, "Study: Up to 95 Percent of 2020 U.S. Riots Are Linked to Black Lives Matter," The Federalist, September 16, 2020, https://thefederalist.com/2020/09/16/study-up-to-95-percent-of-2020-u-s-riots-are-linked-to-black-lives-matter/; Emma Colton, "Conservatives Point Out That Princeton Study on Protests Reveals Violence Was Found at Hundreds of Demonstrations," *Washington Examiner*, September 6, 2020, https://www.washingtonexaminer.com/news/conservatives-point-out-that-princeton-study-on-protests-reveals-violence-was-found-at-hundreds-of-demonstrations; "Fact Check: 48 out of the 50 Major Cities in America Have Seen Violence from the Black Lives Matter Movement," LawEnforcementToday.com, September 8, 2020, https://www.lawenforcementtoday.com/48-out-of-the-50-major-cities-have-seen-violence-from-the-black-lives-matter-movement/.
3. Pullmann, "Study: Up to 95 Percent of 2020 U.S. Riots Are Linked to Black Lives Matter."

4.   Associated Press, "Boston's Peaceful Protests Turn Violent at Night," VOA News, May 31, 2020, https://www.voanews.com/usa/bostons-peaceful -protests-turn-violent-night; Michele Munz, Jeremy Kohler, Christian Gooden, and Colter Peterson, "Peaceful Day of Protests Turns Violent at Night as Ferguson Is Damaged," *St. Louis Post-Dispatch*, May 31, 2020, https://www.stltoday.com/news/local/crime-and-courts/peaceful-day-of -protests-turns-violent-at-night-as-ferguson-is-damaged/article_547e99 80-f6b1-5df9-852a-88ae68833b84.html.

5.   "Seattle BLM Protesters Demand White People 'Give Up' Their Homes," YouTube, August 17, 2020, https://www.youtube.com/watch?v=iBg5T7 KkoZU; Sky News Australia, "Black Lives Matter Protesters Confront White Diners outside D.C. Cafe," YouTube, August 25, 2020, https:// www.youtube.com/watch?v=dSnTTND0UcM; Now This News, "BLM Protesters Block Off Seattle Highway," YouTube, June 17, 2020, https:// www.youtube.com/watch?v=t6-e6PUXnws.

6.   Mercey Livingston, "These Are the Major Brands Donating to the Black Lives Matter Movement," CNet, June 16, 2020, https://www.cnet.com /how-to/companies-donating-black-lives-matter/.

7.   Jeff Wagner, "'It's Real Ugly': Protesters Clash with Minneapolis Police after George Floyd's Death," CBS Minnesota, May 26, 2020, https://min nesota.cbslocal.com/2020/05/26/hundreds-of-protesters-march-in-min neapolis-after-george-floyds-deadly-encounter-with-police/.

8.   Audra D. S. Burch *et al.*, "How Black Lives Matter Reached Every Corner of America," *New York Times*, June 13, 2020, https://www.nytimes.com /interactive/2020/06/13/us/george-floyd-protests-cities-photos.html.

9.   Phil Helsel, "Police Chiefs across U.S. Condemn Officers in Floyd Death," NBC News, May 29, 2020, https://www.nbcnews.com/news/us-news/se veral-police-heads-across-nation-condemn-force-used-floyd-death-n121 7451.

10.   Lou Raguse, Jeremiah Jacobsen, Dana Thiede, and Kiya Edwards, "Judge Considers Decisions on Combined Trial, Venue, Dismissal in George Floyd Case," KARE11, September 11, 2020, https://www.kare11.com/ar ticle/news/local/george-floyd/pre-trial-hearings-begin-for-officers-charged -in-george-floyds-death/89-c9fc14b7-b139-4b49-84de-b0070d882b3d.

11.   Farah Stockman, "'They Have Lost Control': Why Minneapolis Burned," *New York Times*, July 3, 2020, https://www.nytimes.com/2020/07/03/us /minneapolis-government-george-floyd.html; Tom Lyden, "Fall of the Third Precinct: A Minute-by-Minute Account," Fox9, July 9, 2020, https://www.fox9.com/news/fall-of-the-third-precinct-a-minute-by- minute-account; "Minneapolis Police Precinct Burned to Ground in Third Night of Racially Charged Violence," AMNY, May 29, 2020, https://

www.amny.com/nation/minneapolis-police-precinct-burned-to-ground-in-third-night-of-racially-charged-violence/.

12. Lyden, "Fall of the Third Precinct."
13. Mark Reilly, "Twin Cities Businesses Hit by Riots Face Another Shock: Costs of Demolition, Cleanup," *St. Paul Business Journal*, August 31, 2020, https://www.bizjournals.com/twincities/news/2020/08/31/demolition-costs-minneapolis-st-paul-riot-recovery.html.
14. Jenna Curren, "Feds Tell MN Governor to Pound Sand after He Requests Federal Aid for over $500 Million Worth of Damages from Riots," *Law Enforcement Today*, July 11, 2020, https://www.lawenforcementtoday.com/minneapolis-denied-federal-aid-over-500-million-worth-of-damages-from-riots/.
15. Atlas Struggle, "Stephanie Wilford of Minneapolis, Minnesota, Unrest in the Twin Cities, the Aftermath," YouTube, May 30, 2020, https://www.youtube.com/watch?v=f4WDjxCP1Fs.
16. Zachary Crockett, "3 Stories of Black-Owned Businesses Damaged in the Riots," The Hustle, June 6, 2020, https://thehustle.co/black-owned-businesses-riots-george-floyd/.
17. Larry Buchanan, Quoctrung Bui, and Jugal K. Patel, "Black Lives Matter May Be the Largest Movement in U.S. History," *New York Times*, July 3, 2020, https://www.nytimes.com/interactive/2020/07/03/us/george-floyd-protests-crowd-size.html.
18. Burch *et al.*, "How Black Lives Matter Reached Every Corner of America."
19. Ebony Bowden, "More Than 700 Officers Injured in George Floyd Protests across U.S.", *New York Post*, June 8, 2020, https://nypost.com/2020/06/08/more-than-700-officers-injured-in-george-floyd-protests-across-us/; Peter Svab, "Hundreds of Officers Injured Amid Weeks of Rioting, Police Union Says," *Epoch Times*, June 14, 2020, https://www.theepochtimes.com/hundreds-of-police-injured-amid-riots-in-past-weeks-police-union-says_3388254.html; "Deadly Unrest: Here Are the People Who Have Died amid George Floyd Protests across U.S.," Fox6Now, June 8, 2020, https://fox6now.com/2020/06/08/deadly-unrest-here-are-the-people-who-have-died-amid-george-floyd-protests-across-us/.
20. "Retired St. Louis Police Captain Killed during Unrest Sparked by George Floyd Death," CBSNews, June 3, 2020, https://web.archive.org/web/20200618040729/https://www.cbsnews.com/news/david-dorn-retired-st-louis-police-captain-killed-unrest-george-floyd-death/.
21. William La Jeunesse, "George Floyd Protests Could Be Most Expensive Civil Disturbance in U.S. History, Experts Say," Fox News, June 29, 2020, https://www.foxnews.com/politics/george-floyd-protests-expensive-civil-disturbance-us-history.

22. Alan L. Anderson, "On Those 'Mostly Peaceful' Protests," *Catholic World Report*, August 8, 2020, https://www.catholicworldreport.com /2020/08/08/on-those-mostly-peaceful-protests/.

23. Stockman, "'They Have Lost Control': Why Minneapolis Burned."

24. Douglas Ernst, "'Fiery but Mostly Peaceful Protests': CNN Chyron Stuns Viewers," *Washington Times*, August 27, 2020, https://www.washington times.com/news/2020/aug/27/cnns-fiery-but-mostly-peaceful-protests-ch yron-as-/; Joe Concha, "CNN Ridiculed for 'Fiery but Mostly Peaceful' Caption with Video of Burning Building in Kenosha," *The Hill*, August 27, 2020, https://thehill.com/homenews/media/513902-cnn-ridiculed-for -fiery-but-mostly-peaceful-caption-with-video-of-burning.

25. David Jackson and Michael Collins, "Calling Violent Protests 'Acts of Domestic Terror,' Trump Says He'll Send in Military If They Aren't Controlled," *USA Today*, June 1, 2020, https://www.usatoday.com/story /news/politics/2020/06/01/george-floyd-donald-trump-order-additional -help-cities-amid-protests/5312338002/.

26. Dan Friedell, "D.C. Police Added to ACLU Lawsuit Alleging 'Excessive Force' against Protesters on June 1," WTOP News, July 9, 2020, https:// wtop.com/dc/2020/07/dc-police-added-to-aclu-lawsuit-alleging-excessive -force-against-protesters-on-june-1/; Spencer S. Hsu and Peter Hermann, "Civil Rights Groups Say D.C. Police Aided Clearing of Lafayette Square on June 1," *Washington Post*, June 1, July 8, 2020, https://www.washing tonpost.com/local/legal-issues/civil-rights-groups-claim-dc-police-aided -clearing-of-lafayette-square-protesters-on-june-1/2020/07/08/47fcfb68 -c136-11ea-b178-bb7b05b94af1_story.html.

27. Gregory Wallace, "Park Police Chief Says Officers Used 'Tremendous Restraint' Removing Lafayette Square Protesters," CNN, July 28, 2020, https://www.cnn.com/2020/07/28/politics/protest-hearing-washington -dc/index.html; Rebecca Tan *et al.*, "Night of Destruction across D.C. after Protesters Clash with Police outside White House," *Washington Post*, June 1, 2020, https://www.washingtonpost.com/local/dc-braces-for -third-day-of-protests-and-clashes-over-death-of-george-floyd/2020/05 /31/589471a4-a33b-11ea-b473-04905b1af82b_story.html.

28. Stephanie Ebbs and Benjamin Siegel, "Police Did Not Clear Lafayette Square So Trump Could Hold 'Bible' Photo Op: Watchdog," ABC News, June 10, 2021, https://abcnews.go.com/Politics/police-clear-lafayette-pa rk-area-trump-hold-bible/story?id=78171712.

29. Dalton Bennett *et al.*, "The Crackdown before Trump's Photo-Op," *Washington Post*, June 8, 2020, https://www.washingtonpost.com/invest igations/2020/06/08/timeline-trump-church-photo-op/?arc404=true; Greg Sargent, "New Questions about Trump's Ugly Bible Stunt," *Washington Post*, June 15, 2020, https://www.washingtonpost.com/opi

nions/2020/06/15/new-questions-about-trumps-ugly-bible-stunt-hint-so
me-dark-truths/.

30. Katie Rogers, "Protesters Dispersed with Tear Gas So Trump Could Pose at Church," *New York Times*, June 1, 2020, https://www.nytimes.com /2020/06/01/us/politics/trump-st-johns-church-bible.html.

31. Hannah Bleau, "Leftists Rage over President Trump's Church Walk: Trump Is a 'Fascist,'" Breitbart, June 1, 2020, https://www.breitbart.com /politics/2020/06/01/leftists-rage-over-president-trumps-church-walk-tr ump-is-a-fascist/.

32. Adam Shaw, "DHS Chief Slams Pelosi for Calling Federal Law Enforcement 'Stormtroopers,'" Fox News, July 24, 2020, https://www .foxnews.com/politics/dhs-chief-pelosi-federal-law-enforcement-stormtroopers.

33. "June 2 Statement from United States Park Police Acting Chief Gregory T. Monahan about the Actions Taken over the Weekend to Protect Life and Property," National Park Service, June 4, 2020, https://www.nps.gov /subjects/uspp/6_2_20_statement_from_acting_chief_monahan.htm.

34. Ibid.

35. Lauren Aratani, "Washington Mayor Stands Up to Trump and Unveils Black Lives Matter Mural," *The Guardian*, June 6, 2020, https://www.th eguardian.com/us-news/2020/jun/06/washington-mayor-muriel-bowser -trump; Leah Asmelash, "Washington's New Black Lives Matter Street Mural Is Captured in Satellite Image, CNN, June 6, 2020, https://www .cnn.com/2020/06/06/us/black-lives-matter-dc-street-mural-space-trnd /index.html; Rachel Sadon, Hannah Schuster, and Matt Blitz, "Activists Added 'Defund the Police' to the New Black Lives Matter Mural," June 7, 2020, DCist, https://dcist.com/story/20/06/07/activists-added-defund -the-police-to-the-new-black-lives-matter-mural-so-far-d-c-officials-have -let-it-stay/.

36. Muriel Bowser (@MayorBowser) "Breonna Taylor, on your birthday....," Twitter, June 5, 2020, 12:30 p.m., https://twitter.com/mayorbowser/ status/1268943214268030978.

37. "Mayor Inaugurates 'Black Lives Matter Plaza' in D.C. with Giant Yellow Letters," France24, June 6, 2020, https://www.france24.com/en/20200 606-mayor-inaugurates-black-lives-matter-plaza-in-dc-with-giant-yellow -letters.

38. Jorge Fitz-Gibbon, "Black Lives Matter Organizer Calls Chicago Looting 'Reparation,'" *New York Post*, August 11, 2020, https://nypost.com/20 20/08/11/black-lives-matter-organizer-calls-chicago-looting-reparation/.

39. Rob Wildeboer and Chip Mitchell, "'Winning Has Come through Revolts': A Black Lives Matter Activist on Why She Supports Looting,"

WBEZ Chicago, August 12, 2020, https://www.wbez.org/stories/winning -has-come-through-revolts-a-black-lives-matter-activist-on-why-she-sup ports-looting/398d0f3f-73d0-4f2e-ae32-04cceba0d322.

40. Camille Caldera, "Fact Check: Kamala Harris Said Protests Aren't Going to Stop, but Condemns Violence," *USA Today*, September 1, 2020, https:// www.usatoday.com/story/news/factcheck/2020/09/01/fact-check-kama la-harris-said-protests-arent-going-stop/5678687002/.

41. Brie Stimson, "Ayanna Pressley Calls for 'Unrest in the Streets' over Trump-Allied Politicians Ignoring Americans' Concerns," *Black Enterprise*, August 16, 2020, https://www.blackenterprise.com/rep-ayan na-pressley-calls-for-unrest-in-the-streets-over-the-failures-of-the-trump -administration/.

42. Paul Conner, "*New York Times* Editor Resigns after Backlash over Tom Cotton 'Send in the Troops' Op-Ed," Fox Business, June 7, 2020, https:// www.foxbusiness.com/lifestyle/new-york-times-editor-resigns-tom-cot ton-send-in-the-troops-op-ed.

43. Craig R. McCoy, "Stan Wischnowski Resigns as *The Philadelphia Inquirer*'s Top Editor," *Philadelphia Inquirer*, June 5, 2020, https://www .inquirer.com/news/stan-wischnowski-resigns-philadelphia-inquirer-202 00606.html.

44. Bonny Johnson, "Kings Announcer Resigns after 'Black Lives Matter' Dispute with DeMarcus Cousins," BasketballForever, June 3, 2020, https://basketballforever.com/2020/06/03/sacramento-kings-announcer -resigns-after-all-lives-matter-comment; Mark Fischer, "NBA Announcer Grant Napear Fired over 'All Lives Matter' Comment," *New York Post*, June 2, 2020, https://nypost.com/2020/06/02/nba-announcer-grant-nape ar-fired-over-all-live-matter-comment/.

45. "UCLA Professor on Leave after Students Blast Response to Request to Postpone Final Exam as 'Woefully Racist,'" CBSN Los Angeles, June 10, 2020, https://losangeles.cbslocal.com/2020/06/10/ucla-professor-on-lea ve-gordon-klein/.

46. Ibid.

47. Alexis Clark, "Why Eisenhower Sent the 101st Airborne to Little Rock after Brown v. Board," History, April 8, 2020, https://www.history.com /news/little-rock-nine-brown-v-board-eisenhower-101-airborne; Andrew Glass, "Marshals Escort James Meredith onto Ole Miss Campus, September 30, 1962," *Politico*, September 30, 2014, https://www.politico .com/story/2014/09/marshals-escort-james-meredith-onto-ole-miss-cam pus-sept-30-1962-111431; Paul Taylor and Carlos Sanchez, "Bush Orders Troops into Los Angeles," *Washington Post*, May 2, 1992, https://www .washingtonpost.com/archive/politics/1992/05/02/bush-orders-troops-in to-los-angeles/4c4711a6-f18c-41ed-b796-6a8a50d6120d/.

48. Oli Mould, "Revolutionary Ideals of the Paris Commune Live on in Black Lives Matter Autonomous Zone in Seattle," The Conversation, June 15, 2020, https://theconversation.com/revolutionary-ideals-of-the-paris-com mune-live-on-in-black-lives-matter-autonomous-zone-in-seattle-140673; Joseph Klein, "Leftist Tyrants Occupy Seattle Neighborhood," FrontPage Magazine, June 12, 2020, https://www.frontpagemag.com/fpm/2020/06 /leftist-tyrants-occupy-seattle-neighborhood-joseph-klein/?utm_campai gn=1285031&utm_content=1790857%27.

49. Gene Johnson, "Seattle Mayor Meets with Protesters over Dismantling Zone," Associated Press, June 27, 2020, https://apnews.com/8e961202c 8e0b6228181765bb64dd078; Ian Schwartz, "Seattle Mayor Durkan: CHAZ Has a 'Block Party Atmosphere,' Could Turn into 'Summer of Love,'" RealClearPolitics, June 12, 2020, https://www.realclearpolitics .com/video/2020/06/12/seattle_mayor_durkan_chaz_has_a_block_par ty_atmosphere_could_turn_into_summer_of_love.html.

50. Free Capitol Hill, "The Demands of the Collective Black Voices at Free Capitol Hill to the Government of Seattle, Washington," Medium, June 9, 2020, https://medium.com/@seattleblmanon3/the-demands-of-the-col lective-black-voices-at-free-capitol-hill-to-the-government-of-seattle-dda ee51d3e47.

51. Kevin Flower, Artemis Moshtaghian, Elle Reeve, and Susannah Cullinane, "Shooting in Seattle Protest Zone Leaves One Dead. Police Say 'Violent Crowd' Denied Them Entry," CNN, June 21, 2020, https://www.cnn .com/2020/06/20/us/seattle-capitol-hill-chop-chaz-shooting/index.html.

52. Hannah Bleau, "Volunteer Medic in Seattle's Autonomous Zone Says CHOP Security Shot at Black Teen Killed in Monday's Shooting," Breitbart, June 30, 2020, https://www.breitbart.com/politics/2020/06/30 /volunteer-medic-in-seattles-autonomous-zone-says-chop-security-shot-at -black-teen-killed-in-mondays-shooting/.

53. Elle Reeve and Samantha Guff, "They Envisioned a World without Police," CNN, July 6, 2020, https://www.cnn.com/2020/07/05/us/chop -seattle-police-protesters-public-safety/index.html; Brendan Kiley, Ryan Blethen, Sydney Brownstone, and Daniel Beekman, "Seattle Cops Dismantle 'Occupied' Zone, Arrest More Than 30," *Spokesman Review*, July 1, 2020, https://www.spokesman.com/stories/2020/jul/01/seattle-co ps-start-clearing-occupied-zone-make-arr/.

54. "Portland Protests: Nonviolent Gatherings and Unlawful Assemblies in the Wake of George Floyd's Death," KGW, May 29 to June 15, 2020, https://www.kgw.com/article/news/local/protests/protests-in-portland /283-21d67e10-4b33-46d4-a81e-7d3b437a7519.

55. Ibid.; Andy Giegerich, "Wheeler, Hardesty Blast Violence as City Delves into the Riot," *Portland Business Journal*, May 30, 2020, https://www

.bizjournals.com/portland/news/2020/05/30/wheeler-hardesty-blast-pro testers.html.

56. "Portland Protests: Nonviolent Gatherings and Unlawful Assemblies in the Wake of George Floyd's Death," KGW, May 29–June 15, 2020, https://www.kgw.com/article/news/local/protests/protests-in-portland/283-21d 67e10-4b33-46d4-a81e-7d3b437a7519; Nick Budnick, "A Timeline of the Portland Protests and Police Clashes," Pamplin Media, July 22 2020, https://pamplinmedia.com/pt/9-news/474579-383427-a-timeline-of-the -portland-protests-and-police-clashes; Penny Starr, "Portland Rioters Threaten Homes.: 'Come Out, into Streets,' 'Stolen Land, Stolen People," Breitbart, August 22, 2020, https://www.breitbart.com/politics/2020/08/22/portland-rioters-threaten-homes-come-out-into-streets-stolen-land-stolen-people/.

57. Ibid.

58. Katherine Rodriguez, "Portland Riots Cause More than 60 Local 911 Calls to Go Unanswered," Breitbart, August 16, 2020, https://www.bre itbart.com/law-and-order/2020/08/16/portland-riots-cause-more-than -60-local-911-calls-go-unanswered/.

59. Lee Brown, "BLM Mob Beats White Man Unconscious after Making Him Crash Truck: Video," *New York Post*, August 17, 2020, https://nyp ost.com/2020/08/17/blm-mob-beat-white-man-unconscious-after-making -him-crash-truck/.

60. Nick Givas, "Apparent Antifa Member in Portland Overheard Saying She's 'Not Sad That a F—ing Fascist Died Tonight,' After Patriot Prayer Backer Killed," Fox News, August 30, 2020, https://www.foxnews.com /us/i-am-not-sad-that-a-fing-fascist-died-tonight-overheard-at-antifa-gat hering-in-portland-after-patriot-prayer-backer-is-shot-to-death; Gregory Hoyt, "Rioters Celebrate Murder of Trump Supporter in Portland: 'Our Community Took Out the Trash,'" Law Enforcement Today, August 30, 2020, https://www.lawenforcementtoday.com/update-trump-supporter -murdered-in-portland-rioters-celebrate-his-death-on-camera/.

61. The Source Weekly, "Mayor Ted Wheeler and Black Lives Matter Demonstrators at the Justice Center in Portland July 22," YouTube, July 23, 2020, https://www.youtube.com/watch?v=czgkqx-GZmw.

62. Joel B. Pollak, "Rioters Loot Stores, Set Fires at Portland Mayor Ted Wheeler's Condo," Breitbart, September 1, 2020, https://www.breitbart .com/law-and-order/2020/09/01/rioters-loot-stores-set-fires-at-portland -mayor-ted-wheelers-condo/; Lee Brown, "Portland Mayor Ted Wheeler Moving to Avoid Rioters Targeting His Home," *New York Post*, September 2, 2020, https://nypost.com/2020/09/02/portland-mayor-wh eeler-moving-to-avoid-rioters-targeting-building/; Lee Brown, "Riot Declared in Portland after Fire Started in Apartment Building," *New York*

Post, September 1, 2020, https://nypost.com/2020/09/01/riot-declared-in -portland-after-fire-in-mayors-building/; Jamie Hale and Beth Nakaruma, "March to Portland Mayor Ted Wheeler's Home Declared Riot Monday as Burning Debris Thrown into Building," OregonLive, August 31, 2020, https://www.oregonlive.com/portland/2020/09/protesters-march-to-por tland-mayor-ted-wheelers-residence-monday-throw-birthday-party-dema nd-resignation-live-updates.html.

63. Tess Riski, "Mayor Ted Wheeler Directs Portland Police Bureau to Stop Using Tear Gas at Protests," *Willamette Week,* September 10, 2020, https://www.wweek.com/news/city/2020/09/10/mayor-ted-wheeler-dire cts-portland-police-bureau-to-stop-using-tear-gas-at-protests/.

64. Edgar Sandoval, "Protests Flare in Brooklyn over Floyd Death as de Blasio Appeals for Calm," *New York Times,* May 30, 2020, https://www.nyt imes.com/2020/05/30/nyregion/nyc-protests-george-floyd.html; "Protests in George Floyd's Death Turn Violent in Brooklyn; Cops Injured, Hundreds Arrested," ABC7NY, May 29, 2020, https://abc7ny.com/621 8834/.

65. Sydney Pereira, "Cuomo Says Attorney General Will Investigate NYPD's 'Inexplicable' Policing of George Floyd Protests," The Gothamist, May 31, 2020, https://web.archive.org/web/20200603154733/https:/gothamist .com/news/cuomo-says-attorney-general-will-investigate-nypds-inexpl icable-policing-george-floyd-protests; Alan Feuer and Azi Paybarah, "Thousands Protest in NYC, Clashing with Police across All Five Boroughs," *New York Times,* May 30, 2020, https://www.nytimes.com /2020/05/30/nyregion/protests-nyc-george-floyd.html

66. Jake Offenhartz and Gwynne Hogan, "SoHo 'Gutted' by Looting as NYPD Continues Aggressive Crackdown on Protests," The Gothamist, June 1, 2020, https://web.archive.org/web/20200603040330/https:/got hamist.com/news/soho-gutted-looting-nypd-continues-aggressive-crack down-protests.

67. Michael Corkery and Sapna Maheshwari, "Macy's Damage Is Limited, but Looting Deals a Symbolic Blow," *New York Times,* June 2, 2020, https://www.nytimes.com/2020/06/02/business/macys-herald-square-pr otests.html; Sydney Pereira and Jake Offenhartz, "Protesters March during NYC's First Curfew in Decades, Looting Continues Despite Police Increase," The Gothamist, June 2, 2020, https://web.archive.org/web/20 200603140233/https://gothamist.com/news/protesters-march-during-ny cs-first-curfew-decades-looting-continues-despite-police-increase.

68. Wilson Wong and Dennis Romero, "Video Shows Car Plowing through Protesters in Times Square," Yahoo News, September 4, 2020, https://ne ws.yahoo.com/video-shows-car-plowing-protesters-180501097.html; Noah Manskar, "450 NYC Businesses Damaged during George Floyd

Protests," *New York Post*, June 12, 2020, https://nypost.com/2020/06/12 /450-nyc-businesses-damaged-during-george-floyd-protests/.

69. Kate King, "Hundreds of New York City Businesses Were Damaged, Looted in Recent Unrest," *Wall Street Journal*, June 12, 2020, https:// www.wsj.com/articles/hundreds-of-new-york-city-businesses-were-dama ged-looted-in-recent-unrest-11591993138; "De Blasio: NYC 'Took a Step Forward' Last Night, but Curfew to Stay in Place This Week," 1010 WINS Radio, June 3, 2020, https://1010wins.radio.com/articles/nyc-rally-kicks -off-6th-day-off-george-floyd-protests.

70. Emily Zanotti, "New York City Rioters Vandalized 303 NYPD Police Cars, Cost City at Least $1 Million In Damages," The Daily Wire, July 28, 2020, https://www.dailywire.com/news/new-york-city-rioters-vanda lized-303-nypd-police-cars-cost-city-at-least-1-million-in-damages.

71. Kyle Morris, "Nearly 500 NYPD Cops Injured since May Due to Anti-Police Protests," Breitbart, September 27, 2020, https://www.breitbart .com/politics/2020/09/27/nearly-500-nypd-cops-injured-since-may-due -anti-police-protests/.

72. Bernadette Hogan and Bruce Golding, "Suspects in Nonviolent Crimes May Walk Free under State Budget Deal," *New York Post*, March 31, 2019, https://nypost.com/2019/03/31/suspects-of-nonviolent-crimes-may -walk-free-under-state-budget-deal/.

73. Editorial Board, "Gov. Andrew Cuomo's Full of It on Looters and the No-Bail Law," *New York Post*, June 4, 2020, https://nypost.com/20 20/06/04/gov-andrew-cuomos-full-of-it-on-looters-and-the-no-bail-law/.

74. Daniella Diaz, "Bill de Blasio: Black Lives Matter Changed Discussion 'for the Better,'" CNN, July 11, 2016, https://www.cnn.com/2016/07/11 /politics/bill-de-blasio-chirlane-mccray-black-lives-matter/.

75. Trent Baker, "De Blasio Doubles Down on Threat to Paint 'Black Lives Matter' in Front of Trump Tower—Vows to Use Defunded Police Money to Pay for It," Breitbart, July 1, 2020, https://www.breitbart.com/clips/20 20/07/01/de-blasio-doubles-down-on-threat-to-paint-black-lives-matter -in-front-of-trump-tower-vows-to-use-defunded-police-money-to-pay-for -it/; Vincent Barone, "NYC Black Lives Matter Marches Can Continue despite Large-Event Ban, de Blasio Says," *New York Post*, July 9, 2020, https://nypost.com/2020/07/09/nyc-allows-black-lives-matter-marches -despite-ban-on-large-events/.

76. Barone, "NYC Black Lives Matter Marches Can Continue."

77. "Detroit Action/BLM Demands," Every Action, https://secure.everyac tion.com/Z24AA6iV5UuRJdW5B1tTag2?fbclid=IwAR3EszQcA5QY5 eb-FbKQCZElpL4Ch0Q8OD8sglNonN5FjO6wWCAhtjB4rX8; Monique Geannelis, "Another Suggestion: 'All Are Welcome,'"

BenningtonBanner.com, August 9, 2020, https://www.benningtonbann
er.com/stories/letter-another-suggestion-all-are-welcome,611071.

78.   Tonya Mosley, "Defunding the Police Can Achieve 'Real Accountability
and Justice,' Black Lives Matter Co-Founder Says," WBUR, June 3, 2020,
https://www.wbur.org/hereandnow/2020/06/03/black-lives-matter-co-fo
under

79.   John Binder, "Minneapolis Officials Vow to 'Dismantle' Police
Department," Breitbart, June 4, 2020, https://www.breitbart.com/polit
ics/2020/06/04/minneapolis-officials-dismantle-police-department/; Ben
Feuerherd, "Minneapolis City Council Approves Measure to Abolish
Police Force," New York Post, June 26, 2020, https://nypost.com/2020
/06/26/minneapolis-city-council-approves-measure-to-abolish-police-for
ce/.

80.   Katie Honan and Leslie Brody, "De Blasio Agrees to Cut NYPD Funding
by $1 Billion," Wall Street Journal, June 29, 2020, https://www.wsj.com
/articles/de-blasio-agrees-to-cut-nypd-funding-by-1-billion-
11593472369.

81.   Jorge L. Ortiz and N'dea Yancey-Bragg, "Seattle Police Chief Blames City
Council as She Steps Down after Vote to Cut $4 Million in Budget, 100
Officers," USA Today, August 11, 2020, https://www.usatoday.com/sto
ry/news/nation/2020/08/11/seattle-police-chief-resign-following-nearly
-4-million-budget-cuts/3342382001/; Jemima McEvoy, "At Least 13
Cities Are Defunding Their Police Departments," Forbes, August 13,
2020, https://www.forbes.com/sites/jemimamcevoy/2020/08/13/at-least
-13-cities-are-defunding-their-police-departments/?sh=1b0696d429e3.

82.   Brakkton Booker, "Seattle's Police Chief Resigns after Council Votes to
Cut Department Funds," NPR, August 11, 2020, https://www.npr.org
/sections/live-updates-protests-for-racial-justice/2020/08/11/901280451/
seattles-police-chief-resigns-after-council-votes-to-cut-department-funds.

83.   Rich Morin, Kim Parker, Renee Stepler, and Andrew Mercer, "Behind
the Badge," Pew Research, January 11, 2017, https://www.pewsocialtren
ds.org/2017/01/11/behind-the-badge/.

84.   Jon Hilsenrath, "Homicide Spike Hits Most Large U.S. Cities," Wall
Street Journal, August 2, 2020, https://www.wsj.com/articles/homicide
-spike-cities-chicago-newyork-detroit-us-crime-police-lockdown-corona
virus-protests-11596395181; Heather Mac Donald, "The 'Ferguson
Effect' Is Fueling a Growing Crime Wave," New York Post, May 24, 2016,
https://nypost.com/2016/05/24/the-ferguson-effect-is-fueling-a-growing
-crime-wave/; Heather Mac Donald, "The Ferguson Effect," The
Washington Post, July 20, 2016, https://www.washingtonpost.com/news
/volokh-conspiracy/wp/2016/07/20/the-ferguson-effect/; Mark Berman,
"'We Have a Problem.' Homicides Are Up Again This Year in More Than

Two Dozen Major U.S. Cities," *Washington Post*, May 14, 2016, https://www.washingtonpost.com/news/post-nation/wp/2016/05/14/we-have-a-problem-homicides-are-up-again-this-year-in-more-than-two-dozen-major-u-s-cities/; Heather Mac Donald, "The New Nationwide Crime Wave," *Wall Street Journal*, May 29, 2015, https://www.wsj.com/articles/the-new-nationwide-crime-wave-1432938425.

85. Bill Hutchinson, "Chicago Sees 18 Homicides in Deadliest Day in 60 Years," ABC News, June 9, 2020, https://abcnews.go.com/US/chicago-sees-18-homicides-deadliest-day-60-years/story?id=71150234; Matthew Hendrickson, "18 Murders in 24 Hours: Inside the Most Violent Day in 60 Years in Chicago," *Chicago Sun-Times*, June 8, 2020, https://chicago.suntimes.com/crime/2020/6/8/21281998/chicago-deadliest-day-violence-murder-history-police-crime.

86. Bob Chiarito, "Chicago Sees Its Most Violent Month in 28 Years as Murders, Shootings Skyrocket," Block Club Chicago, August 3, 2020, https://blockclubchicago.org/2020/08/03/chicago-sees-its-most-violent-month-in-28-years-as-murders-shootings-skyrocket/.

87. Stephanie Pagones, "NYC Daylight Shootings from May to July More Than Doubled in 2020, Data Shows," Fox News, August 11, 2020, https://www.foxnews.com/us/nyc-daylight-shootings-double-may-to-july-year-over-year.

88. "NYPD Announces Citywide Crime Statistics for June 2020," New York City Police Department, July 6, 2020, https://www1.nyc.gov/site/nypd/news/pr0706/nypd-citywide-crime-statistics-june-2020.

89. Jackie Salo, "NYPD Blames Reform, 'Animosity towards Police' for Spike in Shootings," *New York Post*, June 28, 2020, https://nypost.com/2020/06/28/nypd-animosity-towards-police-is-driving-spike-in-shootings/; Sara Dorn and Dean Balsamini, "Shootings Soar 205 Percent after NYPD Disbands Anti-Crime Unit," *New York Post*, July 4, 2020, https://nypost.com/2020/07/04/shootings-soar-205-percent-after-nypd-disbands-anti-crime-unit/.

90. "Impact Report: COVID-19 and Crime," National Commission on COVID-19 and Criminal Justice, January 31, 2021, https://covid19.counciloncj.org/2021/01/31/impact-report-covid-19-and-crime-3/; Horus Alas, "2020 a 'Perfect Storm' for Homicide Surge," *U.S. News & World Report*, February 4, 2021, https://www.usnews.com/news/national-news/articles/2021-02-04/2020-homicide-rates-spike-amid-pandemic-police-protests.

91. "Honoring Officers Killed in 2020," Officer Down Memorial Page, https://www.odmp.org/search/year/2020.

92. Craig McCarthy, Tina Moore, Larry Celona, and Bruce Golding, "NYPD Limits Retirement Applications amid 400 Percent Surge This Week," *New*

York Post, July 8, 2020, https://nypost.com/2020/07/08/nypd-limits-reti rement-applications-amid-411-surge-this-week/.

93. Luke Barr, "Why Some Police Officials Believe Crime Is on the Rise in US Cities," ABC News, June 24, 2020, https://abcnews.go.com/US/us-ci ties-increase-violent-crime-police-group/story?id=71411919.

94. Tommy Beer, "Minneapolis City Council Unanimously Votes to Replace Police with Community-Led Model," *Forbes*, June 12, 2020, https://www .forbes.com/sites/tommybeer/2020/06/12/minneapolis-city-council-una nimously-votes-to-replace-police-with-community-led-model/?sh=e96df db71a52.

95. John Eligon, "Minneapolis Police Experience Surge of Departures in Aftermath of George Floyd Protests," *New York Times*, July 21, 2020, https://www.nytimes.com/2020/07/21/us/minneapolis-police-george-flo yd-protests.html.

96. Joshua Caplan, "Video: Kenosha Protesters Shout 'Death to America!' and 'Kill the Police!'" Breitbart, August 25, 2020, https:// www.breitbart.com/law-and-order/2020/08/25/video-kenosha-protesters-shout-death-to-america-kill-the-police/.

97. Emma Colton, "Video of BLM Protesters Chanting Popular Iranian Phrase 'Death to America' Goes Viral," *Washington Examiner*, September 1, 2020, https://www.washingtonexaminer.com/news/video-of-blm-pro testers-chanting-popular-iranian-phrase-death-to-america-goes-viral.

98. Ryan Gaydos, "Colin Kaepernick Mocked for Tweet Calling Fourth of July 'Celebration of White Supremacy,'" Fox News, July 6, 2020, https:// www.foxnews.com/sports/colin-kaepernick-mocked-hypocritical-tweet -fourth-of-july.

99. Thomas Sowell, "'Legacy of Slavery' a Legacy of Cliches and Lazy Thinking," Len Connect, July 20, 2015, https://www.lenconnect.com/ar ticle/20150720/OPINION/150729955.

100. Annie Gowen, "As Statues of Founding Fathers Topple, Debate Rages over Where Protesters Should Draw the Line," *Washington Post*, July 7, 2020, https://www.washingtonpost.com/national/as-statues-of-founding -fathers-topple-debate-rages-over-where-protesters-should-draw-the-line /2020/07/07/5de7c956-bfb7-11ea-b4f6-cb39cd8940fb_story.html; "List of Monuments and Memorials Removed during the George Floyd Protests," Wikipedia, https://en.wikipedia.org/wiki/List_of_monuments _and_memorials_removed_during_the_George_Floyd_protests#United _States.

101. "Robert E. Lee Statue Toppled in Montgomery; Confederate Statue Vandalized in Mobile," ABC News, June 2, 2020, https://abc3340.com /news/local/robert-e-lee-statue-toppled-in-montgomery-confederate-sta tue-vandalized-in-mobile.

102. Alan Taylor, "The Statues Brought Down since the George Floyd Protests Began," *The Atlantic*, July 2, 2020, https://www.theatlantic.com/photo /2020/07/photos-statues-removed-george-floyd-protests-began/613774/.

103. Ibid.

104. Ibid.

105. Ibid.

106. David Williams, "Protesters Tore Down a George Washington Statue and Set a Fire on Its Head," CNN, June 19, 2020, https://www.cnn.com/20 20/06/19/us/portland-george-washington-statue-toppled-trnd/index.html.

107. Ella Torres, "Protesters Bring Down Statue of Francis Scott Key," ABC News, June 20, 2020, https://abcnews.go.com/US/protesters-bring-statue -francis-key-scott/story?id=71359718.

108. Robin Pogrebin, "Roosevelt Statue to Be Removed from Museum of Natural History," *New York Times*, June 21, 2020, https://www.nytimes .com/2020/06/21/arts/design/roosevelt-statue-to-be-removed-from-muse um-of-natural-history.html; Nora McGreevy, "The Racist Statue of Theodore Roosevelt Will No Longer Loom Over the American Museum of Natural History," Smithsonian Mag, June 23, 2020, https://www.smi thsonianmag.com/smart-news/statue-theodore-roosevelt-removed-reexa mination-racist-acts-180975154/.

109. Talk of the Nation, "Teddy Roosevelt's 'Shocking' Dinner with Washington," NPR, May 14, 2012, https://www.npr.org/2012/05/14/15 2684575/teddy-roosevelts-shocking-dinner-with-washington.

110. Lee Brown, "Shaun King's Calls to Remove White Jesus Statues Leads to Ridicule, Outrage, Threats," *New York Post*, June 23, 2020, https://nyp ost.com/2020/06/23/shaun-kings-calls-to-remove-jesus-statues-lead-to -death-threats/.

111. Taylor, "Statues Brought Down.".

112. "Emancipation Memorial," Washington.org, https://washington.org/find -dc-listings/emancipation-memorial-freedmans-memorial.

113. Scottie Andrew and Anna Sturla, "A Statue of Frederick Douglass Was Toppled over the Fourth of July Weekend, the Anniversary of His Famous Speech," CNN, July 6, 2020, https://www.cnn.com/2020/07/06/us/freder ick-douglass-statue-toppled-trnd/index.html.

114. "31 Celebrities Who Have Gone Above and Beyond to Support Black Lives Matter," *Harper's Bazaar*, June 10, 2010, https://www.harpersba zaar.com.sg/life/celebrities-gone-above-beyond-support-blm/; Diandra Malivindi, "All the Celebrities Protesting in Solidarity with Black Lives Matter," *Elle Australia*, June 9, 2020, https://www.elle.com.au/celebrity /celebrities-protest-black-lives-matter-23600.

115. Marina Pitofsky, "Kim Kardashian West: 'I Am Infuriated and I Am Disgusted' over George Floyd Death," *The Hill*, May 30, 2020, https://th

ehill.com/blogs/in-the-know/in-the-know/500295-kim-kardashian-west
-i-am-infuriated-and-i-am-disgusted-over#.

116. Mike Oz, "MLB to Feature Social Justice Uniform Patches and 'Black
Lives Matter' Mound Stencil on Opening Day," Yahoo! Sports, July 22,
2020, https://sports.yahoo.com/report-mlb-players-may-wear-social-jus
tice-patches-on-their-uniforms-for-opening-day-204420464.html.

117. Broderick Turner and Dan Woike, "NBA, Players Agree to 'Black Lives
Matter' and Other Messages to Wear on Jerseys," *Tampa Bay Times*, July
5, 2020, https://www.tampabay.com/news/2020/07/05/nba-players-agree
-to-black-lives-matter-and-other-messages-to-wear-on-jerseys/; Zach
Lowe and Ramona Shelburne, "Sources: NBA, Union Plan to Paint 'Black
Lives Matter' on Courts in Orlando," ESPN, June 29, 2020, https://www
.espn.com/nba/story/_/id/29384944/nba-plans-paint-black-lives-matter
-courts-orlando; Richard Haver, "'Power to the People': John Lennon's
Revolutionary Statement," UDiscoverMusic, March 13, 2020, https://
www.udiscovermusic.com/stories/power-to-the-people/;
"Powernomics—27 Ways You Can Practice Group Economics,"
PanAfricanAlliance, https://www.panafricanalliance.com/group-econo
mics/.

118. "Message from Commissioner Roger Goodell," Vimeo, June 5, 2020,
https://vimeo.com/426391664; Rachel Treisman, "The NFL Will Play
'Lift Every Voice and Sing' before Each Season-Opener Game," NPR,
July 2, 2020, https://www.npr.org/sections/live-updates-protests-for-ra
cial-justice/2020/07/02/886936096/the-nfl-will-play-lift-every-voice-and
-sing-before-each-season-opener-game; Hemal Jhaveri, "NFL Planning
to Use 'End Racism' and 'It Takes All Of Us' in End Zones Misses the
Mark," *USA Today*, September 1, 2020, https://ftw.usatoday.com/2020
/09/nfl-planning-to-use-end-racism-and-it-takes-all-of-us-in-end-zones
-misses-the-mark; Geoffrey C. Arnold, "NFL to Allow Names of Victims
of Systemic Racism and Police Brutality on Helmet Padding: Report,"
Oregonian, August 31, 2020, https://www.oregonlive.com/nfl/2020/08
/nfl-to-allow-names-of-victims-of-systemic-racism-and-police-brutality
-on-helmet-padding-report.html.

119. Buchanan, Bui, and Patel, "Black Lives Matter May Be the Largest
Movement in U.S. History."

PART TWO: Black Lives Martyrs

1. Lee Stranahan, "Video—Black Lives Matter Founder Rants at Netroots:
'Burn Everything Down!'" Breitbart, July 27, 2015, https://www.breitbart.
com/politics/2015/07/27/video-black-lives-matter-founder-rants-at-netroots-
burn-everything-down/.

The Cause

1.   "HerStory," Black Lives Matter, https://blacklivesmatter.com/herstory/.

2.   Christopher Brito, "LeBron James Condemns Killing of Ahmaud Arbery, Says 'We're Literally Hunted Everyday,'" CBS News, May 7, 2020, https://www.cbsnews.com/news/lebron-james-ahmaud-arbery-statment-killing-twitter/.

3.   Chauvin's knee was actually on Floyd's neck for nine minutes and twenty-nine seconds, as explained in Eric Levenson, "Former Officer Knelt on George Floyd for 9 Minutes and 29 Seconds—Not the Infamous 8:46," CNN, March 30, 2021, https://www.cnn.com/2021/03/29/us/george-floyd-timing-929-846/index.html.

4.   Bill Russell, "Racism Is Not a Historical Footnote," Players' Tribune, September 14, 2020, https://www.theplayerstribune.com/en-us/articles/bill-russell-nba-racial-injustice.

5.   Sarah DeGue, Katherine A. Fowler, and Cynthia Calkins, "Deaths Due To Use of Lethal Force by Law Enforcement: Findings from the National Violent Death Reporting System, 17 U.S. States, 2009–2012," American Journal of Preventive Medicine 5, no. 1, supplement 3 (November 1, 2016): S173–S187, https://www.ncbi.nlm.nih.gov/pmc/articles/PMC6080222/; John Sullivan, Zane Anthony, Julie Tate, and Jennifer Jenkins, "Nationwide, Police Shot and Killed Nearly 1,000 People in 2017," Washington Post, January 6, 2018, https://www.washingtonpost.com/investigations/nationwide-police-shot-and-killed-nearly-1000-people-in-2017/2018/01/04/4eed5f34-e4e9-11e7-ab50-621fe0588340_story.html; Michael Harriot, "Here's How Many People Police Killed in 2018," The Root, January 3, 2019, https://www.theroot.com/here-s-how-many-people-police-killed-in-2018-1831469528; Heather Mac Donald, "The Myth of Systemic Police Racism," Wall Street Journal, June 2, 2020, https://www.wsj.com/articles/the-myth-of-systemic-police-racism-11591119883; Heather Mac Donald, "There Is No Epidemic of Fatal Police Shootings against Unarmed Black Americans," USA Today, July 3, 2020, https://www.usatoday.com/story/opinion/2020/07/03/police-black-killings-homicide-rates-race-injustice-column/3235072001/.

6.   Ibid.; PragerU (@prageru), "14 Unarmed Blacks Were Fatally Shot by Police in 2019," Twitter, July 15, 2020, 1:29 p.m., https://twitter.com/prageru/status/1283453676577681409?lang=en.

7.   Jodi M. Brown and Patrick A. Langan, "Policing and Homicide, 1976–98: Justifiable Homicide by Police, Police Officers Murdered by Felons," U.S. Department of Justice, Bureau of Justice Statistics, March 2001, https://bjs.gov/content/pub/pdf/ph98.pdf.

8.   John R. Lott Jr. and Carlisle E. Moody, "Do White Police Officers Unfairly Target Black Suspects?" Crime Prevention Research Center,

July 21, 2017, https://papers.ssrn.com/sol3/papers.cfm?abstract_id=2870189.

9. Tom Jacobs, "Black Cops Are Just as Likely as White Cops to Kill Black Suspects," Pacific Standard, August 9, 2018, https://psmag.com/social-justice/black-cops-are-just-as-likely-as-whites-to-kill-black-suspects.

10. Alana Wise, "Oprah Winfrey Commissions 26 Billboards Demanding Arrests in Breonna Taylor's Killing," NPR, August 7, 2020, https://www.npr.org/sections/live-updates-protests-for-racial-justice/2020/08/07/900192570/oprah-winfrey-commissions-26-billboards-demanding-arrests-in-breonna-taylors-kil.

11. "Department of Justice Report Regarding the Criminal Investigation into the Shooting Death of Michael Brown by Ferguson, Missouri, Police Officer Darren Wilson," Justice.gov, March 4, 2015, https://www.justice.gov/sites/default/files/opa/press-releases/attachments/2015/03/04/doj_report_on_shooting_of_michael_brown_1.pdf.

Chapter 1: Face of the Movement: George Floyd

1. Eric Levenson, "Former Officer Knelt on George Floyd for 9 Minutes and 29 Seconds—Not the Infamous 8:46," CNN, March 30, 2021, https://www.cnn.com/2021/03/29/us/george-floyd-timing-929-846/index.html.

2. "Rest in Power, Beautiful," Black Lives Matter, https://blacklivesmatter.com/rest-in-power-beautiful/.

3. Heather Mac Donald, "There Is No Epidemic of Fatal Police Shootings against Unarmed Black Americans," Manhattan Institute, July 3, 2020, https://www.manhattan-institute.org/police-black-killings-homicide-rates-race-injustice.

4. Sachin Jangra, "George Floyd Criminal Past Record/Arrest History/Career Timeline: Baggie, Gun Pregnant and All Details," Courier Daily, June 11, 2020, https://www.thecourierdaily.com/george-floyd-criminal-past-record-arrest/20177/; Jessica Lee, "Background Check: Investigating George Floyd's Criminal Record," Snopes, June 12, 2020, https://www.snopes.com/news/2020/06/12/george-floyd-criminal-record/.

5. "Factbox: After Chauvin, Minnesota Set to Prosecute Three Other Officers in Floyd Murder," Reuters, April 20, 2021, https://www.reuters.com/world/us/after-chauvin-minnesota-set-prosecute-three-other-officers-floyd-death-2021-04-20/.

6. KARE 11, "RAW: Released George Floyd Body Cam Footage from Former Officers Thomas Lane and J. Alexander Kueng," YouTube, August 10, 2020, https://www.youtube.com/watch?v=NjKjaCvXdf4.

7. "George Floyd: What We Know about the Officers Charged over His Death," BBC, June 8, 2020, https://www.bbc.com/news/world-us-canada-52969205; Bill Hutchinson and Alex Perez, "George Floyd's Relatives

Watch as 4 Officers Charged in Killing Appear in Court," ABC News, June 29, 2020, https://abcnews.go.com/US/george-floyds-relatives-watch -officers-charged-killing-court/story?id=71510706.

8. Charlie Wiese, "Autopsy Report: George Floyd Died from Cardiopulmonary Arrest, Was Positive for COVID-19," KSTP, June 3, 2020, https://kstp.com/news/george-floyd-autopsy-report-shows-george -floyd-died-from-cardiopulmonary-arrest-was-positive-for-covid-19/575 0262/.

9. "Hennepin County Medical Examiner's Office Autopsy Report," Hennepin County, https://www.hennepin.us/, May 26, 2020, https://www .hennepin.us/-/media/hennepinus/residents/public-safety/documents/flo yd-autopsy-6-3-20.pdf.

10. "Fentanyl," Centers for Disease Control and Prevention, https://www.cdc .gov/niosh/topics/fentanyl/.

11. Don Brown, "Who Killed George Floyd?" American Thinker, September 18, 2020, https://www.americanthinker.com/articles/2020/09/who_kil led_george_floyd.html#ixzz6YUn2xRxl.

12. George Parry, "Who Killed George Floyd?" American Spectator, August 6, 2020, https://spectator.org/george-floyd-death-toxicology-report/; "State of Minnesota v. Derek Michael Chauvin," Prosecutor File No. 20A06620, https://assets.documentcloud.org/documents/6933246/Derek -Chauvin-Complaint.pdf.

13. Parry, "Who Killed George Floyd?"

14. "Ellison Tweet on Antifa Handbook and Trump Draws Criticism," Associated Press, January 4, 2018, https://apnews.com/b95cf2336ba348 1d88fc971ce347c940/Ellison-tweet-on-Antifa-handbook-and-Trump-dr aws-criticism.

15. For a detailed account of the contents of the videos, see Brown, "Who Killed George Floyd?"

16. "George Floyd," Stark Times, https://starktimes.com/george-floyd-death -wiki-family-age-height-weight-facts-more/; Ivan Pereira, "George Floyd Remembered by Friends and Family as Hardworking 'Gentle Giant,'" ABC News, June 3, 2020, https://abcnews.go.com/US/george-floyd -remembered-friends-family-hardworking-gentle-giant/story?id=7095 4744; Wendy Grossman Kantor, "Friend of George Floyd Says He Would Have Stopped Any Looting or Riots: 'That's Not Him,'" People, June 3, 2020, https://people.com/crime/friend-says-george-floyd-would-have-st opped-the-looting-and-riots./.

17. 10 Tampa Bay, "RAW: George Floyd Minneapolis Police Body Camera Footage," YouTube, August 10, 2020, https://www.youtube.com/watch ?v=0gQYMBALDXc.

18. Stephen Groves, "How Long Did It Take Medics to Reach Floyd?" Associated Press, April 6, 2021, https://apnews.com/article/minneapolis-archive-trials-death-of-george-floyd-racial-injustice-4311fb3090f071c5c2f838a6f14e5d58; 10 Tampa Bay, "RAW: George Floyd Minneapolis Police Body Camera Footage," YouTube, August 10, 2020, https://www.youtube.com/watch?v=0gQYMBALDXc.

19. 10 Tampa Bay, "RAW: George Floyd Minneapolis Police Body Camera Footage," YouTube, August 10, 2020, https://www.youtube.com/watch?v=0gQYMBALDXc.

20. Emily R. Siegel, Andrew W. Lehren, and Andrew Blankstein, "Minneapolis Police Rendered 44 People Unconscious with Neck Restraints in Five Years," NBC News, https://www.nbcnews.com/news/us-news/minneapolis-police-rendered-44-people-unconscious-neck-restraints-five-years-n1220416.

21. CNN, "Unarmed Man Begs for Life, Shot by Police," YouTube, December 10, 2017, https://www.youtube.com/watch?v=7Ooa7wOKHhg&t=67s.

22. "George Floyd's Knee Restraint Death Is Reminder of Tony Timpa's Killing, His Family Says," Inside Edition, June 11, 2020, https://www.insideedition.com/george-floyds-knee-restraint-death-is-reminder-of-tony-timpas-killing-his-family-says-60089.

23. Erin Donaghue, "Disturbing Video Shows Dallas Officers Joking as They Restrain Man Who Died," CBS News, August 1, 2019, https://www.cbsnews.com/news/tony-timpa-disturbing-video-shows-dallas-officers-joking-as-they-restrain-man-who-died/; *Dallas Morning News*, "Dallas Police Body Cameras Show Moment Tony Timpa Stopped Breathing," YouTube, July 30, 2019, https://www.youtube.com/watch?v=_c-E_i8Q5G0.

24. Cary Aspinwall and Cassandra Jaramillo, "Deadly Conduct Charges Dismissed against Dallas Cops in 2016 Death of Tony Timpa, Who Sought 911 Help," *Dallas Morning News*, March 18, 2019, https://www.dallasnews.com/news/2019/03/18/deadly-conduct-charges-dismissed-against-dallas-cops-in-2016-death-of-tony-timpa-who-sought-911-help/.

25. "Reverend Al Sharpton Eulogy Transcript at George Floyd's Memorial Service," Rev, June 4, 2020, https://www.rev.com/blog/transcripts/reverend-al-sharpton-eulogy-transcript-at-george-floyd-memorial-service.

26. "The African American Population," Black Demographics, 2019, https://blackdemographics.com/households/middle-class/.

27. Orlando Patterson, "Race, Gender, and Liberal Fallacies," *New York Times*, October 20, 1991 https://www.nytimes.com/1991/10/20/opinion/op-ed-race-gender-and-liberal-fallacies.html.

28. "Trial of Derek Chauvin," Wikipedia, https://en.wikipedia.org/wiki/State_v._Chauvin; Oliver O'Connell and Nathan Place, "Who Were the Key Witnesses Who Helped Determine the Outcome in Derek Chauvin Trial?"

Independent, April 21, 2021, https://www.independent.co.uk/news/wor
ld/americas/us-politics/derek-chauvin-trial-witnesses-floyd-b1834846
.html.

29. Griff Witte, Joyce Koh, Kim Bellware, and Silvia Foster-Frau, "The
Chauvin Verdict Had Cities Nationwide Braced for Unrest," *Washington
Post*, April 20, 2021, https://www.washingtonpost.com/national/derek
-chauvin-verdict-reaction/2021/04/20/58086c4a-a21d-11eb-85fc-06664
ff4489d_story.html.

30. Adam Barnes, "Derek Chauvin Claims Jury Was Threatened and
Intimidated into Guilty Verdict of Murdering George Floyd," *The Hill*,
April 5, 2021, https://thehill.com/changing-america/respect/
equality/551883-derek-chauvin-claims-jury-was-threatened-and-
intimidated; Kevin McCoy, "Alternate Juror in the Derek Chauvin Trial
Speaks Out: 'I Felt He Was Guilty,'" *USA Today*, April 22, 2021, https://
www.usatoday.com/story/news/nation/2021/04/22/
derek-chauvin-verdict-alternate-juror-speaks-out/7332593002/.

31. Joel B. Pollak, "Maxine Waters: Derek Chauvin Must Be 'Guilty, Guilty,
Guilty' or We Take to the Streets," Breitbart, April 17, 2021, https://www
.breitbart.com/politics/2021/04/17/maxine-waters-derek-chauvin-must
-be-guilty-guilty-guilty-or-we-take-to-the-streets/.

32. Caroline Kelly, "Judge in Derek Chauvin Trial Says Rep. Maxine Waters'
Comments May Be Grounds for Appeal," CNN, April 20, 2021, https://
www.cnn.com/2021/04/19/politics/judge-derek-chauvin-maxine-waters
-mistrial-appeal/index.html.

33. Ibid.

34. Tami Abdollah, "Historic Civil Settlement for George Floyd's Family
Brings Uncertainty to Derek Chauvin's Criminal Trial," *USA Today*,
March 15, 2021, https://www.usatoday.com/story/news/2021/03/15/his
toric-civil-settlement-george-floyds-death-impact/4705076001/.

35. Matthew Williams, "Report: Biden DOJ Planned on Arresting Chauvin
for 'Civil Rights Violations' in Court if He Was Found Innocent,"
American Action News, April 29, 2021, https://americanactionnews.com
/government/2021/04/29/report-biden-doj-planned-on-arresting-chauvin
-for-civil-rights-violations-in-court-if-he-was-found-innocent/; Andy
Mannix, "Feds Plan to Indict Chauvin, Other Three Ex-Officers on Civil
Rights Charges," *Minneapolis Star Tribune*, April 29, 2021, https://www
.startribune.com/feds-plan-to-indict-chauvin-other-three-ex-officers-on
-civil-rights-charges/600051374/?refresh=true.

36. Gustaf Kilander, "First Chauvin Juror Speaks Out and Says Hours Were
Spent Convincing Only Jury Member Uncertain of Guilt," Yahoo! News,
April 28, 2021, https://news.yahoo.com/first-juror-speak-chauvin-trial-14
5029791.html; WCCO-TV staff, "Derek Chauvin Guilty on All 3 Counts

in George Floyd's Death," CBS Minnesota, April 20, 2021, https://min nesota.cbslocal.com/2021/04/20/derek-chauvin-guilty-verdict-george-flo yd-death-trial/.

37. Ibid.

38. Scott Pelley, "*60 Minutes* Interviews the Prosecutors of Derek Chauvin," CBS News, April 26, 2021, https://www.cbsnews.com/news/derek-chau vin-prosecutors-george-floyd-death-60-minutes-2021-04-25/.

Chapter 2: How the Movement Began

1. Jamil Smith, "The Power of Black Lives Matter," *Rolling Stone*, June 16, 2020, https://www.rollingstone.com/culture/culture-features/black-lives -matter-jamil-smith-1014442/.

2. Ibid.

3. Ibid.

4. Jonathan Capehart, "Five Myths about the Killing of Trayvon Martin," *Washington Post*, July 3, 2013, https://www.washingtonpost.com/opin ions/five-myths-about-the-killing-of-trayvon-martin/2013/07/03/0d76c1 76-e368-11e2-80eb-3145e2994a55_story.html; Hank Berrien, "Trayvon Martin: Here's Everything You Need to Know," The Daily Wire, February 5, 2016, https://www.dailywire.com/news/trayvon-martin-review-hank -berrien.

5. "Sanford Cops Sought Warrant to Arrest George Zimmerman in Trayvon Martin Shooting," *Tampa Bay Times*, March 28, 2012, https://www.tam pabay.com/news/publicsafety/crime/sanford-cops-sought-warrant-to-ar rest-george-zimmerman-in-trayvon-martin/1222259/; Trymaine Lee, "Trayvon Martin Case: Police Chief Bill Lee under Fire with 'No Confidence' Vote," HuffPo, March 22, 2012, https://www.huffpost.com /entry/trayvon-martin-case-george-zimmerman-bill-lee_n_1371635.

6. "Trayvon Martin Protests—in Pictures," *The Guardian*, April 13, 2012, https://www.theguardian.com/world/gallery/2012/apr/13/trayvon-mar tin-killing-protests-justice.

7. Tracy Martin and Sybrina Fulton, "Prosecute the Killer of Our Son, 17-year-old Trayvon Martin," Change.org, 2012, https://www.change .org/p/prosecute-the-killer-of-our-son-17-year-old-trayvon-martin; Ruth McCambridge, "Biggest Yet Petition on Change.org is on Trayvon Martin," *Nonprofit Quarterly*, April 4, 2012, https://nonprofitquarterly .org/biggest-yet-petition-on-changeorg-is-on-trayvon-martin/.

8. Elizabeth Flock, "Trayvon Martin 'Million Hoodie March': A Short History of the Hoodie," *Washington Post*, March 22, 2012, https://www .washingtonpost.com/blogs/blogpost/post/trayvon-martin-million-hoo die-march-a-short-history-of-the-hoodie/2012/03/22/gIQAeGCnTS_bl og.html; Casey Glynn, "Trayvon Martin Shooting Sparks 'Hoodie'

Movement," CBS News, April 2, 2012, https://www.cbsnews.com/pictu res/trayvon-martin-shooting-sparks-hoodie-movement/; Lucy Madison, "Dem Rep. Bobby Rush Escorted from House Floor for Wearing Hoodie in Honor of Trayvon Martin," CBS News, March 28, 2012, https://www .cbsnews.com/news/dem-rep-bobby-rush-escorted-from-house-floor-for -wearing-hoodie-in-honor-of-trayvon-martin/.

9. Dashiell Bennett, "Scenes from the 'Million Hoodie March' for Trayvon Martin," *The Atlantic*, March 22, 2012, https://www.theatlantic.com /national/archive/2012/03/scenes-million-hoodie-march-trayvon-martin /330269/.

10. Lisa Orkin Emmanuel, "List of Schools Staging Walkouts for Trayvon Martin," NBC Miami, March 23, 2012, https://www.nbcmiami.com/ne ws/local/list-of-schools-staging-walkouts-for-trayvon-martin/2033257/.

11. John King, "George Zimmerman Charged in Trayvon Martin Case; Martin's Parents React to Charges," CNN (Transcripts), April 11, 2012, http://transcripts.cnn.com/TRANSCRIPTS/1204/11/jkusa.01.html.

12. Steven Nelson, "Jesse Jackson Says Trayvon Martin 'Murdered and Martyred,'" The Daily Caller, March 26, 2012, https://news.yahoo.com /jesse-jackson-says-trayvon-martin-murdered-martyred-162408127.html; Rene Lynch, "Trayvon Martin Case: 'Blacks Are under Attack,' Says Jesse Jackson," *Los Angeles Times*, March 23, 2012, https://www.latimes.com /nation/la-xpm-2012-mar-23-la-na-nn-trayvon-martin-case-jesse-jackson -20120323-story.html.

13. Tina Moore, "Group Offers $10,000 to 'Capture' Trayvon Martin's Killer," *New York Daily News*, March 24, 2012, https://www.nydailyn ews.com/news/national/black-panther-rage-10g-capture-trayvon-killer-ar ticle-1.1050370#ixzz1qI2aVkXd.

14. Roque Planas, "CNN's 'White Hispanic' Label for George Zimmerman Draws Fire," HuffPo, July 7, 2013, https://www.huffpost.com/entry/cnn -white-hispanic_n_3588744; Erik Wemple, "Why Did *New York Times* Call George Zimmerman 'White Hispanic'?" *Washington Post*, March 28, 2012, https://www.washingtonpost.com/blogs/erik-wemple/post/why -did-new-york-times-call-george-zimmerman-white-hispanic/2012/03/28 /gIQAW6fngS_blog.html.

15. Barack Obama, "Remarks by the President on the Nomination of Dr. Jim Kim for World Bank President," The White House, March 23, 2012, https://obamawhitehouse.archives.gov/the-press-office/2012/03/23/rema rks-president-nomination-dr-jim-kim-world-bank-president.

16. Frank Rosario, "Ex-NAACP Big Rips Al & Jesse for Handling of Trayvon Martin Shooting," *New York Post*, March 27, 2012, https://nypost.com /2012/03/27/ex-naacp-big-rips-al-jesse-for-handling-of-trayvon-martin -shooting/.

17. William J. Bennett, "Rush to Judgment in Trayvon Martin Case," CNN, March 30, 2012, https://www.cnn.com/2012/03/30/opinion/bennett-tr ayvon-martin/index.html.

18. Shelby Steele: "The Exploitation of Trayvon Martin," *Wall Street Journal*, April 6, 2012, https://www.wsj.com/articles/SB100014240527023033025 04577323691134926300.

19. Jamil Smith, "The Power of Black Lives Matter," *Rolling Stone*, June 16, 2020, https://www.rollingstone.com/culture/culture-features/black-lives -matter-jamil-smith-1014442/.

20. Linda Deutsch, "Bystander Officer Says Powell Shouted King Was 'Dusted' With PM-LA Mayor, Bjt," Associated Press, March 18, 1993, https://apnews.com/article/c0bf75886bd4b783e844c781588250e2; "Hallucinogen Presentation," Riverside Community College District, Summer 2019, http://websites.rcc.edu/estrada/files/2019/07/Hallucino gens-Summer-2019.pdf.

21. Douglas O. Linder, "LAPD and the Use of Force," Famous Trials, https:// famous-trials.com/lapd/574-kingforce..

22. "Riots Erupt in Los Angeles after Police Officers Are Acquitted in Rodney King Trial," History.com, March 3, 2010, https://www.history.com/this -day-in-history/riots-erupt-in-los-angeles.

23. Carolina A. Miranda, "Of the 63 People Killed during '92 Riots, 23 Deaths Remain Unsolved," *Los Angeles Times*, April 28, 2017, https:// www.latimes.com/entertainment/arts/miranda/la-et-cam-la-riots-jeff-be all-los-angeles-uprising-20170427-htmlstory.html.

24. "Rodney King Timeline: Life after the Los Angeles Riots: A Timeline of Events in King's Life Beginning with the Beating Incident," ABC News, June 17, 2012, https://abcnews.go.com/US/rodney-king-dies-timeline-life -los-angeles-riots/story?id=16589879.

25. United Press International, "Milwaukee Officer Won't Face Charges for Killing Mentally Ill Man," Breitbart, December 22, 2014, https://www .breitbart.com/news/milwaukee-officer-wont-face-charges-for-killing -mentally-ill-man/; Meg Kissinger and Ashley Luthern, "More Training Sought after Fatal Shooting by Milwaukee Police," *Milwaukee Journal Sentinel*, May 2, 2014, https://archive.jsonline.com/news/milwaukee/au topsy-planned-thursday-on-man-shot-by-police-at-red-arrow-park-b992 60307z1-257512561.html/; Ben Handelman, "Former MPD Officer Christopher Manney Breaks His Silence: 'I'm Not Some Monster,'" Fox 6 Milwaukee, February 12, 2016, https://www.fox6now.com/news/for mer-mpd-officer-christopher-manney-breaks-his-silence-im-not-some-mo nster; Ashley Luthern, "Ex-Milwaukee Officer Won't Be Charged in Dontre Hamilton Shooting," *Milwaukee Journal Sentinel*, December 22, 2014, https://archive.jsonline.com/news/milwaukee/former-officer-wont

-be-charged-in-fatal-shooting-of-dontre-hamilton-b99398655z1-286559
211.html/; Bruce Vielmetti, "Appeals Court Affirms Firing of Milwaukee
Officer in Dontre Hamilton Killing," *Milwaukee Journal Sentinel*, August
22, 2017, https://www.jsonline.com/story/news/crime/2017/08/22/chris
topher-manneys-firing-upheld-court-appeals/589337001/.

26. "Documents Describe Dontre Hamilton's Battle with Mental Illness, His
Family's Efforts to Get Him Help," Fox 6 Milwaukee, December 24,
2014, https://www.fox6now.com/news/documents-describe-dontre-ha
miltons-battle-with-mental-illness-his-familys-efforts-to-get-him-help;
Kissinger and Luthern, "More Training Sought."

27. Max Seigle, "Many Participate in 'Black Lives Matter' Rally Downtown,"
WISN.com, December 14, 2014, https://www.wisn.com/article/many-par
ticipate-in-black-lives-matter-rally-downtown/6324601; "Jackson Leads
Milwaukee Protest of Police Killing of Dontre Hamilton," NBC News,
January 2, 2015, https://www.nbcnews.com/news/us-news/jackson-leads
-milwaukee-protest-police-killing-dontre-hamilton-n278646; Tea Krulos,
"New Black Lives Matter Mural Depicts Dontre Hamilton, Sandra Bland
and Syville Smith," ShepherdExpress.com, June 29, 2020, https://www
.newsbreak.com/news/1591893921081/new-black-lives-matter-mural-de
picts-dontre-hamilton-sandra-bland-and-syville-smith.

28. Ashley Sears, "Estimated 1,200, Including Dontre Hamilton's Family,
Take Part in Protests during GOP Debate," Fox 6 Milwaukee, November
10, 2015, https://www.fox6now.com/news/estimated-1200-including-do
ntre-hamiltons-family-take-part-in-protests-during-gop-debate.

29. Seigle, "Many Participate in 'Black Lives Matter' Rally Downtown."

30. Ibid.

31. Ashley Luthern, "City of Milwaukee Reaches Tentative $2.3 Million
Settlement in Dontre Hamilton Case," *Milwaukee Journal Sentinel*, May
9, 2017, https://www.jsonline.com/story/news/crime/2017/05/09/city-mil
waukee-reaches-tentative-23-million-settlement-dontre-hamilton-case/10
1487358/.

32. Associated Press, "Milwaukee Council OKs $2.3 Million Settlement in
Dontre Hamilton Shooting," NBC News, May 31, 2017, https://www.nb
cnews.com/news/us-news/milwaukee-council-oks-2-3-million-settlement
-dontre-hamilton-shooting-n766876.

33. Associated Press, "No Federal Charges for Milwaukee Officer Who Killed
Man," Breitbart, November 10, 2015, https://www.breitbart.com/news/
no-federal-charges-for-milwaukee-officer-who-killed-man/.

34. "Police Officer Kevin Dorian Jordan," Officer Down Memorial Page,
https://www.odmp.org/officer/22088-police-officer-kevin-dorian-jordan.

35. Jim Meyers, "11 Facts about the Eric Garner Case the Media Won't Tell You," Newsmax, December 4, 2014, https://www.newsmax.com/News front/eric-garner-chokehold-grand-jury-police/2014/12/04/id/611058/.
36. WKBN27, "Eric Garner Death," YouTube, December 3, 2014, https://www.youtube.com/watch?v=19uR8-fErzE.
37. Barry Latzer, "An Officer Doing His Job," *City Journal*, September 18, 2017, https://www.city-journal.org/html/officer-doing-his-job-15449.html.
38. Ben Shapiro, "The Actual Facts of the Eric Garner Case," Breitbart, December 3, 2014, https://www.breitbart.com/politics/2014/12/03/actu al-facts-eric-garner/; Ian Fisher, "Kelly Bans Choke Holds by Officers," *New York Times*, November 24, 1993, https://www.nytimes.com/1993/11/24/nyregion/kelly-bans-choke-holds-by-officers.html.
39. Barry Latzer, "An Officer Doing His Job," *City Journal*, September 18, 2017, https://www.city-journal.org/html/officer-doing-his-job-15449.html.
40. Larry Celona and Kathianne Boniello, "Man in Chokehold Death Had No Throat Damage: Autopsy," *New York Post*, July 19, 2014, https://ny post.com/2014/07/19/man-in-chokehold-death-had-no-throat-damage-autopsy/; G. Wesley Clark, "A Medical Perspective on the Garner Tragedy," American Thinker, December 8, 2014, https://www.american thinker.com/articles/2014/12/a_medical_perspective_on_the_garner_tr agedy.html.
41. Krav Maga Street Defence, "Carotid Artery Choke," YouTube, June 8, 2010, https://www.youtube.com/watch?v=gP5ccHbgUi4.
42. "'I Can't Breathe': Eric Garner Put in Chokehold by NYPD Officer—Video," *The Guardian*, December 4, 2014, https://www.theguardian.com/us-news/video/2014/dec/04/i-cant-breathe-eric-garner-chokehold-death-video.
43. Ashley Southall, "'I Can't Breathe': 5 Years after Eric Garner's Death, an Officer Faces Trial," *New York Times*, May 12, 2019, https://www.nyt imes.com/2019/05/12/nyregion/eric-garner-death-daniel-pantaleo-choke hold.html; Clark, "A Medical Perspective on the Garner Tragedy."
44. Caroline Bankoff, "Cop Who Put Staten Island Man in Fatal Chokehold Stripped of Badge and Gun," *New York Magazine*, July 20, 2014, https://nymag.com/intelligencer/2014/07/cop-who-choked-garner-stripped-of-badge-and-gun.html.
45. Daudi Abe, "Eric Garner, 1970–2014," Black Past, July 21, 2016, https://www.blackpast.org/african-american-history/garner-eric-1970-2014/; Shapiro, "The Actual Facts."
46. Ali Winston, "Medical Examiner Testifies Eric Garner Died of Asthma Caused by Officer's Chokehold," *New York Times*, May 15, 2019, https://

www.nytimes.com/2019/05/15/nyregion/eric-garner-death-daniel-panta leo-chokehold.html.

47. Clark, "A Medical Perspective on the Garner Tragedy."

48. Ibid.

49. Josh Margolin, Ron Claiborne, and Mark Crudele, "NYPD Cop's Chokehold May Not Have Caused Serious Injury to Man's Throat," ABC News, July 20, 2014, https://abcnews.go.com/US/nypd-cops-chokehold -caused-injury-mans-throat/story?id=24640347; Mike Hayes, Meg Wagner, and Veronica Rocha, "NYPD Officer in Eric Garner Case Fired," CNN, August 19, 2019, https://www.cnn.com/us/live-news/daniel-panta leo-eric-garner-nypd/h_02f8f93e1b782e85c738c7d5fded8897.

50. Zed Collective and Page May, "We're Assata's Daughters," Zed, October 19, 2016, https://www.zedbooks.net/blog/posts/getting-free/.

51. Vivian Ho, Peter Fimrite, and Kale Williams, "Oakland, S.F. Protesters Denounce Police Killing of Eric Garner," *San Francisco Chronicle*, December 3, 2014, https://www.sfchronicle.com/bayarea/article/Bay-Area -protesters-denounce-police-killing-of-5933671.php; Peniel E. Joseph, "'I Can't Breathe': Why Eric Garner Protests Are Gaining Momentum," Reuters, December 5, 2014, http://blogs.reuters.com/great-debate/2014 /12/05/i-cant-breathe-why-eric-garner-protests-are-gaining-momentum/.

52. Chelsia Rose Marcius, Joe Stepansky, and Kerry Burke, "Protesters Flood NYC in Second Night of Demonstrations Opposing Ruling Not to Indict NYPD Cop in Eric Garner's Death," *New York Daily News*, December 5, 2014, https://www.nydailynews.com/new-york/nyc-protests-eric-gar ner-case-resume-night-article-1.2033891; Brandt Williams, "Protests Shut Down Part of I-35W for over an Hour," MPR News, December 4, 2014, https://www.mprnews.org/story/2014/12/04/protesters-close-i35w; Evan Sernoffsky, Greta Kaul, and Hamed Aleaziz, "Police Use Tear Gas on Berkeley Protesters," *San Francisco Chronicle*, December 7, 2014, https:// www.sfgate.com/bayarea/article/Protesters-march-again-in-S-F-and-Ber keley-5940498.php; Adam Janos, Thomas MacMillan, Joe Jackson, and Pervaiz Shallwani, "300 Arrests after 2 Days of Eric Garner Protests, More Demonstrations Planned," *Wall Street Journal*, December 5, 2014, https://www.wsj.com/articles/more-than-200-arrested-in-second -night-of-new-york-city-protests-1417792930; "Eric Garner Death: 76 Arrested at London Westfield Demo," BBC News, December 11, 2014, https://www.bbc.com/news/uk-england-london-30424338.

53. News Wires, "#BlackLivesMatter: NYPD Sacks Officer over 2014 Death of Eric Garner," France24, August 19, 2019, https://www.france24.com /en/20190819-usa-blacklivesmatter-nypd-sacks-officer-pantaleo-over-20 14-death-eric-garner; Jenée Desmond-Harris, "'Black Lives Matter,' Again: New Yorkers Protest Eric Garner Decision," *Vox*, December 3,

2014, https://www.vox.com/xpress/2014/12/3/7329005/eric-garner-pro tests-photos; "It Took Only Five Years for Eric Garner to Get Justice—If It Even Lasts," *Washington Post*, August 24, 2019, https://www.washing tonpost.com/opinions/it-took-only-five-years-for-eric-garner-to-get-justi ce—if-it-even-lasts/2019/08/24/a17075aa-c5d1-11e9-9986-1fb3e4397b e4_story.html.

54. Joseph Goldstein and Nate Schweber, "Man's Death after Chokehold Raises Old Issue for the Police," *New York Times*, July 18, 2014, https:// www.nytimes.com/2014/07/19/nyregion/staten-island-man-dies-after-he -is-put-in-chokehold-during-arrest.html.

55. Denis Hamill, "Widow of Staten Island Dad Who Died after Cop Put Him in Chokehold Remembers Husband as 'Gentle Giant,'" *New York Daily News*, July 18, 2014, https://www.nydailynews.com/new-york/ha mill-widow-staten-island-dad-died-chokehold-remembers-husband-gent le-giant-article-1.1872618.

56. Matt Zapotosky and Devlin Barrett, "Justice Dept. Will Not Charge Police in Connection with Eric Garner's Death," *Washington Post*, July 16, 2019, https://www.washingtonpost.com/national-security/justice-de pt-will-not-charge-police-in-connection-with-eric-garners-death/2019/07 /16/f5188d84-a761-11e9-86dd-d7f0e60391e9_story.html.

57. J. David Goodman, "Eric Garner Case Is Settled by New York City for $5.9 Million," *New York Times*, July 13, 2015, https://www.nytimes.com /2015/07/14/nyregion/eric-garner-case-is-settled-by-new-york-city-for-5-9 -million.html.

Chapter 3: How the Movement Grew

1. Elisa Crouch, "Michael Brown Remembered As a 'Gentle Giant,'" *St. Louis Post-Dispatch*, August 11, 2014, https://www.stltoday.com/news /local/crime-and-courts/michael-brown-remembered-as-a-gentle-giant/ar ticle_cbafa12e-7305-5fd7-8e0e-3139f472d130.html.

2. TDC, "Surveillance Video of Michael Brown's 'Strong-Arm' Robbery," YouTube, https://www.youtube.com/watch?v=38K36LBVT9o. A video of the officer's account of what happened in an interview with ABC's George Stephanopoulos is available here: ABC News, "Officer Darren Wilson Says He Struggled with Brown, Feared for His Life," YouTube, November 26, 2014, https://www.youtube.com/watch?v=YVVmn14NnII.

3. Ben Shapiro, "The Myth or the True Story of Michael Brown, Gentle Giant," FrontPage Magazine, October 28, 2014, https:// archives.frontpagemag.com/fpm/ben-shapiro-myth-or-true-story- michael-brown-truthrevoltorg/.

4. "The Death of Michael Brown," *New York Times*, August 12, 2014, https://www.nytimes.com/2014/08/13/opinion/racial-history-behind-the-ferguson-protests.html.

5. Ibid.

6. Ibid.

7. Pamela Engel, "Here's Everything We Know about the Day Michael Brown Was Killed," *Business Insider*, August 15, 2014, https://www.businessinsider.com/timeline-of-the-day-michael-brown-was-shot-2014-8; Associated Press, "Timeline of Events in Shooting of Michael Brown in Ferguson," ABC News, August 8, 2019, https://abcnews.go.com/US/wireStory/timeline-events-shooting-michael-brown-ferguson-64846365.

8. Rachel Clarke and Christopher Lett, "What Happened When Michael Brown Met Officer Darren Wilson," CNN, November 11, 2014, https://www.cnn.com/interactive/2014/08/us/ferguson-brown-timeline/.

9. News Direct, "Michael Brown Shooting: Timeline," YouTube, September 17, 2014, https://www.youtube.com/watch?v=DYjGLXLka2g.

10. Alberto Cuadra, Lazaro Gamio, Kimbriell Kelly, and Scott Higham, "Chaos in a Police Vehicle," *Washington Post*, December 6, 2014, https://www.washingtonpost.com/wp-srv/special/national/ferguson-reconstruction/.

11. Kimberly Kindi and Sari Horwitz, "Evidence Supports Officer's Account of Shooting in Ferguson," *Washington Post*, October 23, 2014, https://www.washingtonpost.com/politics/new-evidence-supports-officers-account-of-shooting-in-ferguson/2014/10/22/cf38c7b4-5964-11e4-bd61-346aee66ba29_story.html.

12. "Department of Justice Report Regarding the Criminal Investigation into the Shooting Death of Michael Brown by Ferguson, Missouri, Police Officer Darren Wilson," U.S. Department of Justice, March 4, 2015, https://www.justice.gov/sites/default/files/opa/press-releases/attachments/2015/03/04/doj_report_on_shooting_of_michael_brown_1.pdf.

13. Jim Salter and David Lieb, "No Charges in Ferguson Case; Chaos Fills Streets," Associated Press, November 25, 2014, https://apnews.com/eb63bd63c7464573a2a1b8e11375de9f; "Documents from the Ferguson Grand Jury," CNN, November 25, 2014, https://www.cnn.com/interactive/2014/11/us/ferguson-grand-jury-docs/index.html; Kindi and Horwitz, "Evidence Supports Officer's Account of Shooting in Ferguson"; Cuadra, Gamio, Kelly, and Higham, "Chaos in a Police Vehicle"; Shapiro, "The Myth or the True Story of Michael Brown, Gentle Giant"; Wesley Lowery and Darryl Fears, "Michael Brown and Dorian Johnson, the Friend Who Witnessed His Shooting," *Washington Post*, August 31, 2014, https://www.washingtonpost.com/politics/michael-brown-and-dorian-johnson

-the-friend-who-witnessed-his-shooting/2014/08/31/bb9b47ba-2ee2-11 e4-9b98-848790384093_story.html.

14. Dorian Johnson, "The Boy Who Cried Wolf," *Investor's Business Daily*, August 22, 2014, https://www.investors.com/politics/editorials/dorian-jo hnson-the-boy-who-cried-wolf/.

15. "Herstory," BlackLivesMatter.com, https://blacklivesmatter.com/herst ory/.

16. Patrisse Cullors and Asha Bandele, *When They Call You a Terrorist: A Black Lives Matter Memoir* (New York: St. Martin's Press, 2018), https:// books.google.com/books?id=6l4mDwAAQBAJ&pg=PT17&lpg=#v=0 nepage&q&f=false.

17. Associated Press, "Michael Brown's Family Received $1.5 Million Settlement with Ferguson," NBC News, June 23, 2017, https://www.nb cnews.com/storyline/michael-brown-shooting/michael-brown-s-family-re ceived-1-5-million-settlement-ferguson-n775936.

18. "Herstory," BlackLivesMatter.com, https://blacklivesmatter.com/herst ory/; Akiba Solomon, "Get on the Bus: Inside the Black Life Matters 'Freedom Ride' to Ferguson," ColorLines, September 5, 2014, https:// www.colorlines.com/articles/get-bus-inside-black-life-matters-freedom-ri de-ferguson.

19. Darnell L. Moore and Patrisse Cullors, "5 Ways to Never Forget Ferguson—and Deliver Real Justice for Michael Brown," *The Guardian*, September 4, 2014, https://www.theguardian.com/commentisfree/2014 /sep/04/never-forget-ferguson-justice-for-michael-brown.

20. "Patrisse Cullors," Keywiki, https://keywiki.org/Patrisse_Cullors.

21. The author witnessed Faulkner making this observation.

22. Nassim Benchaabane, "Family, Friends, Activists Rebuild Memorial to Michael Brown on Eve of Fourth Anniversary," *St. Louis Post-Dispatch*, August 9, 2018, https://www.stltoday.com/news/local/crime-and-courts /family-friends-activists-rebuild-memorial-to-michael-brown-on-eve-of -fourth-anniversary/article_8c2957d5-400e-5871-8dbd-17c922538e44 .html; Mark Follman, "Michael Brown's Mom Laid Flowers Where He Was Shot—and Police Crushed Them," *Mother Jones*, August 27, 2014, https://www.motherjones.com/politics/2014/08/ferguson-st-louis-police -tactics-dogs-michael-brown/.

23. "Looting Erupts after Vigil for Slain Missouri Teen Michael Brown," NBC News, August 10, 2014, https://www.nbcnews.com/news/us-news/loo ting-erupts-after-vigil-slain-missouri-teen-michael-brown-n177426; Jeremy Kohler, "Ferguson by the Numbers: Breakdown since Protests Began," *St. Louis Post-Dispatch*, November 22, 2014, https://www.stlt oday.com/news/local/crime-and-courts/ferguson-by-the-numbers-break down-since-protests-began/article_5ec448a4-3f08-5861-813c-d03bed1c

9784.html; Tim Barker, "Ferguson-Area Businesses Cope with Aftermath of Weekend Riot," *St. Louis Post-Dispatch*, August 11, 2014, https://www.stltoday.com/news/local/ferguson-area-businesses-cope-with-aftermath-of-weekend-riot/article_4a310ec3-94de-57dd-95f7-4e350f6a6fa2.html.

24.   Associated Press, "Police, Protesters Again Clash outside St. Louis," *Arkansas Democrat Gazette*, August 12, 2014, https://www.arkansasonline.com/news/2014/aug/12/police-protesters-again-clash-outside-st-louis/; Ryan J. Reilly and Christine Conetta, "State Senator to Ferguson Police: 'Will I Get Tear-Gassed Again?'" HuffPo, August 13, 2014, https://www.huffpost.com/entry/state-senator-ferguson_n_5676766; "West Florissant Explodes in Protest of Police Shooting, More Than 30 Arrests," *St. Louis American*, August 11, 2014, http://www.stlamerican.com/news/local_news/article_554e1212-2159-11e4-9dee-001a4bcf887a.html.

25.   Associated Press, "Ferguson Protests Erupt in Violence as People Lob Molotov Cocktails, Police Use Tear Gas" Cleveland.com, August 14, 2014, https://www.cleveland.com/nation/2014/08/ferguson_protests_erupt_in_vio.html; Dylan Byers and Hadas Gold, "Reporters Arrested in Ferguson," *Politico*, August 13, 2014, https://www.politico.com/blogs/media/2014/08/reporters-arrested-in-ferguson-193914; "Obama Urges Ferguson Protesters to Unite under Common Values," America.Aljazeera, August 13, 2014, http://america.aljazeera.com/articles/2014/8/13/2nd-shooting-ferguson.html; Barack Obama, "Statement by the President," Obama White House Archives, August 14, 2014, https://obamawhitehouse.archives.gov/the-press-office/2014/08/14/statement-president.

26.   Charles Pulliam-Moore and Margaret Myers, "Timeline of Events in Ferguson," *The Nation*, August 20, 2014, https://www.pbs.org/newshour/nation/timeline-events-ferguson.

27.   Margaret Hartmann, "National Guard Deployed after Chaotic, Violent Night in Ferguson," *New York Magazine*, August 18, 2014, https://nymag.com/intelligencer/2014/08/national-guard-called-after-more-ferguson-chaos.html; Kevin McDermott, "Ferguson Protests Cool Down after Holder's Visit," I24 News, August 21, 2014, https://web.archive.org/web/20140826130419/http:/www.i24news.tv/en/news/international/americas/40984-140821-ferguson-protests-cool-after-holder-s-visit; "Tense Rally in Ferguson Includes Fires, Shootings and 31 Arrests," *St. Louis Post-Dispatch*, August 19, 2014, https://www.stltoday.com/news/local/metro/tense-tally-in-ferguson-includes-fires-shootings-and-arrests/article_32463afe-f868-564a-9533-9d8ae0b8df14.html; Alan Scher Zagier, "Gov. Nixon Taking National Guard out of Ferguson," *Philadelphia Inquirer*, August 21, 2014, https://web.archive.org/web/20140826183735/http:

/www.philly.com/philly/news/nation_world/20140821_ap_7c413f03c50
84fffb320803ae7713dec.html#RMDYOAuh00Y26Id8.99.

28. Scott Neuman, "Ferguson Timeline: Grief, Anger, and Tension," NPR, November 24, 2014, https://www.npr.org/sections/thetwo-way/2014/11/24/364103735/ferguson-timeline-grief-anger-and-tension.

29. Heather Mac Donald, "The 'Ferguson Effect' Is Fueling a Growing Crime Wave," *New York Post*, May 24, 2016, https://nypost.com/2016/05/24/the-ferguson-effect-is-fueling-a-growing-crime-wave/; Heather Mac Donald, "The Ferguson Effect," *Washington Post*, July 20, 2016, https://www.washingtonpost.com/news/volokh-conspiracy/wp/2016/07/20/the-ferguson-effect/; Mark Berman, "'We Have a Problem.' Homicides Are Up Again This Year in More Than Two Dozen Major U.S. Cities," *Washington Post*, May 14, 2016, https://www.washingtonpost.com/news/post-nation/wp/2016/05/14/we-have-a-problem-homicides-are-up-again-this-year-in-more-than-two-dozen-major-u-s-cities/; Heather Mac Donald, "The New Nationwide Crime Wave," *Wall Street Journal*, May 29, 2015, https://www.wsj.com/articles/the-new-nationwide-crime-wave-1432938425.

30. Jim Suhr, "Mourners Urge Black Americans to Take Action," *Kansas City Star*, August 25, 2014, https://web.archive.org/web/20140826114854if_/http:/www.kansascity.com/news/state/missouri/article1290626.html.

31. "Ferguson Riots: Ruling Sparks Night of Violence," BBC News, November 25, 2014, https://www.bbc.com/news/world-us-canada-30190224.

32. Adam McDonald, "Unrest in Ferguson Cost Missouri Residents This Much," KMOV4, March 19, 2015, https://www.kmov.com/news/unrest-in-ferguson-cost-missouri-residents-this-much/article_755ba32d-13c3-5311-b3c6-95e1780f33b9.html; "Total Cost of Ferguson Riots," HoosierEcon, March 7, 2015, https://hoosierecon.com/2015/03/07/total-cost-of-ferguson-riots/.

33. Josh Hafner, "How Michael Brown's Death, Two Years Ago, Pushed #BlackLivesMatter into a Movement," *USA Today*, August 8, 2016, https://www.usatoday.com/story/news/nation-now/2016/08/08/how-michael-browns-death-two-years-ago-pushed-blacklivesmatter-into-movement/88424366/; Jim Salter and David Lieb, "No Charges in Ferguson Case; Chaos Fills Streets," Associated Press, November 25, 2014, https://apnews.com/eb63bd63c7464573a2a1b8e11375de9f; "Timeline of Events in Shooting of Michael Brown in Ferguson," Associated Press, August 8, 2019, https://apnews.com/9aa32033692547699a3b61da8fd1fc62.

Chapter 4: How the Movement Became National

1. Ruben Vives, Kate Mather, and Richard Winton, "Parents of Man Slain by LAPD Say His Mental Illness Was Well Known," *Los Angeles Times*, August 13, 2014, https://www.latimes.com/local/lanow/la-me-ln-lapd-sh ooting-man-mental-illness-20140813-story.html.

2. Elizabeth Chou, "LAPD Officers Shot Ezell Ford in Self-Defense and Won't Be Charged, Says DA's Office," *Los Angeles Daily News*, January 24, 2017, https://www.dailynews.com/2017/01/24/lapd-officers-shot-eze ll-ford-in-self-defense-and-wont-be-charged-says-das-office/; Awr Hawkins, "LA County District Attorney Clears Officers in Ezell Ford Shooting," Breitbart, January 27, 2017, https://www.breitbart.com/local /2017/01/27/la-county-district-attorney-clears-officers-ezell-ford-shoo ting/.

3. Frank Stoltze, "Ezell Ford Shooting: LAPD Officer Had History in Neighborhood," SCPR, January 30, 2015, https://www.scpr.org/news/20 15/01/30/49567/ezell-ford-shooting-lapd-officer-had-history-in-ne/; Elizabeth Chou, "LAPD Officers Shot Ezell Ford in Self-Defense and Won't Be Charged, Says DA's Office," *Los Angeles Daily News*, January 24, 2017, https://www.dailynews.com/2017/01/24/lapd-officers-shot-eze ll-ford-in-self-defense-and-wont-be-charged-says-das-office/; Matt Hamilton, "Parents of Ezell Ford, Who Was Fatally Shot by LAPD Officers, Settle Lawsuit with City," *Los Angeles Times*, November 2, 2016, https://www.latimes.com/local/lanow/la-me-ln-ezell-ford-lawsuit -20161101-story.html.

4. Jenna Chandler, "LAPD Says Man Slain by Police Reached for Officer's Holstered Gun," *Los Angeles Register*, August 13, 2014, https://web.arc hive.org/web/20140815042810/http://www.losangelesregister.com/artic les/police-603353-officers-shooting.html; Robert Wilde, "Attorney for Ezell Ford Family Calls LAPD Officers 'Animalistic,'" Breitbart, December 30, 2014, https://www.breitbart.com/local/2014/12/30/attorney-for-eze ll-ford-family-calls-lapd-officers-animalistic/; Scott Glover, "Ezell Ford Autopsy Experts," *Los Angeles Times*, December 29, 2014, https://www .latimes.com/local/lanow/la-me-ln-ezell-ford-autopsy-experts-20141229 -story.html.

5. Jenna Chandler, "LAPD Says Man Slain by Police Reached for Officer's Holstered Gun," *Los Angeles Register*, August 13, 2014, https://web.arc hive.org/web/20140815042810/http://www.losangelesregister.com/artic les/police-603353-officers-shooting.html.

6. KCETSoCalConnected, "Black Lives Matter," YouTube, https://youtu.be /D9Bn3h9qiMA?t=21.

7. A. W. R. Hawkins, "LA County District Attorney Clears Officers in Ezell Ford Shooting," Breitbart, January 27, 2017, https://www.breitbart.com

/local/2017/01/27/la-county-district-attorney-clears-officers-ezell-ford-sh ooting/.

8. Wilde, "Attorney for Ezell Ford Family Calls LAPD Officers 'Animalistic.'"

9. Ibid.

10. Robert Wilde, "Autopsy Report: Ezell Ford Grabbed Officer's Gun before Being Killed," Breitbart, December 29, 2021, https://www.breitbart.com /local/2014/12/29/autopsy-report-ezell-ford-grabbed-police-officers-gun/; "Ezell Ford Family Lawsuit: $1.5M Settlement Reached," ABC7, February 8, 2017, https://abc7.com/news/ezell-ford-family-lawsuit-$15m-settlement -reached/1744227/.

11. "Black Lives Matter Actions: Baltimore, Chicago, Oakland, Los Angeles," *News & Letters*, June 30, 2015, https://newsandletters.org/black-lives -matter-actions-baltimore-chicago-oakland-los-angeles/.

12. Associated Press, "Los Angeles Police Panel: 1 Officer Unjustified in Death," *Epoch Times*, June 9, 2015, https://www.theepochtimes.com/los -angeles-police-panel-1-officer-unjustified-in-death_1386618.html; Robert Wilde, "Commission Overrules LAPD Investigation in Fatal Shooting of Ezell Ford," Breitbart, June 10, 2015, https://www.breitbart.com/politics /2015/06/10/commission-over-rules-lapd-investigation-in-fatal-shooting -of-ezell-ford/.

13. Kate Mather, James Queally, and Marisa Gerber, "No Charges against LAPD Officers Who Shot and Killed Ezell Ford, D.A. Says," *Los Angeles Times*, January 24, 2017, https://www.latimes.com/local/lanow/la-me-ln -ezell-ford-no-charges-20170124-story.html.

14. Black Lives Matter–Los Angeles, "Ezell Ford Was Murdered by LAPD Officers," Facebook, https://www.facebook.com/blmla/photos/today-we -honor-the-spirit-of-ezell-ford-who-was-murdered-by-lapd-officers-shar lt/2920139408058357/.

15. Tom McCarthy, "Tamir Rice: Video Shows Boy, 12, Shot 'Seconds' after Police Confronted Child," *The Guardian*, November 26, 2014, https:// www.theguardian.com/us-news/2014/nov/26/tamir-rice-video-shows-boy -shot-police-cleveland.

16. A. W. R. Hawkins, "Cleveland Officers Claim Tamir Rice Lifted Shirt, Reached into Waistband," Breitbart, December 1, 2015, https://www.bre itbart.com/politics/2015/12/01/cleveland-officers-claim-tamir-rice-lifted -shirt-reached-waistband/; Wesley Lowery and Afi Scruggs, "Cleveland Officers Say Tamir Rice Reached into Waistband and Pulled Toy Gun before One of Them Shot Him," *Washington Post*, December 2, 2015, https://www.washingtonpost.com/news/post-nation/wp/2015/12/01/cle veland-officers-say-tamir-rice-reached-into-waistband-and-pulled-toy-gun -before-one-of-them-shot-him/; "911 Dispatcher, Police Officer Disciplined in Connection with Tamir Rice Case," *Inside Edition*, March 15, 2017,

https://www.insideedition.com/headlines/22207-911-dispatcher-police
-officer-disciplined-in-connection-with-tamir-rice-case; News 5
Cleveland, "Tamir Rice Shooting/Cleveland Police Dispatch Radio,"
YouTube, November 24, 2014, https://www.youtube.com/watch?v=kqB
qg43WN34.

17. "Cleveland Prosecutor's Report: Tamir Rice Borrowed Pellet Gun from
Friend," NPR, June 13, 2015, https://www.npr.org/sections/thetwo-way
/2015/06/13/414235596/cleveland-prosecutors-report-tamir-rice-borro
wed-pellet-gun-from-friend.

18. Zola Ray, "This Is the Toy Gun That Got Tamir Rice Killed 3 Years Ago
Today," *Newsweek*, November 22, 2017, https://www.newsweek.com/ta
mir-rice-police-brutality-toy-gun-720120; "Cleveland Prosecutor's
Report: Tamir Rice Borrowed Pellet Gun from Friend," NPR, June 13,
2015, https://www.npr.org/sections/thetwo-way/2015/06/13/414235596
/cleveland-prosecutors-report-tamir-rice-borrowed-pellet-gun-from-fr
iend.

19. "Cop Says He Told Tamir Rice to Show Hands before Fatal Shots," CBS
News, December 1, 2015, https://www.cbsnews.com/news/cop-says-he
-told-tamir-rice-to-show-hands-before-fatal-shots/; DW News, "Tamir
Rice Video Adds to Anger in U.S.," YouTube, November 27, 2014, https://
www.youtube.com/watch?v=NPeqDXqMvqg; Cleveland.com, "Full
Surveillance Video Captures a Cleveland Police Officer Fatally Shooting
12-Year-Old Tamir Rice," YouTube, November 26, 2014, https://www
.youtube.com/watch?v=Vki8SU6Oz6Q.

20. Hawkins, "Cleveland Officers Claim Tamir Rice Lifted Shirt, Reached
into Waistband."

21. "Cleveland Prosecutor's Report: Tamir Rice Borrowed Pellet Gun from
Friend," NPR, June 13, 2015, https://www.npr.org/sections/thetwo-way
/2015/06/13/414235596/cleveland-prosecutors-report-tamir-rice-borro
wed-pellet-gun-from-friend.

22. Jenell Walton, "Black Lives Matter Rally Shows Support for Tamir Rice's
Family," WLTW, November 21, 2015, https://www.wlwt.com/article/bl
ack-lives-matter-rally-shows-support-for-tamir-rice-s-family/3560146#.

23. "Family of Tamir Rice, 12-Year-Old Shot by Cop, Files Wrongful Death
Suit," NBC News, December 5, 2015, https://www.nbcnews.com/news
/us-news/family-tamir-rice-12-year-old-shot-cop-files-
wrongful-n262661.

24. Ashley Fantz, Steve Almasy, and Catherine E. Shoichet, "Tamir Rice
Shooting: No Charges for Officers," CNN, December 28, 2015, https://
www.cnn.com/2015/12/28/us/tamir-rice-shooting/index.html.

25. Ibid.

26. "Activist Says Tamir Rice Grand Jury Decision 'Devastating' for Family,"
     NPR, December 28, 2015, https://www.npr.org/2015/12/28/461322342
     /black-lives-matter-activist-weighs-in-on-tamir-rice-investigation.

27. Denisse Moreno, "Family of Tamir Rice Will Receive $6 Million from
     City of Cleveland," *Epoch Times*, April 25, 2016, https://www.theepoch
     times.com/family-of-tamir-rice-will-receive-6-million-from-city-of-cleve
     land_2038452.html.

28. "Video Shows NYC Protesters Chanting for 'Dead Cops,'" NBCNewYork.
     com, December 15, 2014, https://www.nbcnewyork.com/news/local/eric
     -garner-manhattan-dead-cops-video-millions-march-protest/2015303/;
     "Last Week: NYC Protesters Chant 'What Do We Want? Dead Cops!
     When Do We Want It? Now!,'" RealClearPolitics, December 22, 2014,
     https://www.realclearpolitics.com/video/2014/12/22/last_week_nyc_pr
     otesters_chant_what_do_we_want_dead_cops_when_do_we_want_it
     _now.html.

29. Larry Celona *et al.*, "Gunman Executes 2 NYPD Cops in Garner
     'Revenge,'" *New York Post*, December 20, 2014, https://nypost.com/20
     14/12/20/2-nypd-cops-shot-execution-style-in-brooklyn/; Benjamin
     Mueller and Al Baker, "2 N.Y.P.D. Officers Killed in Brooklyn Ambush;
     Suspect Commits Suicide," *New York Times*, December 20, 2014, https://
     www.nytimes.com/2014/12/21/nyregion/two-police-officers-shot-in-the
     ir-patrol-car-in-brooklyn.html.

30. "Brooklyn Protesters Demand Justice for Akai Gurley," UK.Screen,
     https://web.archive.org/web/20150104080937/https://uk.screen.yahoo
     .com/storyful-trending-videos/brooklyn-protesters-demand-justice-akai
     -081243047.html.

31. J. Weston Phippen, "Why Was Officer Peter Liang Convicted?" *The
     Atlantic*, March 3, 2016, https://www.theatlantic.com/national/archive
     /2016/03/peter-liang-police-shooting/471687/.

32. Pervaiz Shallwani and Thomas MacMillan, "NYPD Officer Pleads Not
     Guilty in Shooting Death of Unarmed Man," *Wall Street Journal*,
     February 11, 2015, https://www.wsj.com/articles/nypd-officer-surrende
     rs-after-indictment-in-death-of-unarmed-man-1423668909.

33. Ibid.

34. "New York Cop Peter Liang Convicted of Manslaughter for Ricochet
     Shooting of Black Man," *South China Morning Post*, February 12, 2016,
     https://www.scmp.com/news/world/article/1912284/new-york-cop-peter
     -liang-convicted-manslaughter-ricochet-shooting-black.

35. Chris Fuchs, "In Tears on Stand, NYPD Cop Recalls Fatal Shooting of
     Akai Gurley," NBC News, February 8, 2016, https://www.nbcnews.com
     /news/asian-america/tears-stand-nypd-cop-recalls-fatal-shooting-akai-gur
     ley-n514216.

36. Phippen, "Why Was Officer Peter Liang Convicted?"

37. Thomas Tracy *et al.*, "NYPD Officer Peter Liang Found Guilty of Manslaughter in Fatal Shooting of Akai Gurley in Brooklyn Housing Development," *New York Daily News*, February 12, 2016, https://www.nydailynews.com/new-york/nyc-crime/nypd-peter-liang-guilty-fatal-shooting-akai-gurley-article-1.2528827; Emily Saul, Kevin Fasick, and Kate Sheehy, "NYPD Cop Peter Liang Dodges Prison for Killing Akai Gurley," *New York Post*, April 19, 2016, https://nypost.com/2016/04/19/nypd-cop-peter-liang-gets-community-service-for-killing-akai-gurley/.

38. "A Message from the Trayvon Martin Organizing Committee," New Inquiry, December 22, 2014, https://thenewinquiry.com/a-message-from-the-trayvon-martin-organizing-committee/.

39. "Police Report: Tony Robinson, Man Killed by Madison Officer, High on Mushrooms," Breitbart, May 12, 2015, https://www.breitbart.com/politics/2015/05/12/police-report-tony-robinson-man-killed-by-madison-officer-high-on-mushrooms/; Annie Wu, "Public Awareness of Police Shootings Post-Ferguson Keeps #BlackLivesMatter Going," *Epoch Times*, March 9, 2015, https://www.theepochtimes.com/public-awareness-of-police-shootings-post-ferguson-keeps-blacklivesmatter-going_1277952.html.

40. "The Estate of Robinson Ex Rel. Irwin v. the City of Madison," Leagle, February 13, 2017, https://www.leagle.com/decision/infdco20170214d64.

41. Paul Mirengoff, "Demonstrators Protest Obviously Justified Shooting in Madison," Powerline, May 13, 2015, https://www.powerlineblog.com/archives/2015/05/demonstrators-protest-obviously-justified-shooting-in-madison.php; Mary Spicuzza and Jason Stein, "Family of Tony Robinson, Man Shot by Madison Police, to Receive $3.35 Million," *Milwaukee Journal Sentinel*, February 23, 2017, https://www.jsonline.com/story/news/local/milwaukee/2017/02/23/family-tony-robinson-man-shot-madison-police-receive-335-million-lawyers-say/98292352/; Wisconsin Division of Criminal Investigation, Case/Report Number 15-1188/145, "Report of Investigation, Officer Involved Death (OID) of Tony Terrell Robinson, Jr.," 2015, https://www.doj.state.wi.us/sites/default/files/MADISON%20-%20TONY%20T.%20ROBINSON%20JR.%20INVESTIGATION%2C%20MARCH%202015.pdf.

42. "Estate of Robinson Ex Rel. Irwin v. City of Madison," Leagle; "Police Report: Tony Robinson, Man Killed by Madison Officer, High on Mushrooms," Breitbart.

43. Mary Spicuzza, "Madison Police Clear Officer of Wrongdoing in Tony Robinson Shooting," *Milwaukee Journal Sentinel*, June 3, 2015, https://archive.jsonline.com/news/crime/madison-police-clear-officer-of-disciplinary-charges-in-tony-robinson-shooting-b99512882z1-306029091.html.

44. Alex Johnson, "Tony Robinson Shooting: No Charges for Wisconsin Police Officer," NBC News, May 12, 2015, https://www.nbcnews.com /news/us-news/tony-robinson-shooting-no-charges-lawful-use-force-n35 7876.

45. German Lopez, "What We Know about the Police Shooting of Unarmed 19-Year-Old Tony Robinson in Madison, WI," Justice Policy Institute, March 9, 2015, http://www.justicepolicy.org/news/8839.

46. Black Lives Matter Portland, "19-Year-Old Tony Robinson Was Murdered," Facebook, 2015, https://www.facebook.com/blacklivesmatt erpdx/posts/19-year-old-tony-robinson-was-murdered-by-madison-wi-po lice-officer-matt-kenny-a/852538868176182/.

47. Wu, "Public Awareness of Police Shootings Post-Ferguson."

48. Mary Spicuzza, "Leaders Call for Change as Teen Killed by Madison Cop Is Remembered," *Milwaukee Journal Sentinel*, March 14, 2015, https:// archive.jsonline.com/news/wisconsin/hundreds-gather-for-the-funeral-of -teen-killed-by-madison-officer-as-community-leaders-call-for-chan-296 328181.html.

49. Ibid.

50. United Press International, "Dashcam Footage Shows Tony Robinson Fatal Shooting by Police," Breitbart, May 13, 2015, https://www.breitba rt.com/news/dashcam-footage-shows-tony-robinson-fatal-shooting-by-po lice/.

51. Mary Spicuzza and Jason Stein, "Family of Tony Robinson, Man Shot by Madison Police, to Receive $3.35 Million," *Milwaukee Journal Sentinel*, February 23, 2017, https://www.jsonline.com/story/news/local/milwau kee/2017/02/23/family-tony-robinson-man-shot-madison-police-receive -335-million-lawyers-say/98292352/.

52. "Sergeant Robert Francis Wilson, III," Officer Down Memorial Page, https://www.odmp.org/officer/22401-sergeant-robert-francis-wilson-iii.

53. "Knife-Wielding Woman Fatally Shot by Officers in Oxnard," CBS Los Angeles, March 28, 2015, https://losangeles.cbslocal.com/2015/03/28/kn ife-wielding-woman-fatally-shot-by-officers-in-oxnard/; "Report on the March 28, 2015 Shooting of Meagan Hockaday by Oxnard Police Officer Roger Garcia," Office of the District Attorney, August 18, 2016, https:// www.vcdistrictattorney.com/wp-content/uploads/2016/08/Hockaday -OIS-Report-FINAL-PDF.pdf; Tonika Reed, "Let's Scream Our Sister's Name: The Story of Meagan Hockaday," Edhat, August 12, 2020, https:// www.edhat.com/news/let-s-scream-our-sister-s-name-the-story-of-mea gan-hockaday.

54. "Report on the March 28, 2015 Shooting of Meagan Hockaday," Office of the District Attorney.

55. Cheri Carlson and Megan Diskin, "DA's Office Finds Officer Justified in Fatal Shooting of Oxnard Woman," VC Star, August 18, 2016, http://ar chive.vcstar.com/news/local/oxnard/das-office-finds-officer-justified-in -fatal-shooting-of-oxnard-woman-3a5b3b30-0bab-627d-e053-0100007 -390622791.html.

56. Carrie Hutchinson, "No More Hollow Statements: The Time for Black Respect Is Now," *Santa Barbara Independent*, June 3, 2020, https://www .independent.com/2020/06/03/no-more-hollow-statements/; "Black Lives Matter Los Angeles Brings Together Black Families of Those Killed by the Police in Historic First," *L.A. Watts Times*, July 28, 2016, https://www .lawattstimes.com/index.php?option=com_content&view=article&id=3 707:black-lives-matter-los-angeles-brings-together-black-families-of-tho se-killed-by-the-police-in-historic-first; Carlson and Diskin, "DA's Office Finds Officer Justified."

57. Hutchinson, "No More Hollow Statements."

58. Sebastian Murdock, "Michael Slager Pleads Guilty in Killing of Unarmed, Fleeing Black Man Walter Scott," HuffPo, May 2, 2017, https://www.hu ffpost.com/entry/michael-slager-cop-who-killed-fleeing-black-man-wal ter-scott-pleads-guilty-to-tk_n_59089734e4b02655f840c8f1; Michael Schmidt and Matt Apuzzo, "South Carolina Officer Is Charged with Murder of Walter Scott," *New York Times*, April 7, 2015, https://www .nytimes.com/2015/04/08/us/south-carolina-officer-is-charged-with-mur der-in-black-mans-death.html.

59. Michael Martinez, "South Carolina Cop Shoots Unarmed Man: A Timeline," CNN, April 9, 2015, https://www.cnn.com/2015/04/08/us/so uth-carolina-cop-shoots-black-man-timeline/index.html.

60. Alan Blinder, "Ex-Officer Who Shot Walter Scott Pleads Guilty in Charleston," *New York Times*, May 2, 2017, https://www.nytimes.com /2017/05/02/us/michael-slager-walter-scott-north-charleston-shooting .html.

61. Catherine E. Shoichet and Mayra Cuevas, "Walter Scott Shooting Case: Court Documents Reveal New Details," CNN, September 10, 2015, https://www.cnn.com/2015/09/08/us/south-carolina-walter-scott-shoo ting-michael-slager.

62. Michael Schmidt and Matt Apuzzo, "South Carolina Officer Is Charged with Murder of Walter Scott."

63. Shoichet and Cuevas, "Walter Scott Shooting Case."

64. Mark Berman, Wesley Lowery, and Kimberly Kindy, "South Carolina Police Officer Charged with Murder after Shooting Man during Traffic Stop," *Washington Post*, April 7, 2015, https://www.washingtonpost.com /news/post-nation/wp/2015/04/07/south-carolina-police-officer-will-be -charged-with-murder-after-shooting/.

65. Darran Simon, Keith O'Shea, and Emanuella Grinberg, "Judge Declares Mistrial in Michael Slager Trial," CNN, December 6, 2016, https://www.cnn.com/2016/12/05/us/michael-slager-murder-trial-walter-scott-mistri al/index.html; Blinder, "Ex-Officer Who Shot Walter Scott Pleads Guilty in Charleston."

66. Philip Weiss, "'Black Lives Matter' Hold Rallies in N. Charleston for Walter Scott," Live5News.com, April 8, 2015, https://www.live5news.com /story/28747410/civil-rights-groups-schedule-rally-presser-in-wake-of-wal ter-scotts-murder/.

67. Liz Fields, "After Walter Scott Killing, Black Lives Matter Movement Calls for Citizen Oversight of Police," Vice News, April 10, 2015, https://www.vice.com/en_us/article/8x7wxa/after-walter-scott-killing-black-lives-mat ter-movement-calls-for-citizen-oversight-of-police.

68. "Killing of Walter Scott," Wikipedia, https://en.wikipedia.org/wiki/Sho oting_of_Walter_Scott, citing Blinder, "Ex-Officer Who Shot Walter Scott Pleads Guilty"; *Sebastian Murdock*, "Michael Slager Pleads Guilty in Killing Of Unarmed, Fleeing Black Man Walter Scott," HuffPo, May 2, 2017, https://www.huffpost.com/entry/michael-slager-cop-who-killed -fleeing-black-man-walter-scott-pleads-guilty-to-tk_n_59089734e4b02 655f840c8f1; Meridith Edwards and Dakin Andone, "Ex-Carolina Cop Michael Slager Gets 20 Years for Walter Scott Killing," CNN, December 7, 2017, https://www.cnn.com/2017/12/07/us/michael-slager-sentencing /index.html.

69. Blinder, "Ex-Officer Who Shot Walter Scott Pleads Guilty."

70. Eliott C. McLaughlin, Ben Brumfield, and Dana Ford, "Freddie Gray Death: Questions Many, Answers Few, Emotions High in Baltimore," CNN, April 20, 2015, https://www.cnn.com/2015/04/20/us/baltimore-fr eddie-gray-death/index.html.

71. "Timeline: What We Know about the Freddie Gray Arrest," NPR, May 1, 2015, https://www.npr.org/sections/thetwo-way/2015/05/01/4036291 04/baltimore-protests-what-we-know-about-the-freddie-gray-arrest.

72. David Mikkelson, "Freddie Gray Arrest Record, Criminal History, and Rap Sheet," Snopes, April 2015, https://www.snopes.com/fact-check/fred die-gray-rap-sheet/.

73. Kevin Rector, "The 45-Minute Mystery of Freddie Gray's Death," *Baltimore Sun*, April 25, 2015, https://www.baltimoresun.com/news/cri me/bs-md-gray-ticker-20150425-story.html#page=1.

74. Ibid.

75. Larry Elder (@larryelder), "Freddie Gray Died (2015)," Twitter, June 6, 2020, 8:49 p.m., https://twitter.com/larryelder/status/126943134456980 2752?lang=en.

76. Associated Press, Baltimore "Police Might Have Ignored Seat Belt Policy with Freddie Gray," *Denver Post*, April 23, 2015, https://www.denverpo st.com/2015/04/23/baltimore-police-might-have-ignored-seat-belt-policy -with-freddie-gray/.

77. Associated Press, "Thousands Expected at Monday's Funeral for Freddie Gray," Breitbart, April 27, 2015, https://www.breitbart.com/news/thousa nds-expected-at-mondays-funeral-for-freddie-gray/; German Lopez, "The Baltimore Protests over Freddie Gray's Death, Explained," *Vox*, August 18, 2016, https://www.vox.com/2016/7/27/18089352/freddie-gray-bal timore-riots-police-violence.

78. Matt Ford, "Protesters and Police Clash in Baltimore," *The Atlantic*, April 27, 2015, https://www.theatlantic.com/politics/archive/2015/04/a-state-of -emergency-in-baltimore/391607/.

79. Philip Klein, "How the Baltimore Mayor's Office Explains Her Infamous 'Space to Destroy' Remark," *Washington Examiner*, April 27, 2015, https://www.washingtonexaminer.com/how-the-baltimore-mayors-office -explains-her-infamous-space-to-destroy-remark.

80. Kate Raddatz, "#BlackLivesMatter Protesters March through Minneapolis," CBS Minnesota, April 29, 2015, https://minnesota.cbslo cal.com/2015/04/29/blacklivesmatter-to-protest-at-gold-medal-park/.

81. Paulina Dedaj, "Six Officers Acquitted in Freddie Gray Case Now Back at Work," Fox News, December 1, 2017, https://www.foxnews.com/us/ six-officers-acquitted-in-freddie-gray-case-now-back-at-work.

82. Sheryl Gay Stolberg, "Baltimore Announces $6.4 Million Settlement in the Death of Freddie Gray," *New York Times*, September 8, 2015, https:// www.nytimes.com/2015/09/09/us/freddie-gray-baltimore-police-death .html.

83. Patrisse Cullors and Asha Bandele, *When They Call You a Terrorist: A Black Lives Matter Memoir* (New York: St. Martin's Press, 2018), https:// books.google.com/books?id=6l4mDwAAQBAJ&pg=PT18&lpg=#v=o nepage&q&f=false.

84. Elder (@larryelder), "Freddie Gray Died (2015)."

85. "'Suspect Down': Video Footage, Dispatch Tape from Alton Sterling Police Shooting Released," RT, July 6, 2016, https://www.rt.com/usa/349787 -anton-sterling-video-dispatch/; Joshua Berlinger, Nick Valencia, and Steve Almasy, "Alton Sterling Shooting: Homeless Man Made 911 Call, Source Says," CNN, July 8, 2016, https://www.cnn.com/2016/07/07/us/baton-ro uge-alton-sterling-shooting/.

86. Jason Silverstein, "Who Was Alton Sterling?" *New York Daily News*, July 6, 2016, https://www.nydailynews.com/news/national/alton-sterling -article-1.2700893; Jack Phillips, "Alton Sterling Was Arrested in 2009 after Similar Confrontation with Police Officer," *Epoch Times*, July 14,

2016, https://www.theepochtimes.com/alton-sterling-was-arrested-in-20
09-after-similar-confrontation-with-police-officer_2115532.html; Emily
Shapiro, "Alton Sterling Was Arrested in '09 after Confrontation with
Baton Rouge Cop, Police Report Says," ABC News, July 13, 2016, https://
abcnews.go.com/US/alton-sterling-arrested-09-confrontation-baton-rou
ge-cop/story?id=40555802; Jack Phillips, "5 Things to Know about the
Alton Sterling Shooting," *Epoch Times*, July 6, 2016, https://www.thee
pochtimes.com/5-things-to-know-about-the-alton-sterling-shooting_21
08192.html.

87.   John Bacon, and Melanie Eversley, "Who Was Alton Sterling? Residents
Mourn Salesman, Father," *USA Today*, July 6, 2016, https://www.usato
day.com/story/news/2016/07/06/who-alton-sterling/86767354./

88.   Shapiro, "Alton Sterling Was Arrested in '09."

89.   "Federal Officials Close Investigation into Death of Alton Sterling,"
Department of Justice, Office of Public Affairs, May 3, 2017, https://www
.justice.gov/opa/pr/federal-officials-close-investigation-death-alton-ster
ling.

90.   Ibid.

91.   Nicole Chavez, "Body Camera Shows Officer Threatened to Shoot Alton
Sterling within Seconds," CNN, March 31, 2018, https://www.cnn.com
/2018/03/31/us/alton-sterling-police-videos-hearings/index.html.

92.   "Black Lives Matter: No Charges for Louisiana Police Who Shot Alton
Sterling," ABC News, March 27, 2018, https://www.abc.net.au/news/20
18-03-28/no-charges-for-louisiana-police-who-shot-alton-sterling/959
5404.

93.   Elizabeth Vowell, "Medical Expert Weighs in on Sterling Toxicology
Report," WAFB, March 27, 2018, https://www.wafb.com/story/378230
44/medical-expert-weighs-in-on-sterling-toxicology-report/.

94.   Department of Justice, "Federal Officials Close Investigation."

95.   Christopher Brennan, Nicole Hensley and Denis Slattery, "Alton Sterling
Shot, Killed by Louisiana Cops during Struggle after He Was Selling
Music outside Baton Rouge Store," *New York Daily News*, July 6, 2016,
https://www.nydailynews.com/news/national/la-cops-shoot-kill-man-sel
ling-music-baton-rouge-store-article-1.2700548.

96.   Michael Edison Hayden and David Caplan, "Protests Continue in Baton
Rouge and St. Paul Following Night of Arrests," ABC News, July 10, 2016,
https://abcnews.go.com/US/protests-continue-baton-rouge-st-paul-night
-arrests/story?id=40467365; Ken Daley, "43 of 102 Arrested Protesters
from Outside Baton Rouge, Police Say," *Times-Picayune*, July 11, 2016,
https://www.nola.com/news/crime_police/article_57022895-66eb-58c0
-b034-9bb62029bf59.html.

97. Peniel E. Joseph, "For Change to Happen, Americans Must Confront the Pain of Black History," *Globe and Mail*, July 9, 2016, https://www.theg lobeandmail.com/opinion/for-change-to-happen-americans-must-confr ont-the-pain-of-black-history/article30831352/.

98. Trey Schmaltz and Chris Nakamoto, "Police ID Suspects Arrested after Federal Raid at BR Home Tied to Murder Plot against Police," WBRZ2, July 12, 2016, https://www.wbrz.com/news/federal-raid-at-br-home-tied -to-murder-plot-against-police/.

99. "Local Groups and the ACLU of Louisiana Sue Baton Rouge Police for First Amendment Violations at Alton Sterling Protest," ACLU, July 13, 2016, https://www.aclu.org/press-releases/local-groups-and-aclu-louisia na-sue-baton-rouge-police-first-amendment-violations.

100. Jessica Contrera, "Officer Brad Garafola's Wife Arrived to Pick Him Up from Work. He Would Never Make It Home," *Washington Post*, July 17, 2016, https://www.washingtonpost.com/news/post-nation/wp/2016/07 /17/officer-brad-garafolas-wife-arrived-to-pick-him-up-from-work-he-wo uld-never-make-it-home/.

101. Jaweed Kaleem, "Louisiana Will Not Charge Officers in Alton Sterling Shooting Death," *Los Angeles Times*, March 27, 2018, https://www.la times.com/nation/la-na-alton-sterling-20180327-story.html.

102. Matt Furber and Mitch Smith, "'I Had No Choice': Minnesota Officer Testifies on Shooting," *New York Times*, June 9, 2017, https://www.nyt imes.com/2017/06/09/us/jeronimo-yanez-philando-castile-minnesota-sh ooting.html.

103. Ibid.; Lana Shadwick, "Minnesota Cop Found Not Guilty in Philando Castile Shooting Trial," Breitbart, June 16, 2017, https://www.breitbart .com/border/2017/06/16/minnesota-cop-found-not-guilty-philando-casti le-shooting-trial/.

104. "'Philando Can Be Any of Us': Black Lives Matter Protests Acquittal of Officer in Minnesota Killing," Democracy Now!, June 19, 2017, https:// www.democracynow.org/2017/6/19/philando_can_be_any_of_us.

Chapter 5: Five Dead Cops in Dallas

1. Louis Casiano, "81% of Black Americans Want Police to Maintain or Increase Local Presence, Poll Reveals," Fox News, August 5, 2020, https:// Www.Foxnews.Com/Us/81-Black-Americans-Police-Retain-Increase-Pr esence.

2. Patrick McGee, Manny Fernandez, and Jonah Engel Bromwich, "Snipers Kill 5 Dallas Officers at Protest against Police Shootings," *New York Times*, July 7, 2016, https://www.nytimes.com/2016/07/08/us/dallas-po lice-officers-killed.html.

3.   Ibid.; Terri Langford, "Dallas Police Chief: Suspect 'Wanted to Kill White People,'" *Texas Tribune*, July 8, 2016, https://www.texastribune.org/20 16/07/08/dallas-police-chief-suspect-wanted-kill-white-peop/.

4.   "Sniper Ambush Kills 5 Officers, Injures 7 in Dallas Following Peaceful Protest," NBCDFW, July 6, 2016, https://www.nbcdfw.com/news/local /protests-in-dallas-over-alton-sterling-death/88950/; "Who Are the Dallas Police Shooting Victims? Michael Smith, Lorne Ahrens, Brent Thompson, Patrick Zamarripa, Michael Krol," *Oxford Eagle*, July 11, 2016, https:// www.oxfordeagle.com/2016/07/11/who-are-the-dallas-police-shooting -victims-michael-smith-lorne-ahrens-brent-thompson-patrick-zamarripa -michael-krol-and-more/.

5.   Daniel Politi, "Dallas Shooter Had Plans for Larger Attack, Says Police Chief," Slate, July 10, 2016, https://slate.com/news-and-politics/2016/07 /dallas-shooter-micah-xavier-johnson-had-plans-for-larger-attack.html

6.   "New Details on Robot That Killed Ambush Suspect," CBS DFW, July 11, 2016, http://dfw.cbslocal.com/2016/07/11/details-on-robot-that-killed -ambush-suspect/; Jason Kravarik and Sara Sidner, "The Dallas Shootout, in the Eyes of Police," CNN, July 15, 2016, https://www.cnn.com/2016 /07/15/health/dallas-shootout-police-perspective/.

7.   Patrisse Cullors and Asha Bandele, *When They Call You a Terrorist: A Black Lives Matter Memoir* (New York: St. Martin's Griffin, 2018), 6.

8.   Jamiles Lartey, "Obama on Black Lives Matter: They Are 'Much Better Organizers Than I Was,'" *The Guardian*, February 18, 2016, https://www .theguardian.com/us-news/2016/feb/18/black-lives-matter-meet-president -obama-white-house-justice-system.

9.   Kirsten West Savali, "'Whereas' #BlackLivesMatter Did Not Accept Crumbs from the DNC's Table," The Root, https://www.theroot.com/wh ereas-blacklivesmatter-did-not-accept-crumbs-from-1790861011; Matthew Vadum, "Infiltrating the #BlackLivesMatter Cult," American Thinker, September 17, 2015, https://www.americanthinker.com/articles /2015/09/infiltrating_the_blacklivesmatter_cult.html; Paul Bedard, "War: Black Lives Matter Slams Dems, Party Stops 'Black People's Efforts to Liberate Ourselves,'" *Washington Examiner*, August 31, 2015, https:// www.washingtonexaminer.com/war-black-lives-matter-slams-dems-par ty-stops-black-peoples-efforts-to-liberate-ourselves.

10. Charlie Spiering, "Valerie Jarrett Meets with Black Lives Matter Leaders at the White House," Breitbart, September 17, 2015, https://www.breitba rt.com/politics/2015/09/17/valerie-jarrett-meets-black-lives-matter-leade rs-white-house/.

11. Lucia Abbamonte, *"Black Lives Matter": Cross-Media Resonance and the Iconic Turn of Language* (Newcastle upon Tyne, England: Cambridge

Scholars Publishing, 2018), 27, https://books.google.com/books?id=_mF 6DwAAQBAJ&pg=PA27&lpg=#v=onepage&q&f=false.

12. Manny Fernandez, Richard Pérez-Peña, and Jonah Engel Bromwich, "Five Dallas Officers Were Killed as Payback, Police Chief Says," *New York Times*, July 8, 2016, https://www.nytimes.com/2016/07/09/us/dallas-po lice-shooting.html.

13. Cullors and Bandele, *When They Call You a Terrorist*, 92.

14. Ibid.

Chapter 6: The Target Is the Law

1. Michael Graczyk and Jamie Stengle, "Experts: Report Shows Sandra Bland May Have Used Pot in Jail," *Seattle Times*, July 28, 2015, https:// www.seattletimes.com/nation-world/experts-report-shows-sandra-bland -may-have-used-pot-in-jail/.

2. Michael Graczyk and Jason Keyser, "No Evidence of Homicide in Autopsy of Woman Who Died in Texas Cell: Prosecutor," CTV News, July 23, 2015, https://www.ctvnews.ca/world/no-evidence-of-homicide-in-autop sy-of-woman-who-died-in-texas-cell-prosecutor-1.2483490.

3. St. John Barned-Smith, "Officials: Sandra Bland Spoke of Previous Suicide Attempt," *Houston Chronicle*, July 22, 2015, https://www.chron.com /houston/article/Sandra-Bland-dash-cam-video-appears-to-have-been-63 99017.php.

4. Evan Blake, "Murky Death of Sandra Bland Points to Possible Police Lynching," World Socialist, July 17, 2015, https://www.wsws.org/en/artic les/2015/07/17/poli-j17.html.

5. Tom Dart, "'What Happened to Sandy?': Protesters Tie Sandra Bland Case to U.S. Race Tensions," *The Guardian*, July 18, 2015, https://www .theguardian.com/us-news/2015/jul/17/sandra-bland-texas-protest-racial -tensions.

6. Janell Ross, "Nine Grieving Mothers Came to the Democratic National Convention Stage," *Washington Post*, July 26, 2016, https://www.was hingtonpost.com/news/the-fix/wp/2016/07/26/nine-grieving-mothers-ca me-to-the-democratic-national-convention-stage/.

7. Adeel Hassan, "The Sandra Bland Video: What We Know," *New York Times*, May 7, 2019, https://www.nytimes.com/2019/05/07/us/sandra-bl and-brian-encinia.html.

8. Alice Barr, "City Council Votes to Keep Sandra Bland Parkway," Khou, September 22, 2015, https://web.archive.org/web/20150927072022/htt p://www.khou.com/story/news/local/2015/09/22/city-council-votes-keep -sandra-bland-parkway/72655080/.

9. Jamiles Lartey, "Sandra Bland: Behind a Poignant Documentary of Her Life and Death," *The Guardian*, December 3, 2018, https://www.thegu

ardian.com/tv-and-radio/2018/dec/03/sandra-bland-behind-a-poignant -documentary-of-her-life-and-death.

10. "Sparks Honoring Black Lives Matter: Sandra Bland," Los Angeles Sparks, August 10, 2020, https://sparks.wnba.com/news/sparks-honoring -black-lives-matter-sandra-bland/.

11. Jonathan Silver, "Texas Gov. Abbott Signs 'Sandra Bland Act' into Law," *Texas Tribune*, June 15, 2017, https://www.texastribune.org/2017/06/15 /texas-gov-greg-abbott-signs-sandra-bland-act-law/; "The Life and Death of Sandra Bland," April 4, 2020, https://vlmckay.wordpress.com/2020/04 /04/the-life-and-death-of-sandra-bland/.

12. Ibid.

13. Merrit Kennedy, "Sandra Bland's Family Reaches $1.9 Million Settlement, Lawyer Says," NPR, September 15, 2016, https://www.npr.org/sections /thetwo-way/2016/09/15/494071469/sandra-blands-family-reportedly-re aches-1-9-million-settlement.

14. Kurt Chirbas, Erik Ortiz, and Corky Siemaszko, "Baltimore County Police Fatally Shoot Korryn Gaines, 23, Wound 5-Year-Old, Son," NBC News, August 2, 2016, https://www.nbcnews.com/news/us-news/baltimo re-county-police-fatally-shoot-korryn-gaines-boy-5-hurt-n621461; Meg Wagner, "Korryn Gaines, Mom Killed by Baltimore Police in Standoff, Was Wanted after Telling Cop 'You Will Have to Murder Me' during Traffic Stop," *New York Daily News*, August 3, 2016, https://www.nyd ailynews.com/news/national/korryn-gaines-wanted-failing-court-article -1.2736844; Paul Mirengoff, "Another Implausible Black Lives Matter Martyr," Powerline, August 15, 2016, https://www.powerlineblog.com /archives/2016/08/another-implausible-black-lives-matter-martyr.php; Colin Campbell, Christiana Amarachi Mbakwe, and Jessica Anderson, "Woman Killed by Baltimore County Police Ignored Pleas from Boyfriend to Surrender, Mother Says," *Baltimore Sun*, August 2, 2016, https://www .baltimoresun.com/news/crime/bs-md-korryn-gaines-tuesday-20160802 -story.html.

15. Mirengoff, "Another Implausible Black Lives Matter Martyr."

16. Ibid.

17. Ibid.

18. Alison Knezevich and Kevin Rector, "'Investigative Files Provide New Insights into Korryn Gaines' 6-Hour Standoff with Baltimore County Police," *Baltimore Sun*, November 5, 2016, https://www.baltimoresun .com/news/investigations/bs-md-co-korryn-gaines-timeline-20161103-st ory.html.

19. "The Shooting of Violent Criminal, Korryn Gaines: The Actual Details," Blue Lives Matter, August 4, 2016, https://archive.bluelivesmatter.blue/ko rryn-gaines-shooting-details/.

20. Ibid.; Jamiles Lartey, "Black Woman Shot Dead by Police during Alleged Standoff while Holding Son," *The Guardian*, August 2, 2016, https://www.theguardian.com/us-news/2016/aug/02/korryn-gaines-black-wo man-killed-by-police-son-injured; "Korryn Gaines: The 6-Hour Police Standoff," *Baltimore Sun*, August 2016, http://data.baltimoresun.com/ne ws/korryn-gaines/.

21. Kwegyirba Croffie, "Jury Awards More Than $37 Million to Family of Maryland Woman Killed in Police Standoff," CNN, February 18, 2018, https://www.cnn.com/2018/02/17/us/baltimore-jury-award-korryn-ga ines-shooting/index.html; Alison Knezevich, "Judge Overturns $38M Verdict in Lawsuit over Baltimore County Police Killing of Korryn Gaines," *Baltimore Sun*, February 15, 2019, https://www.baltimoresun .com/maryland/baltimore-county/bs-md-co-gaines-overturned-201902 15-story.html; Knezevich and Rector, "Investigative Files Provide New Insights."

22. Pamela Wood and Alison Knezevich, "Jury Awards More Than $37 Million to Family of Maryland Woman Killed in Police Standoff," *Baltimore Sun*, February 16, 2018, https://www.baltimoresun.com/mar yland/baltimore-county/bs-md-co-korryn-gaines-civil-deliberate-20180 216-story.html

23. Knezevich, "Judge Overturns $38M Verdict in Lawsuit."

24. Justin George, "Small Group Protests Korryn Gaines' Death," *Baltimore Sun*, August 27, 2016, https://www.baltimoresun.com/maryland/bs-md -gaines-protest-20160827-story.html; "NYC Shut It Down in Abolition Square: The Police Are Assassinating Protesters," It's Going Down, August 9, 2016, https://itsgoingdown.org/nyc-shut-abolition-square-po lice-assassinating-protesters/; "Black Lives Matter Protest in Downtown Portland, MAX Trains Blocked," KOMO News, August 13, 2016, https:// komonews.com/news/local/black-lives-matter-protest-in-downtown-por tland-max-delays-reported; Dalvin Hollins and Loreal Tsignine, "ANWO Phoenix Organizes Protest for Korryn Gaines," African National Women's Organization, August 7, 2016, https://anwouhuru.org/anwo-ph oenix-organizes-protest-for-korryn-gaines-dalvin-hollins-and-loreal-tsig nine/.

25. Faith Karimi, Eric Levenson, and Justin Gamble, "Tulsa Officer Acquitted in Fatal Shooting of Terence Crutcher," CNN, May 18, 2017, https://www .cnn.com/2017/05/17/us/tulsa-police-shooting-trial/index.html.

26. Associated Press, "Attorney: Man Ignored Officer's Commands before Shooting," *Epoch Times*, September 20, 2016, https://www.theepocht imes.com/attorney-man-ignored-officers-commands-before-shooting_21 58988.html; Derek Hawkins, "Black Man Shot by Tulsa Police Had Hands 'In the Air,' Says Pastor Who Reviewed Video of the Shooting,"

Washington Post, September 19, 2016, https://www.washingtonpost.com /news/morning-mix/wp/2016/09/19/black-man-shot-by-tulsa-police-had -hands-in-the-air-says-pastor-who-reviewed-video-of-the-shooting/; Karimi, Levenson, and Gamble, "Tulsa Officer Acquitted in Fatal Shooting of Terence Crutcher"; "Terence Crutcher Shooting: Minute-by- Minute Timeline," *Tulsa World*, September 20, 2016, https://tulsawo rld.com/news/local/terence-crutcher-shooting-minute-by-minute-timeli ne/article_623c7127-23b4-56b1-a450-243984a8e47f.html; "Timeline: Fatal Shooting of Unarmed Man, Terence Crutcher, by Tulsa Police Officer," KJRH, September 19, 2016, https://www.kjrh.com/news/timel ine-tpd-fatal-officer-involved-shooting.

27. "Tulsa Shooting: Family of Man Killed by Police Call for Protests," BBC News, September 20, 2016, https://www.bbc.com/news/world-us-cana da-37413558.

28. "Tulsa Police Release Graphic Footage of Fatal Shooting of Terence Crutcher," TPBS, September 19, 2016, https://www.pbs.org/newshour /nation/tulsa-police-release-graphic-footage-of-fatal-shooting-of-terence -crutcher.

29. Samantha Vicent, "Update: Finding of PCP in Terence Crutcher's System Called 'Immaterial' by Family's Attorneys," *Tulsa World*, October 12, 2016, https://tulsaworld.com/news/local/autopsy-report-terence-crutcher -had-pcp-in-his-system-when/article_d41e00a2-88ac-55ba-81c4-c89bea 961414.html.

30. "Toxicology Reports Show Terence Crutcher Had PCP in System at Time of Death," Fox23, October 12, 2016, https://www.fox23.com/news/toxic ology-reports-show-terence-crutcher-had-pcp-in-system-at-time-of-death /456111947/.

31. Samantha Vincent, "Not Guilty: Betty Shelby Acquitted; Jurors in Tears; Crutcher's Sister Says Police Tried to Cover up Her Brother's 'Murder,'" *Tulsa World*, May 17, 2017, https://tulsaworld.com/news/local/not-guil ty-betty-shelby-acquitted-jurors-in-tears-crutchers-sister-says-police-tried -to-cover/article_cfdc970b-2b10-5f15-b4c1-711c5da4cc03.html.

32. Emma Keith and Anna Mayer, "Black Lives Matter Protesters Hold Die-in for Terence Crutcher, Speak Out against Police Brutality," *Oklahoma Daily*, September 22, 2016, http://www.oudaily.com/news/black-lives-mat ter-protesters-hold-die-in-for-terence-crutcher-speak-out-against-police -brutality/article_f2807e38-811c-11e6-b8f1-eb0c9ef0819c.html.

33. Harrison Grimwood, "Several Tulsa Houses of Worship Display 'Black Lives Matter' on Anniversary of Terence Crutcher's Death," *Tulsa World*, September 17, 2020, https://tulsaworld.com/news/local/several-tulsa -houses-of-worship-display-black-lives-matter-on-anniversary-of-terence -crutchers-death/article_afec005e-f84d-11ea-92b8-172be6fa0708.html.

34. Mitchell Shaw, "Keith Lamont Scott: Armed and Dangerous," *New American*, September 29, 2016, https://thenewamerican.com/keith-lamont-scott-armed-and-dangerous/.

35. Associated Press, "Police Chief: Officers Warned Black Man to Drop Gun," *Epoch Times*, September 21, 2016, https://www.theepochtimes.com/police-chief-officers-warned-black-man-to-drop-gun_2159718.html; Sarah Larimer, "Read the Charlotte Police Department's Investigative Summary on the Keith Lamont Scott Shooting," *Washington Post*, September 24, 2016, https://www.washingtonpost.com/news/post-nation/wp/2016/09/24/read-the-charlotte-police-report-on-the-fatal-shooting-of-keith-lamont-scott/.

36. Associated Press, "Police Chief: Officers Warned Black Man to Drop Gun."

37. Holly Yan, Rolando Zenteno, and Brian Todd, "Keith Scott Killing: No Charges against Officer," CNN, November 30, 2016, https://www.cnn.com/2016/11/30/us/keith-lamont-scott-case-brentley-vinson/index.html.

38. Jack Phillips, "Report: Charlotte Rioters Try to Throw Photographer into Fire," *Epoch Times*, September 22, 2016, https://www.theepochtimes.com/report-charlotte-rioters-try-to-throw-photographer-into-fire_2160560.html.

39. Rory Devine and R. Stickney, "Who Was Alfred Olango?" NBC San Diego, September 28, 2016, https://www.nbcsandiego.com/news/local/who-was-alfred-olango-el-cajon-police-shooting-san-diego/93431/.

40. James Cook, "U.S. Police Shooting: Alfred Olango 'Pointed E-cigarette,'" BBC News, September 29, 2016, https://www.bbc.com/news/world-us-canada-37503048; Abdi Latif Dahir, "He Fled Uganda, Grew up in a Refugee Camp, Loved Cooking and Soccer. And Then He Was Shot by American Police," Quartz Africa, October 1, 2016, https://qz.com/africa/797655/he-fled-uganda-grew-up-in-a-refugee-camp-loved-cooking-and-soccer-and-then-he-was-shot-by-american-police/; Alex Riggins, "Jury Finds El Cajon Officer Not Negligent in Alfred Olango's Shooting Death," *San Diego Union-Tribune*, July 31, 2019, https://www.sandiegouniontribune.com/news/courts/story/2019-07-31/jury-finds-el-cajon-officer-not-negligent-in-alfred-olangos-shooting-death.

41. Rebeca Partida Montes, "Shooting in El Cajon Sparks Black Lives Matter Protests," *Mesa Press*, October 9, 2016, https://www.mesapress.com/news/2016/10/09/shooting-in-el-cajon-sparks-black-lives-matter-protests/?print=true; "Suspect in Deadly Church Rampage Back in Charleston," CBS News, June 18, 2015, https://www.cbsnews.com/news/charleston-shooting-suspect-dylann-storm-roof-caught-north-carolina/.

42. Kristina Davis and Dana Littlefield, "Dumanis Rules El Cajon Police Shooting of Alfred Olango Justified," *San Diego Union-Tribune*, January

10, 2017, https://www.sandiegouniontribune.com/news/courts/sd-me
-olango-ruling-20170109-story.html.

43. Associated Press, "Police Took over 1 Hour to Respond, about 1 Minute
to Shoot," Breitbart, September 29, 2016, https://www.breitbart.com/ne
ws/police-took-over-1-hour-to-respond-about-1-minute-to-shoot/.

44. Alex Riggins, "Jury Finds El Cajon Officer Not Negligent in Alfred
Olango's Shooting Death," *San Diego Union-Tribune*, July 31, 2019,
https://www.sandiegouniontribune.com/news/courts/story/2019-07-31
/jury-finds-el-cajon-officer-not-negligent-in-alfred-olangos-shooting
-death.

45. "Video: Protests in the Weeks Following Olango Shooting," *San Diego
Union-Tribune*, November 2, 2016, https://www.sandiegouniontribune
.com/91827247-132.html; Montes, "Shooting in El Cajon"; Associated
Press, "Police Took over 1 Hour."

46. Lauren Lowrey, "Metro Officer Who Shot Jocques Clemmons to Resign,"
WSMV, October 14, 2019, https://www.wsmv.com/news/davidson_coun
ty/metro-officer-who-shot-jocques-clemmons-to-resign/article_c3fa4620
-eedd-11e9-bffa-53676c9acb4f.html; "Video: San Diego Police Officer
Won't Face Charges for Shooting Dead Weaponless 'Mentally Ill' Black
Man Who Was Holding an E-Cigarette," *Daily Mail*, https://www.daily
mail.co.uk/video/news/video-1335322/This-video-shows-seconds-Alfred
-Olango-shot-dead.html.

47. Ariana Maia Sawyer, "Justice for Jocques Coalition Demonstrates outside
Nashville Mayor's Home," *Tennessean*, May 12, 2017, https://www.ten
nessean.com/story/news/local/2017/05/12/justice-jocques-coalition-hold
-silent-protest-after-no-charges-brought-against-officer/320433001/.

48. Adam Tamburin and Anita Wadhwani, "Jocques Clemmons' Family,
Community Leaders Call for Officer's Firing," *Tennessean*, May 11, 2017,
https://www.tennessean.com/story/news/2017/05/11/community-reaction
-no-prosecution-nashville-officer-involved-shooting/318462001/.

49. Ibid.

50. Ibid.

Chapter 7: The Summer of George Floyd

1. "Killing of Ahmaud Arbery," Wikipedia, https://en.wikipedia.org/wiki/
Killing_of_Ahmaud_Arbery.

2. Richard Fausset, "Suspects in Ahmaud Arbery's Killing Are Indicted on
Murder Charges," *New York Times*, June 24, 2020, https://www.nytimes
.com/2020/06/24/us/ahmaud-arbery-shooting-murder-indictment.html.

3. "New Evidence Reveals Ahmaud Arbery Claimed to Be a 'Jogger' as an
Alibi for Criminal Activity," The Post Millennial, April 1, 2021, https://

thepostmillennial.com/new-evidence-reveals-ahmaud-arbery-claimed-to
-be-a-jogger-as-an-alibi-for-criminal-activity.

4.   Troy Closson and Ed Shanah, "Black Man Died of Suffocation after
Officers Put Hood on Him," *New York Times*, September 2, 2020,
https://www.nytimes.com/2020/09/02/nyregion/daniel-prude-rochester
-police.html.

5.   Ibid.

6.   Will Cleveland, "How Did Daniel Prude Die? What We Know about
Rochester Homicide," *Rochester Democrat and Chronicle*, September 2,
2020, https://www.democratandchronicle.com/story/news/2020/09/02
/daniel-prude-rochester-ny-death-police-custody-what-known/5684856
002/.

7.   Taylor Romine, Benjamin Norbitz, and Madeline Holcombe, "7 Rochester
Police Officers Suspended over Daniel Prude's Death, Mayor Says," CNN,
September 4, 2020, https://www.cnn.com/2020/09/03/us/rochester-po
lice-daniel-prude-death/index.html.

8.   Ibid.; Closson and Shanahan, "Black Man Died of Suffocation after
Officers Put Hood on Him."

9.   Steve Orr, "Video Released from Arrest of Chicago Man Who Died of
Asphyxiation after Being Pinned to Ground by N.Y. Police," *Chicago
Sun-Times*, September 2, 2020, https://chicago.suntimes.com/2020/9/2/21
419199/daniel-prude-death-rochester-police-chicago;
Closson and Shanahan, "Black Man Died of Suffocation after Officers
Put Hood on Him."

10.   Ibid.; "Family Remembers Daniel Prude, Black Man From Chicago Killed
by Police in Rochester," NBC Chicago, September 3, 2020, https://www
.nbcchicago.com/news/local/family-remembers-daniel-prude-black-man
-from-chicago-killed-by-police-in-rochester/2333595/.

11.   Closson and Shanahan, "Black Man Died of Suffocation after Officers
Put Hood on Him"; Steve Orr, "A Black Man Pinned to the Ground by
NY Police Died Two Months before George Floyd," *USA Today*,
September 2, 2020, https://www.usatoday.com/story/news/nation/2020
/09/02/daniel-prude-death-ruled-homicide-after-rochester-police-incident
/5691797002/.

12.   Michael Hill, "Video in Black Man's Suffocation Shows Cops Put Hood
on Him," Associated Press, September 2, 2020, https://apnews.com/artic
le/virus-outbreak-ap-top-news-ny-state-wire-racial-injustice-il-state-wire
-5c2f0cf366e560b7f41ebb3c964b099c; Gary Craig, "Will Police Be
Charged in Daniel Prude's Death?" *Hays Daily News*, September 6, 2020,
https://www.hdnews.net/zz/news/20200906/will-police-be-charged-in
-daniel-prudes-death-this-evidence-may-be-deciding-factor; Cleveland,

"How Did Daniel Prude Die? What We Know about Rochester Homicide."

13. Wendy Wright, "Medical Examiner Gives His Take on Daniel Prude's Autopsy," *Spectrum News*, September 10, 2020, https://spectrumlocalne ws.com/nys/rochester/news/2020/09/10/expert-reviews-daniel-prude-s-a utopsy.

14. Taylor Romine, Benjamin Norbitz, and Madeline Holcombe, "7 Rochester Police Officers Suspended over Daniel Prude's Death, Mayor Says," CNN, September 4, 2020, https://www.cnn.com/2020/09/03/us/rochester-po lice-daniel-prude-death/index.html.

15. Hill, "Video in Black Man's Suffocation"; Spectrum News Staff and Andrew Freeman, "Protests Thursday in Rochester after Prude's Death," Spectrum News, September 4, 2020, https://spectrumlocalnews .com/nys/rochester/public-safety/2020/09/04/protests-continue-in-roche ster-after-daniel-prude-s-death; Allen Kim and Sheena Jones, "NYPD Investigating Car That Plowed into a Group of BLM Protesters in Times Square," CNN, September 4, 2020, https://www.cnn.com/2020/09/04 /us/car-times-square-protesters-trnd/index.html.

16. Rachel Treisman, Gino Fanelli, and Jeremy Moule, "Rochester, NY Mayor Suspends Officers over Asphyxiation Death of Daniel Prude," NPR, September 3, 2020, https://www.npr.org/sections/live-updates-pro tests-for-racial-justice/2020/09/03/909081869/protesters-in-rochester-n-y -demand-answers-in-asphyxiation-death-of-black-man.

17. Vianne Burog, "Police Reforms Being Pushed in Rochester Following Daniel Prude's Death," *Latin Times*, September 7, 2020, https://www.la tintimes.com/police-reforms-being-pushed-rochester-following-daniel-pr udes-death-461459.

18. Sebastian Murdock, "Rochester Police Chief Retires Following Video Showing Police Killing of Daniel Prude," HuffPo, September 8, 2020, https://www.huffingtonpost.ca/entry/rochester-police-chief-retires-dani el-prude-killing_n_5f579c80c5b6c815e76b2138?utm_hp_ref=ca-us-po litics.

19. Gary Craig and Brian Sharp, "Rochester Mayor Lovely Warren Indicted in Felony Campaign Finance Fraud," *Rochester Democrat and Chronicle*, October 2, 2020, https://www.democratandchronicle.com/story/news/20 20/10/02/lovely-warren-indicted-rochester-mayor-accused-campaign-fi nance-fraud/5892804002/.

20. Crystal Bonvillian, "Breonna Taylor: Family Files Lawsuit after Louisville Police Shoot EMT 8 Times in 'Botched' Drug Raid," ActionNewsJax, May 13, 2020, https://www.actionnewsjax.com/news/trending/breonna -taylor-family-files-lawsuit-after-louisville-police-shoot-emt-8-times-wro ng-house-raid/MCMJQBYNJRCTXE6C7CKDBJ4TFE/.

21. Li Cohen, "Oprah Launches Massive Billboard Campaign to Demand the Cops Who Killed Breonna Taylor Be Arrested and Charged," CBS News, August 7, 2020, https://www.cbsnews.com/news/oprah-billboar ds-breonna-taylor-massive-campaign-to-demand-the-cops-who-killed-tay lor-are-arrested-and-charged/.

22. "Fighting for What We Believe In. Together," Until Freedom, https://unti lfreedom.com/about/; Emma Austin, "Breonna Taylor's Oprah Winfrey Magazine Cover Going Up on Billboards around Louisville," *Louisville Courier Journal*, August 7, 2020, https://www.courier-journal.com/story /news/local/breonna-taylor/2020/08/07/oprah-winfrey-placing-breonna -taylor-billboards-around-louisville/3316770001/.

23. Marianne Garvey, "Oprah Winfrey Wants to Be Marching in Honor of Breonna Taylor," CNN, July 31, 2020, https://www.cnn.com/2020/07 /31/entertainment/oprah-winfrey-breonna-taylor/index.html.

24. Oprah Winfrey, "Why Oprah Gave up Her Cover for the First Time Ever to Honor Breonna Taylor," Oprah Daily, July 30, 2020, https://www.op rahdaily.com/life/a33449982/oprah-breonna-taylor/.

25. Scott Glover, Collette Richards, Curt Devine, and Drew Griffin, "A Key Miscalculation by Officers Contributed to the Tragic Death of Breonna Taylor," CNN, July 23, 2020, https://www.cnn.com/2020/07/23/us/bre onna-taylor-police-shooting-invs/index.html.

26. Tessa Duvall, "Breonna Taylor Shooting: A Minute-by-Minute Timeline of the Events That Led to Her Death," *Louisville Courier Journal*, September 23, 2020, https://www.courier-journal.com/story/news/local /breonna-taylor/2020/09/23/minute-by-minute-timeline-breonna-taylor -shooting/3467112001/; Ann Coulter, "Breonna Taylor—The True Story of a BLM Hero," Breitbart, https://www.breitbart.com/politics/2020/12 /16/ann-coulter-breonna-taylor-the-true-story-of-a-blm-hero/.

27. Rukmini Callimachi, "Breonna Taylor's Life Was Changing. Then the Police Came to Her Door," *New York Times*, August 30, 2020, https:// www.nytimes.com/2020/08/30/us/breonna-taylor-police-killing.html; "Was a Dead Body Found in Breonna Taylor's Rental Car in 2016? Yes," Heavy, September 25, 2020, https://heavy.com/news/breonna-taylor-ren tal-car/; Coulter, "Breonna Taylor—The True Story of a BLM Hero."

28. Andrew C. McCarthy, "A Just Decision Not to File Homicide Charges in the Tragic Breonna Taylor Case," *National Review*, September 24, 2020, https://www.nationalreview.com/2020/09/breonna-taylor-case-just-deci sion-not-to-file-homicide-charges/.

29. Coulter, "Breonna Taylor—The True Story of a BLM Hero."

30. Ibid.; McCarthy, "A Just Decision Not to File Homicide Charges in the Tragic Breonna Taylor Case."

31.   Jason Riley, Travis Ragsdale, and Marcus Green, "New Court Records Reveal Jail Phone Calls after Breonna Taylor Shooting," WDRB, August 27, 2020, https://www.wdrb.com/in-depth/new-court-records-reveal-jail -phone-calls-after-breonna-taylor-shooting/article_7b75f76c-e899-11ea -96de-4bbf9536d026.html.

32.   Ibid.

33.   Ibid.

34.   Coulter, "Breonna Taylor—The True Story of a BLM Hero."

35.   Tessa Duvall, "Fact Check 2.0: Separating the Truth from the Lies in the Breonna Taylor Police Shooting," *Louisville Courier Journal*, June 16, 2020, https://www.courier-journal.com/story/news/crime/2020/06/16/bre onna-taylor-fact-check-7-rumors-wrong/5326938002/; Richard A. Oppel Jr., Derrick Bryson Taylor, and Nicholas Bogel-Burroughs, "What to Know about Breonna Taylor's Death," *New York Times*, January 6, 2021, https://www.nytimes.com/article/breonna-taylor-police.html.

36.   Duvall, "Breonna Taylor Shooting: A Minute-by-Minute Timeline of the Events That Led to Her Death."

37.   Ibid.

38.   Duvall, "Fact Check 2.0."

39.   Oppel, Taylor, and Bogel-Burroughs, "What to Know about Breonna Taylor's Death."

40.   Duvall, "Breonna Taylor Shooting: A Minute-by-Minute Timeline of the Events That Led to Her Death."

41.   Duvall, "Fact Check 2.0."

42.   Glover, Richards, Devine, and Griffin, "A Key Miscalculation by Officers Contributed to the Tragic Death of Breonna Taylor."

43.   Tania Ganguli, "LeBron James on Breonna Taylor: 'We Want the Cops Arrested Who Committed That Crime,'" *Los Angeles Times*, July 23, 2020, https://www.latimes.com/sports/lakers/story/2020-07-23/lebron-ja mes-anthony-davis-discuss-breonna-taylor-social-justice.

44.   Oppel, Taylor, and Bogel-Burroughs, "What to Know about Breonna Taylor's Death."

45.   Ibid.

46.   Ibid.

47.   Dylan Lovan, "'Say Her Name': City to Pay $12M to Breonna Taylor's Family," Associated Press, September 15, 2020, https://apnews.com/artic le/police-lawsuits-louisville-breonna-taylor-archive-42df1f3ebea59ff20a 309b8fe04619df.

48.   Gwen Aviles, "Black Transgender Man Fatally Shot by Florida Police," NBC News, May 29, 2020, https://www.nbcnews.com/feature/nbc-out/ black-transgender-man-fatally-shot-florida-police-n1218156.

49. Trudy Ring, "Black Trans Man Tony McDade Killed by Police in Florida," *Advocate*, May 29, 2020, https://www.advocate.com/crime/2020/5/29/black-trans-man-tony-mcdade-killed-police-florida; Jeff Burlew, "'Somebody Failed Somewhere': Family of Slain Malik Jackson Warned Tony McDade Was Dangerous," *Tallahassee Democrat*, June 29, 2020, https://www.tallahassee.com/story/news/local/2020/06/19/somebody-failed-somewhere-malik-jackson-family-warned-tony-mcdade-dangerous/5341454002/.

50. Ibid.

51. Ibid.

52. Ibid.

53. Blaise Gainey, "What We've Learned about Events prior to the Death of Tony McDade," WFSU Public Media, May 31, 2020, https://news.wfsu.org/wfsu-local-news/2020-05-31/what-weve-learned-about-events-prior-to-the-death-of-tony-mcdade.

54. Burlew, "'Somebody Failed Somewhere': Family of Slain Malik Jackson Warned Tony McDade Was Dangerous."; Ethan Reed, "I'm gonna pull it out. . . ." Facebook, June 1, 2020, https://www.facebook.com/permalink.php?id=113930360325196&story_fbid=121754092876156.

55. Jeff Burlew, "'I Need Help': McDade Struggled with Mental Illness before Fatal Stabbing, Police Shooting," *Tallahassee Democrat*, June 2, 2020, https://www.tallahassee.com/story/news/local/2020/06/02/natosha-tony-mcdade-tallahasssee-protests-protest-mental-illness-fatal-stabbing-police-shooting/5300384002/.

56. E. J. Dickson, "Another Black Man, Tony McDade, Was Shot and Killed by Police Last Week," *Rolling Stone*, June 1, 2020, https://www.rollingstone.com/culture/culture-news/tony-mcdade-shooting-death-tallahassee-1008433/; "Police: Trans Man Fatally Shot by Officer after Pointing Gun," Associated Press, June 1, 2020, https://apnews.com/87d9bb3b1eb5fc49d1c2522165286924.

57. Carmel Kookogey and Andy Humbles, "Black Trans Lives Matter Vigil in Nashville Draws over 500 as Tony McDade Remembered," *Nashville Tennessean*, June 20, 2020, https://www.tennessean.com/story/news/local/davidson/2020/06/20/black-trans-lives-matter-vigil-nashville-honor-tony-mcdade/3207819001/.

58. "Justice for Tony McDade," Change.org, https://www.change.org/p/black-lives-matter-activists-justice-for-tony-mcdade.

59. Chas Danner, "Everything We Know about the Killing of Rayshard Brooks by Atlanta Police," *New York*, June 18, 2020, https://nymag.com/intelligencer/2020/06/what-we-know-about-the-killing-of-rayshard-brooks.html.

60. Malachy Browne, Christina Kelso, and Barbara Marcolini, "How Rayshard Brooks Was Fatally Shot by the Atlanta Police," *New York Times*, June 14, 2020, https://www.nytimes.com/2020/06/14/us/videos-rayshard-brooks-shooting-atlanta-police.html.

61. Laura Collins, "Rayshard Brooks Was on Probation for Four Crimes," *Daily Mail*, June 17, 2020, https://www.dailymail.co.uk/news/article-8431801/Rayshard-Brooks-probation-faced-going-prison-charged-DUI.html.

62. Jessica Lee, "Rayshard Brooks: Another Black Man Smeared in Viral Social Media Posts after His Death," Snopes, June 24, 2020, https://www.snopes.com/news/2020/06/24/rayshard-brooks-criminal-past/; Kevin Riley, "Reporting on the Life of Rayshard Brooks," *Atlanta Journal-Constitution*, June 30, 2020, https://www.ajc.com/news/opinion/opinion-taking-time-tell-fuller-story/HC9QQyt9Z2qFUCxN5ShGxL/; Susan Daniels, "Rayshard Brooks Was a Menace to Society," American Thinker, July 21, 2020, https://www.americanthinker.com/blog/2020/06/rayshard_brooks_was_a_menace_to_society.html.

63. Danner, "Everything We Know about the Killing of Rayshard Brooks by Atlanta Police."

64. Browne, Kelso, and Marcolini, "How Rayshard Brooks Was Fatally Shot"; Justin Carissimo, "Who Is Rayshard Brooks, 27-Year-Old Black Man Killed by Atlanta Police?" CBS News, June 16, 2020, https://www.cbsnews.com/news/rayshard-brooks-killed-atlanta-police-shooting-victim-27-years-old/.

65. Danner, "Everything We Know about the Killing of Rayshard Brooks by Atlanta Police."

66. Doha Madani, "Suspect in Custody in Alleged Arson at Wendy's Where Rayshard Brooks Was Killed," NBC News, June 23, 2020, https://www.nbcnews.com/news/us-news/suspect-custody-alleged-arson-wendy-s-where-rayshard-brooks-was-n1231930.

67. Audrey Washington, "Timeline: Here's How Protests Unfolded Saturday Night," WSB TV, June 13, 2020, https://www.wsbtv.com/news/local/atlanta/child-shot-killed-atlanta-police-say/CLSJOKHUWFBDTH3UUGXQCKDPBA/; Rachel Siegel, "Atlanta Police Chief Resigns after Law Enforcement Fatally Shoots Black Man," *Washington Post*, June 14, 2020, https://www.washingtonpost.com/nation/2020/06/13/atlanta-shooting-police/.

68. Ryan Young, Eric Levenson, Steve Almasy, and Christina Maxouris, "Ex-Atlanta Police Officer Who Killed Rayshard Brooks Charged with Felony Murder," CNN, June 17, 2020, https://www.cnn.com/2020/06/17/us/rayshard-brooks-atlanta-shooting-wednesday/index.html.

69. Zachary Hansen and Christian Boone, "Former Atlanta Cop Charged with Felony Murder in Rayshard Brooks' Death," *Atlanta Journal-Constitution*, June 17, 2020, https://www.ajc.com/news/crime—law/bre aking-atlanta-cop-charged-with-felony-murder-other-charges-rayshard -brooks-death/h0j3W9OZvMgtSf3eE1i2hM/.

70. The Daily Wire, "Rayshard Brooks Was a Violent Criminal, Not a Victim: The Matt Walsh Show Episode 507," Facebook, June 18, 2020, https:// www.facebook.com/watch/?v=2576181922484225.

71. Bill Rankin, "GBI Investigating Fulton DA's Use of Subpoenas in Rayshard Brooks Case," *Atlanta Journal-Constitution*, July 14, 2020, https://www .ajc.com/news/local/gbi-investigating-fulton-use-subpoenas-rayshard-br ooks-case/AvMAZGA5IPVLABwv4K5fXM/.

72. Ryan Saavedra, "Police Body Cam Footage Challenges Narrative on Death of Rayshard Brooks," The Daily Wire, June 14, 2020, https://www .dailywire.com/news/watch-police-body-cam-footage-challenges-nar rative-on-death-of-rayshard-brooks.

73. Brian Freeman, "Stacey Abrams: Police Shooting of Brooks Was Murder," Newsmax, June 15, 2020, https://www.newsmax.com/us/rayshard-broo ks-stacey-abrams-atlanta-police/2020/06/15/id/972289/.

74. Danner, "Everything We Know about the Killing of Rayshard Brooks by Atlanta Police."

75. Safoora, "Black Lives Matter: Atlanta Erupts over Rayshard Brooks Death," The Siasat Daily, June 17, 2020, https://www.siasat.com/black -lives-matter-atlanta-erupts-over-rayshard-brooks-death-1902886/.

76. Kate Brumback, "Atlanta Police Call Out Sick to Protest Charges in Shooting," Associated Press, June 18, 2020, https://apnews.com/article /870f32a425b41ce391f84e1625439ebe; Seth Cohen, "As Atlanta Police Protest, Is 'Blue Flu' the Next Pandemic?" *Forbes*, June 18, 2020, https:// www.forbes.com/sites/sethcohen/2020/06/18/as-atlanta-police-protest-is -blue-flu-the-next-pandemic/#a636b93638f3; Tracey Amick-Peer, "Atlanta Police Sickout Calls Continue for Third Day," 11Alive, June 19, 2020, https://www.11alive.com/article/news/local/protests/officer-sicko ut-blue-flu-third-day-atlanta/85-515886b4-7241-4320-8db3-e257fb27 54a5.

77. Hollie Silverman and Ray Sanchez, "About 170 Atlanta Officers Called Out Sick after Cops Were Charged in Rayshard Brooks' Death," CNN, June 27, 2020, https://www.cnn.com/2020/06/27/us/atlanta-police-rays hard-brooks-shooting-sick-outs/index.html.

78. Amick-Peer, "Atlanta Police Sickout Calls Continue for Third Day."

79. Collin Kelley, "Interim Atlanta Police Chief Addresses Officer Sickout in Wake of Rayshard Brooks Charges," ReporterNewspapers, June 21, 2020, https://www.reporternewspapers.net/2020/06/21/interim-atlanta

-police-chief-addresses-officer-sickout-in-wake-of-rayshard-brooks-char ges/.

80. Richard Belcher, "Crime Numbers across Atlanta Drop Dramatically after Protests, Records Show," WSBTV, June 22, 2020, https://www.ws btv.com/news/local/atlanta/crime-numbers-across-atlanta-drop-dramat ically-ahead-rayshard-brooks-shooting-records-show/7QOMP2UE6BF LRJSWEBX6ST5MIQ/.

81. Christian Boone, Bill Rankin, and Alexis Stevens, "Fulton DA Charges Former APD Cop with Murder in Wendy's Shooting," *Atlanta Journal-Constitution*, June 18, 2020, https://www.ajc.com/news/crime—law/ful ton-charges-former-apd-cop-with-murder-wendy-shooting/Gi2sNmHp B0s2JB3QCk6UDO/; Li Cohen, "Atlanta Police Department Morale 'Is Down Ten-Fold,' Mayor Keisha Lance Bottoms Says," CBS News, June 18, 2020, https://www.cbsnews.com/news/atlanta-police-department-mo rale-down-mayor-keisha-lance-bottoms-says/.

82. John Eligon, Sarah Mervosh, and Richard A. Oppel Jr., "Jacob Blake Was Shackled in Hospital Bed after Police Shot Him," *New York Times*, August 28, 2020, https://www.nytimes.com/2020/08/28/us/jacob-blake -shackles-assault.html; Todd Richmond, "Kenosha Police Union Gives Its Version of Blake Shooting," Associated Press, August 28, 2020, https:// apnews.com/article/48c70ebf843f6018d66bddd4e5112e6f.

83. Nicole Chavez, "What We Know So Far about Jacob Blake's Shooting," CNN, August 27, 2020, https://www.cnn.com/2020/08/27/us/jacob-bla ke-shooting-what-we-know/index.html; Gabrielle Fonrouge, "This Is Why Jacob Blake Had a Warrant Out for His Arrest," *New York Post*, August 28, 2020, https://nypost.com/2020/08/28/this-is-why-jacob-bla ke-had-a-warrant-out-for-his-arrest/; Eligon, Mervosh, and Oppel, "Jacob Blake Was Shackled."

84. Gabrielle Fonrouge, "This Is Why Jacob Blake Had a Warrant Out for His Arrest."

85. "Police: K9 Dozer Helps Subdue Man Who Pulled Gun at Bar," *Racine County Eye*, September 22, 2015, https://racinecountyeye.com/police-k9 -dozer-helps-subdue-man-who-pulled-gun-at-bar/.

86. "Police Association: Jacob Blake Physically Struggled with Officers before Shooting," WBAY, August 28, 2020, https://www.wbay.com/2020/08/28 /jacob-blake-no-longer-in-restraints-in-hospital-more-kenosha-officers -identified/.

87. Jaclyn Peiser *et al.*, "After Video Shows Wisconsin Police Shooting a Black Man Multiple Times, National Guard Is Called to Kenosha," *Washington Post*, August 24, 2020, https://web.archive.org/web/20200825040228 /https://www.washingtonpost.com/nation/2020/08/23/kenosha-police-sh ooting-video-wisconsin/.

88. Associated Press, "Judge Delays Extradition of Alleged Kenosha Gunman," Canadian Broadcasting Company, August 28, 2020, https://www.cbc.ca/news/world/jacob-blake-police-kenosha-wisconsin-1.570 3414.

89. Todd Richmond, "Kenosha Police Union Gives Its Version of Jacob Blake Shooting," KAREII, August 28, 2020, https://www.kare11.com/article /news/nation-world/kenosha-police-union-gives-its-version-of-jacob-bla ke-shooting/507-90ab65b9-8e04-4283-aa07-ba141925928f.

90. Meg Jones and Joe Taschler, "Jacob Blake Shooting Timeline," *Milwaukee Journal Sentinel*, August 25, 2020, https://www.jsonline.com/story/news /2020/08/25/kenosha-police-shot-jacob-blake-3-minutes-after-arrival-au dio-reveals/5628076002/; Clare Proctor, "Jacob Blake's Father Says Son's Paralyzed from Waist Down after Police Shooting in Kenosha," *Chicago Sun-Times*, Aug 25, 2020, https://chicago.suntimes.com/2020/8/25/214 00481/jacob-blake-kenosha-police-shooting-riots-evanston.

91. Daniel Greenfield, "Lynch Mob Lawyer," FrontPage Mag, May 6, 2021 https://www.frontpagemag.com/fpm/2021/05/lynch-mob-lawyer-daniel -greenfield/.

92. Zachary Stieber, "Chaos in Wisconsin City as Rioters Burn Buildings, Attack Police," *Epoch Times*, August 24, 2020, https://www.theepocht imes.com/chaos-in-wisconsin-city-as-rioters-burn-buildings-attack-police _3472915.html.

93. Mark Guarino, Mark Berman, Jaclyn Peiser, and Griff Witte, "17-Year-Old Charged with Homicide after Shooting during Kenosha Protests, Authorities Say," *Washington Post*, August 26, 2020, https://www.was hingtonpost.com/nation/2020/08/26/jacob-blake-kenosha-police-pro tests/; "Riots & Looting in Kenosha, Wisconsin, as Police Reportedly Shoot Black Man in the Back Seven Times," RT News, August 24, 2020, https://www.rt.com/usa/498843-kenosha-police-shooting-curfew/.

94. Lee Brown, "Wisconsin Officer Knocked out by Brick Thrown during Riots in Kenosha," *New York Post*, August 24, 2020, https://nypost.com /2020/08/24/officer-knocked-out-by-brick-thrown-in-kenosha-as-proteste rs-shout-f-k-the-police/.

95. Sophie Carson and Meg Jones, "Kenosha Businesses Damaged and Vehicles Burned after Police Officer Shoots Jacob Blake in the Back," *Milwaukee Journal Sentinel*, August 24, 2020, https://www.jsonline.com /story/news/2020/08/24/kenosha-protests-escalate-after-police-shoot-bla ck-man-jacob-blake/3427941001/; "Jacob Blake Protests: Fresh Clashes after Wisconsin Shooting," BBC News, August 25, 2020, https://www .bbc.com/news/world-us-canada-53897641.

96. "Teenager Arrested over Shooting Deaths of Two People in Wisconsin as Donald Trump Says He Is Sending In Federal Law Enforcement," ABC

News August 26, 2020, https://www.abc.net.au/news/2020-08-26/jacob
-blake-protest-kenosha-wisconsin-shooting-one-dead/12599002.

97. Peiser *et al.*, "After Video Shows Wisconsin Police Shooting a Black Man
Multiple Times, National Guard Is Called to Kenosha"; Victor Jacobo,
"Following Jacob Blake Shooting, Evers Calls Special Session, Vos to Form
Task Force," CBS58.Com, August 23, 2020, https://www.cbs58.com/ne
ws/gov-evers-releases-statement-on-shooting-of-jacob-blake-in-kenosha;
Dylan Gwinn, "Gunshots Ring Out as Armed Rioters Confront Police in
Wisconsin," Breitbart, August 23, 2020, https://www.breitbart.com/poli
tics/2020/08/23/watch-gunshots-ring-out-as-armed-rioters-confront-po
lice-in-wisconsin/.

98. "Three Game 5s Set for Wednesday Postponed after Bucks' Decision to
Not Take Floor," ESPN, August 26, 2020, https://www.espn.com/nba/st
ory/_/id/29747523/bucks-not-taking-court-game-5-vs-magic.

99. Courtney Subramanian and Rebecca Morin, "Biden Focuses on Jacob
Blake, Trump Touts Police, and Other Takeaways from Dueling Kenosha
Visits," *USA Today*, September 3, 2020, https://www.usatoday.com/sto
ry/news/politics/elections/2020/09/03/kenosha-biden-visits-jacob-blakes
-family-and-other-takeaways/5702166002/.

Chapter 8: The Evidence on Police Shootings, Race, and Crime

1. InsaneNutter, "Chris Rock—How Not to Get Your Ass Kicked by the
Police!" YouTube, February 2, 2007, https://www.youtube.com/watch?v=
uj0mtxXEGE8.

2. "QuickFacts: Detroit City, Michigan," U.S. Census Bureau, 2019, https://
www.census.gov/quickfacts/fact/table/detroitcitymichigan,MI/PST04
5219.

3. M. L. Elrick, "Detroit Police Executives Say They Are Fed Up with the
Detroit Will Breathe Movement," *Detroit Free Press*, August 24, 2020,
https://amp.freep.com/amp/3431311001.

4. Ibid.

5. Ibid.

6. Peter C. Myers, "The Mind of Black Lives Matter," *National Affairs*,
Summer 2017, https://www.nationalaffairs.com/publications/detail/the
-mind-of-black-lives-matter.

7. "Herstory," Black Lives Matter, https://blacklivesmatter.com/herstory/.

8. Jodi Brown and Patrick Langan, "Policing and Homicide, 1976–98:
Justifiable Homicide by Police, Police Officers Murdered by Felons," U.S.
Department of Justice, March 2001, https://bjs.gov/content/pub/pdf/ph
98.pdf, 5; "Persons Arrested," Uniform Crime Reports, 1995 (see Table

43), https://ucr.fbi.gov/crime-in-the-u.s/1995/95sec4.pdf; "Persons Arrested," Uniform Crime Reports, 1996 (see Table 43), https://ucr.fbi.gov/crime-in-the-u.s/1996/96sec4.pdf; "Persons Arrested," Uniform Crime Reports, 1997 (see Table 43), https://ucr.fbi.gov/crime-in-the-u.s/1997/97sec4.pdf; "Persons Arrested," Uniform Crime Reports, 1998 (see Table 43), https://ucr.fbi.gov/crime-in-the-u.s/1998/98sec4.pdf.

9.   Andrea M. Burch, "Arrest-Related Deaths, 2003–2009—Statistical Tables, NCJ 235385," U.S. Department of Justice, November 2011, https://www.bjs.gov/content/pub/pdf/ard0309st.pdf. The annual violent-crime arrest statistics for 2003–2009, broken down by race, can be found here: "Crime in the United States, 2003," U.S. Department of Justice, (see Table 43), https://ucr.fbi.gov/crime-in-the-u.s/2003/03sec4.pdf; "Crime in the United States, 2004," U.S. Department of Justice (see Table 43), https://www2.fbi.gov/ucr/cius_04/persons_arrested/table_38-43.html; "Crime in the United States, 2005," U.S. Department of Justice (See Table 43), https://www2.fbi.gov/ucr/05cius/data/table_43.html; "Crime in the United States, 2006," U.S. Department of Justice (see Table 43), https://www2.fbi.gov/ucr/cius2006/data/table_43.html; "Crime in the United States, 2007," U.S. Department of Justice (see Table 43), https://www2.fbi.gov/ucr/cius2007/data/table_43.html; "Crime in the United States, 2008," U.S. Department of Justice (see Table 43), https://www2.fbi.gov/ucr/cius2008/data/table_43.html; "Crime in the United States, 2009," U.S. Department of Justice (see Table 43), https://www2.fbi.gov/ucr/cius2009/data/table_43.html.

10.   Uniform Crime Reports, "Crime in the United States, 2017," Table 43A, https://ucr.fbi.gov/crime-in-the-u.s/2017/crime-in-the-u.s.-2017/topic-pages/tables/table-43; Uniform Crime Reports, "Crime in the United States, 2018," Table 43A, https://ucr.fbi.gov/crime-in-the-u.s/2018/crime-in-the-u.s.-2018/topic-pages/tables/table-43; Uniform Crime Reports, "Crime in the United States, 2019," Table 43A, https://ucr.fbi.gov/crime-in-the-u.s/2019/crime-in-the-u.s.-2019/topic-pages/tables/table-43; Statista.com, "Number of People Shot to Death by the Police in the United States from 2017 to 2021, by Race," https://www.statista.com/statistics/585152/people-shot-to-death-by-us-police-by-race/.

11.   Sarah DeGue, Katherine A. Fowler, and Cynthia Calkins, "Deaths Due To Use of Lethal Force by Law Enforcement: Findings from the National Violent Death Reporting System, 17 U.S. States, 2009–2012," *American Journal of Preventive Medicine* 5, no. 1, supplement 3 (November 1, 2016): S173–S187, https://www.ncbi.nlm.nih.gov/pmc/articles/PMC6080222/; John Sullivan, Zane Anthony, Julie Tate, and Jennifer Jenkins, "Nationwide, Police Shot and Killed Nearly 1,000 People in 2017," *Washington Post*, January 6 2018, https://www

.washingtonpost.com/investigations/nationwide-police-shot-and-killed -nearly-1000-people-in-2017/2018/01/04/4eed5f34-e4e9-11e7-ab50-621 fe0588340_story.html; Michael Harriot, "Here's How Many People Police Killed in 2018," TheRoot.com, January 3, 2019, https://www.th eroot.com/here-s-how-many-people-police-killed-in-2018-1831469528; Heather Mac Donald, "The Myth of Systemic Police Racism," *Wall Street Journal*, June 2, 2020, https://www.wsj.com/articles/the-myth-of-systemic -police-racism-11591119883; Heather Mac Donald, "There Is No Epidemic of Fatal Police Shootings against Unarmed Black Americans," *USA Today*, July 3, 2020, https://www.usatoday.com/story/opinion/20 20/07/03/police-black-killings-homicide-rates-race-injustice-column/323 5072001/.

12. "Number of People Shot to Death by the Police in the United States from 2017 to 2021, by Race," Statista, https://www.statista.com/statistics /585152/people-shot-to-death-by-us-police-by-race/.

13. "Quick Facts: United States," United States Census Bureau, https://www .census.gov/quickfacts/fact/table/US/PST045219, percentages for "Black or African American Alone" and "White Alone, not Hispanic or Latino"; FBI Uniform Crime Reports, "Arrests by Race and Ethnicity, 2019," *Crime in the United States 2019*, Table 43, https://ucr.fbi.gov/crime-in-the-u.s/20 19/crime-in-the-u.s.-2019/topic-pages/tables/table-43.

14. Jamil Smith, "The Power of Black Lives Matter: How the Movement That's Changing America Was Built and Where It Goes Next," *Rolling Stone*, June 16, 2020, https://blog.adafruit.com/2020/06/16/black-lives -matter-from-ferguson-to-now-rolling-stone/.

15. Heather Mac Donald, "There Is No Epidemic of Fatal Police Shootings against Unarmed African Americans," Manhattan Institute, July 3, 2020, https://www.manhattan-institute.org/police-black-killings-homici de-rates-race-injustice; PragerU (@prageru), "Facts: 14 unarmed blacks were fatally shot by police in 2019," Twitter, July 15, 2020, https://twitter .com/prageru/status/1283453676577681409?lang=en.

16. John R. Lott Jr. and Carlisle E. Moody, "Do White Police Officers Unfairly Target Black Suspects?" The Crime Prevention Research Center, July 21, 2017, https://papers.ssrn.com/sol3/papers.cfm?abstract_id=287 0189.

17. Jodi Brown and Patrick Langan, *Policing and Homicide, 1976-98: Justifiable Homicide by Police, Police Officers Murdered by Felons*, U.S. Department of Justice, March 2001, https://bjs.gov/content/pub/pdf/ph 98.pdf.

18. Tom Jacobs, "Black Cops Are Just as Likely as White Cops to Kill Black Suspects," *Pacific Standard*, August 9, 2018, https://psmag.com/social-jus tice/black-cops-are-just-as-likely-as-whites-to-kill-black-suspects.

19. Roland G. Fryer Jr., "An Empirical Analysis of Racial Differences in Police Use of Force," National Bureau of Economic Research, July 2016, revised January 2018, https://www.nber.org/papers/w22399.pdf.
20. David J. Johnson, Trevor Tress, Nicole Burkel, and Carley Taylor, "Officer Characteristics and Racial Disparities in Fatal Officer-Involved Shootings," Proceedings of the National Academy of Sciences of the United States of America, July 22, 2019, https://www.pnas.org/content /116/32/15877; Heather Mac Donald, "There Is No Epidemic of Racist Police Shootings," *National Review*, July 31, 2019, https:// www.nationalreview.com/2019/07/white-cops-dont-commit-mo re-shootings/.
21. Heather Mac Donald, "Academic Research on Police Shootings and Race," *Washington Post*, July 19, 2016, https://www.washingtonpost.com /news/volokh-conspiracy/wp/2016/07/19/academic-research-on-police-sh ootings-and-race/.
22. Heather Mac Donald, "A Platform of Urban Crime," *City Journal*, September 23, 2019, https://www.city-journal.org/democratic-candidat es-racism-crime.
23. Tim Hains, "Stefan Molyneux: Race-Baiting Lies about Cops Do Real Damage to the Black Community," RealClearPolitics, July 8, 2016, https:// www.realclearpolitics.com/video/2016/07/08/stefan_molyneux_lies_abo ut_the_dangers_of_white_racism_do_a_massive_amount_of_damage _to_the_black_community.html; Terry Paulson, "America's Future Rests on Neither White or Black Privilege," Townhall, April 5, 2021, https://to wnhall.com/columnists/terrypaulson/2021/04/05/americas-future-rests -on-neither-white-or-black-privilege-n2587378.
24. Mac Donald, "A Platform of Urban Crime."
25. Ibid.
26. Smith, "The Power of Black Lives Matter."

PART THREE: Black Lives Matter, Inc.

Chapter 9: What Kind of Movement Is This?

1.   "The Black Liberation Army and Homegrown Terrorism in 1970s America," International Centre for the Study of Radicalisation, https://ic sr.info/2012/04/12/the-black-liberation-army-and-homegrown-terrorism -in-1970s-america/.
2.   William Rosenau, "The Dark History of America's First Female Terrorist Group," *Politico*, May 3, 2020, https://www.politico.com/news/magaz ine/2020/05/03/us-history-first-women-terrorist-group-191037.

3. Hollie McKay, "Behind Susan Rosenberg and the Roots of Left-Wing Domestic Extremism," Fox News, November 17, 2020, https://www.fox news.com/us/susan-rosenberg-left-wing-domestic-extremism-roots.

4. Talon Archives, "#BlackLivesMatter Assata Shakur Chant," YouTube, August 7, 2016, https://www.youtube.com/watch?v=SNayoOysBLY; Assata Shakur, "To My People," The Talking Drum, http://www.thetalkingdrum.com/tmp.html; Lee Stranahan, "BlackLivesMatter Pays Homage to Marxist Cop Killer at Every Event It Holds," Breitbart, July 23, 2015, https://www.breitbart.com/politics/2015/07/23/blacklivesmatter-pays-homage-to-marxist-cop-killer-at-every-event-it-holds/.

5. "Lessons from Fidel: Black Lives Matter and the Transition of *El Comandante*," Black Lives Matter Global Network, November 27, 2016, Medium.com, https://medium.com/@BlackLivesMatterNetwork/lessons-from-fidel-black-lives-matter-and-the-transition-of-el-comandante-c11ee5e51fb0.

6. Adelle Banks, "Farrakhan 'Justice or Else' Rally Reaches Beyond 'Black Lives Matter,'" *Washington Post*, October 10, 2015, https://www.washingtonpost.com/national/religion/farrakhan-justice-or-else-rally-reaches-beyond-black-lives-matter/2015/10/10/f14ee6b0-6f95-11e5-91eb-27ad15c2b723_story.html.

7. Deneen Borelli, "Al Sharpton Joins Black Lives Matter Rally to Defend Farrakhan," DeneenBorelli.com, March 19, 2018, https://deneenborelli.com/2018/03/al-sharpton-joins-black-lives-matter-rally-defend-farrakhan/; Valerie Richardson, "Anti-Farrakhan Resolution Prompts Black Delegation Call to Condemn Trump Instead," *Washington Post*, March 19, 2018, https://www.washingtontimes.com/news/2018/mar/19/todd-rokitas-anti-louis-farrakhan-resolution-spurs/.

8. "2019 Hate Crime Statistics," FBI Uniform Crime Reports, https://ucr.fbi.gov/hate-crime/2019/topic-pages/tables/table-1.xls.

9. Daniel Greenfield, "A Farrakhan Supporter Led the L.A. Black Lives Matter Rally That Became a Pogrom," FrontPage Mag, June 19, 2020, https://www.frontpagemag.com/fpm/2020/06/farrakhan-supporter-led-la-black-lives-matter-daniel-greenfield./.

10. Sharon McNary, "Black Lives Matter–L.A. Leader Explains 'Very Deliberate' Choice to Demonstrate in Upscale Neighborhoods," LAist, May 31, 2020, https://laist.com/2020/05/31/melina-abdullah-black-lives-matter-la-protest-police-violence-george-floyd.php.

11. "Over 1,000 People and 39 Organizations Signed the Statement," BlackforPalestine, 2015, http://www.blackforpalestine.com/view-the-signatories.html; "2015 Black Solidarity Statement with Palestine," BlackforPalestine, 2015, http://www.blackforpalestine.com/read-the-sta

tement.html; Dan Diker, "Unmasking BDS: Radical Roots, Extremist Ends," Jerusalem Center for Public Affairs, 2016, https://jcpa.org/pdf/Un masking_.pdf https://jcpa.org/unmasking-bds/.

12. "2015 Black Solidarity Statement with Palestine," Black for Palestine; "Boycott, Divestment & Sanctions Movement," Discover the Networks, https://www.discoverthenetworks.org/organizations/boycott-divestment -sanctions-movement-bds/; Alex Emmons, "Hillary Clinton Attacks Israel Boycott Movement in AIPAC Speech," The Intercept, March 22, 2016, https://theintercept.com/2016/03/22/clinton-attacks-israeli-boycott-mo vement-in-aipac-speech/.

13. "Demonstrators in D.C. Chant 'Israel, We Know You, You Murder Children, Too,'" Jewish Telegraphic Agency, July 2, 2020, https://www .jta.org/quick-reads/black-lives-matter-demonstrators-in-dc-chant-israel -we-know-you-you-murder-children-too.

14. "Pro-Palestinian BLM Rallies in U.S. Call for 'Death to Israel, Death to America,'" Breitbart, July 6, 2020, https://www.breitbart.com/middle-ea st/2020/07/06/pro-palestinian-blm-rallies-in-u-s-call-for-death-to-israel -and-to-america/.

15. Joseph Wulfsohn, "Black Lives Matter Removes 'What We Believe' Website Page Calling to 'Disrupt . . . Nuclear Family Structure,'" Fox News, September 21, 2020, https://www.foxnews.com/media/black-lives -matter-disrupt-nuclear-family-website.

16. Ian Rowe, "The Power of the Two-Parent Home Is Not a Myth," American Enterprise Institute, January 8, 2020, https://www.aei.org/ar ticles/the-power-of-the-two-parent-home-is-not-a-myth/.

17. Thomas Sowell, *Civil Rights: Rhetoric or Reality?* (New York: William Morrow & Company, 1984), 48.

18. Rowe, "The Power of the Two-Parent Home Is Not a Myth."

19. Robert Rector, "The Effects of Welfare Reform," *Heritage Foundation*, March 15, 2001, https://www.heritage.org/testimony/the-effects-welfare -reform.

20. Ibid.

21. Elaine Kamarck, "Fatherless Families: A Violent Link," *Los Angeles Times*, May 7, 1992 https://www.latimes.com/archives/la-xpm-1992-05- 07-me-2237-story.html.

22. Mona Charen, "Liberal Tinkering Has Put Our Civilization at Risk," *Conservative Chronicle*, August 24, 1994, 21.

23. Rector, "The Effects of Welfare Reform."

24. Richard Weikart, "Marx, Engels, and the Abolition of the Family," *History of European Ideas* 18:5 (1994): 657–72, https://www.csus tan.edu/sites/default/files/History/Faculty/Weikart/Marx-Engels-and-the -Abolition-of-the-Family.pdf.

25. Wulfsohn, "Black Lives Matter Removes 'What We Believe' Website Page"; Zachary Stieber, "Black Lives Matter Removes Goal of Disrupting Family Structure from Website," *Epoch Times*, September 21, 2020, https://www.theepochtimes.com/black-lives-matter-removes-goal-of-dis rupting-family-structure-from-website_3508437.html.

26. Kat H., "Trained Marxist Patrisse Cullors, Black Lives Matters BLM," YouTube, June 20, 2020, https://www.youtube.com/watch?v=1noLh25 FbKI; Tom Kertscher, "Is Black Lives Matter a Marxist movement?" Politifact, July 21, 2020, https://www.politifact.com/article/2020/jul/21/ black-lives-matter-marxist-movement/.

27. Kertscher, "Is Black Lives Matter a Marxist Movement?"

28. Michael Ezra, "Karl Marx's Radical Antisemitism," *The Philosophers' Magazine*, March 23, 2015, https://www.philosophersmag.com/opinion /30-karl-marx-s-radical-antisemitism.

29. "Who We Are," Black Lives Matter–L.A., https://www.blmla.org/who -we-are; James Simpson, "Reds Exploiting Blacks: The Roots of Black Lives Matter," AIM, January 12, 2016, https://www.aim.org/special-re port/reds-exploiting-blacks-the-roots-of-black-lives-matter/.

30. Simpson, "Reds Exploiting Blacks: The Roots of Black Lives Matter"; Joshua Klein, "Black Lives Matter Founder Mentored by Ex-Domestic Terrorist Who Worked with Bill Ayers," Breitbart, June 24, 2020, https:// www.breitbart.com/politics/2020/06/24/black-lives-matter -founder-mentored-by-ex-domestic-terrorist-who-worked-with-bill-ayers/.

31. Peter Myers, "How Black Lives Matter Is Moving into the Schools," *New York Post*, August 29, 2019, https://nypost.com/2019/08/29/how-black -lives-matter-is-moving-into-the-schools/.

32. Sara Dogan, "Thousands of Public School Educators Celebrate 'Black Lives Matter At School Week,'" FrontPage Mag, March 25, 2019, http:// www.frontpagemag.com/fpm/2019/03/thousands-public-school-educato rs-celebrate-black-sara-dogan/.

33. Lalena Garcia, "Guiding Principles," Black Lives Matter at NYC Schools, https://blmedu.wordpress.com/guiding-principles/.

34. Dogan, "Thousands of Public School Educators Celebrate 'Black Lives Matter At School Week.'"

35. Fred Lucas, "These 18 Corporations Gave Money to Radical Black Lives Matter Group," The Daily Signal, July 7, 2020, https://www.dailysignal .com/2020/07/07/these-18-corporations-gave-money-to-black-lives-mat ter-group/; Jordan Davidson, "These 'Fortune 500' Companies Donated to the Marxist, Anti-Capitalism Black Lives Matter Foundation," The Federalist, July 13, 2020, https://thefederalist.com/2020/07/13/these-for tune-500-companies-donated-to-the-marxist-anti-capitalism-black-lives -matter-foundation/.

36. Robert Stilson, "The Various Faces of Black Lives Matter," Capital Research Center, June 24, 2020, https://capitalresearch.org/article/the-various-faces-of-black-lives-matter/; Robert Stilson, "The Organizational Structure of Black Lives Matter," Capital Research Center, June 18, 2020, https://capitalresearch.org/article/the-organizational-structure-of-black-lives-matter/.

37. Benjamin Weiser, "Former Terrorist Now Fights for Parole," *New York Times*, November 5, 1999, https://www.nytimes.com/1999/11/05/nyregion/former-terrorist-now-fights-for-parole.html.

38. Scott Walter, "A Terrorist's Ties to a Leading Black Lives Matter Group," Capital Research Center, June 24, 2020, https://capitalresearch.org/article/a-terrorists-ties-to-a-leading-black-lives-matter-group/; "May 19th Communist Organization," GlobalSecurity, https://www.globalsecurity.org/military/world/para/m19co.htm; Andrew C. McCarthy, "Opposed to Holder without Apology," *National Review*, November 25, 2008, https://www.nationalreview.com/2008/11/opposed-holder-without-apology-andrew-c-mccarthy/.

39. Robert Stilson, "Movement for Black Lives Has a New Fiscal Sponsor," Capital Research Center, February 1, 2021, https://capitalresearch.org/article/movement-for-black-lives-has-a-new-fiscal-sponsor/.

40. Hayden Ludwig, "ActBlue: The Left's Favorite 'Dark Money' Machine," Capital Research Center, June 16, 2020, https://capitalresearch.org/article/actblue-the-lefts-favorite-dark-money-machine/; F. William Engdahl, "'Color Revolution' in U.S.: Deep State's 'Regime Change' Plot," Adara Press, June 30, 2020, https://adarapress.com/2020/06/30/color-revolution-in-us-deep-states-regime-change-plot-f-william-engdahl/; "99.64% BLM's Defund the Police Donations Go to Joe Biden Campaign Via ActBlue," GreatGameIndia, June 12, 2020, https://greatgameindia.com/defund-the-police-donations-joe-biden/ .

41. William La Jeunesse, "George Floyd Protests Could Be Most Expensive Civil Disturbance in U.S. History, Experts Say," Fox News, June 29, 2020, https://www.foxnews.com/politics/george-floyd-protests-expensive-civil-disturbance-us-history; Lois Beckett, "At Least 25 Americans Were Killed During Protests and Political Unrest in 2020," *The Guardian*, October 31, 2020, https://www.theguardian.com/world/2020/oct/31/americans-killed-protests-political-unrest-acled#.

42. Becket Adams, "Biden Now Claims That Michael Brown Was a Victim of Systemic Racism," *Washington Examiner*, August 10, 2020, https://www.washingtonexaminer.com/opinion/joe-biden-now-claims-that-michael-brown-was-a-victim-of-systemic-racism.

43. Glenn Kessler, "Harris, Warren Ignore DOJ Report to Claim Michael Brown Was 'Murdered,'" *Washington Post*, August 13, 2019, https://www

.washingtonpost.com/politics/2019/08/13/harris-warren-ignore-doj-repo
rt-claim-that-michael-brown-was-murdered/.

44. Elizabeth Warren (@ewarren), "5 years ago Michael Brown was
    murdered. . . ." Twitter, August 9, 2019, 2:59 p.m., https://
    twitter.com/ewarren/status/1159902078103445507.

45. "Department of Justice Report Regarding the Criminal Investigation into
    the Shooting Death of Michael Brown by Ferguson, Missouri Police
    Officer Darren Wilson," Department of Justice, March 4, 2015, https://
    www.justice.gov/sites/default/files/opa/press-releases/attachments/2015
    /03/04/doj_report_on_shooting_of_michael_brown_1.pdf.

46. "Taking Action on Racial Equity and Justice Learning Challenge Series—
    Discussion Guide and Workbook," Apple, January 9, 2021, https://educ
    ation-static.apple.com/cfc/conversations-discussion-guide.pdf.

47. Kevin Clarke, "Apple Guide to Discuss Racial Justice," Issuu, January 9,
    2021, https://issuu.com/victorybyvalorfinal/docs/conversations-discussi
    on-guide.

48. "Louis Farrakhan," DiscoverTheNetworks.org, https://www.discoverth
    enetworks.org/individuals/louis-farrakhan/.

49. Lydia Saad, "Black Americans Want Police to Retain Local Presence,"
    Gallup, August 5, 2020, https://news.gallup.com/poll/316571/black-amer
    icans-police-retain-local-presence.aspx.

50. "Pandemic, Social Unrest, and Crime in U.S. Cities: 2020 Year-End
    Update," National Commission on COVID-19 and Criminal Justice,
    January 31, 2021, https://covid19.counciloncj.org/2021/01/31/impact-re
    port-covid-19-and-crime-3/; Horus Alas, "2020 a 'Perfect Storm' for
    Homicide Surge," U.S. News & World Report, February 4, 2021, https://
    www.usnews.com/news/national-news/articles/2021-02-04/2020-homi
    cide-rates-spike-amid-pandemic-police-protests.

51. Stephanie Pagones, "America's Murder Rate Increase in 2020 Has 'No
    Modern Precedent,' Crime Analyst Group Finds," Fox News, February
    1, 2021, https://www.foxnews.com/us/murder-rate-increase-2020-no-mo
    dern-precedent-crime-analyst-group-finds.

52. Heather Mac Donald, "Taking Stock of a Most Violent Year," Wall Street
    Journal, January 24, 2021, https://www.wsj.com/articles/taking-stock-of
    -a-most-violent-year-11611525947.

Chapter 10: Whose Future?

1. David Horowitz, Blitz (New York: Humanix Books, 2020), 8–9; Ian
   Schwartz, "Trump to Black Voters: 'What Do You Have to Lose by Trying
   Something New?' Reject Hillary's 'Bigotry,'" RealClearPolitics, August
   19, 2016, https://www.realclearpolitics.com/video/2016/08/19/trump_to

_black_voters_what_do_you_have_to_lose_by_trying_something_new
_reject_hillarys_bigotry.html.

2.   Andy Ngo, *Unmasked: Inside Antifa's Radical Plan to Destroy Democracy* (Nashville, Tennessee: Center Street, 2021), 135.

3.   Jeremy Blum, "Biden Says He'll Be a President for All, Including Pro-Trump 'Chumps' at Rally," HuffPo, October 24, 2020, https://www.huffpost.com/entry/joe-biden-president-for-all-chumps_n_5f949909c5b6a2e1fb61d911.

4.   Joe Concha, "By His Own Definition, Biden Is Already Governing like a Dictator," *The Hill*, January 28, 2021, https://thehill.com/opinion/white-house/536317-by-his-own-definition-biden-is-already-governing-like-a-dictator.

5.   "Letter to President-Elect Joe Biden and Vice President-Elect Kamala Harris," Black Lives Matter, November 9, 2020, https://blacklivesmatter.com/wp-content/uploads/2020/11/blm-letter-to-biden-harris-110720.pdf.

6.   Ibid.

7.   "Executive Order on Advancing Racial Equity and Support for Underserved Communities through the Federal Government," The White House, January 20, 2021, https://www.whitehouse.gov/briefing-room/presidential-actions/2021/01/20/executive-order-advancing-racial-equity-and-support-for-underserved-communities-through-the-federal-government/.

8.   President Biden (@POTUS), "The fact is systemic racism touches every facet of American life. . . ." Twitter, January 26, 2021, 7:15 p.m., https://twitter.com/POTUS/status/1354221331605319681.

9.   Robert Rector, "How the War on Poverty Was Lost," *Wall Street Journal*, January 7, 2014, https://www.wsj.com/articles/SB10001424052702303345104579282760272285556; "How Much the U.S. Spends on Welfare," Myth Detector, June 8, 2020, https://www.mythdetector.ge/en/myth/how-much-us-spends-welfare-and-statistics-spread-politicano.

10.   "Households: Middle Class," Black Demographics: The African American Population, https://blackdemographics.com/households/middle-class/.

11.   Ibid..

12.   "Indian Americans' Household Income Average $120,000 Annually: Report," *Times of India*, January 29, 2021, https://timesofindia.indiatimes.com/world/us/indian-americans-household-income-average-120000-annually-report/articleshow/80574003.cms.

13.   Christine Benz, "100 Must-Know Statistics about Race, Income, and Wealth," Morningstar, June 8, 2020, https://www.morningstar.com/articles/987356/100-must-know-statistics-about-race-income-and-wealth.

14.   "Legal Highlight: The Civil Rights Act of 1964," U.S. Department of Labor, https://www.dol.gov/agencies/oasam/civil-rights-center/statutes/civil-rights-act-of-1964#.

15. Alison Durkee, "Biden Campaign Deploys 600 Lawyers So Trump Can't 'Steal This Election,'" *Forbes*, July 2, 2020, https://www.forbes.com/sites /alisondurkee/2020/07/02/biden-campaign-deploys-600-lawyers-so-tru mp-cant-steal-this-election/?sh=5c7aea291e00.

16. James M. Lindsay, "The 2020 Election by the Numbers," Council on Foreign Relations, December 15, 2020, https://www.cfr.org/blog/2020 -election-numbers; Brooke Singman, "Trump Claims Mail-in Voting Will Lead to 'Most Corrupt Election' in U.S. History," Fox News, July 21, 2020, https://www.foxnews.com/politics/trump-mail-in-voting-will-lead -to-most-corrupt-election-in-us-history.

17. "Building Confidence in U.S. Elections," Report of the Commission on Federal Election Reform," September 2005, https://www.legislationline .org/download/id/1472/file/3b50795b2d0374cbef5c29766256.pdf; Fred Lucas, "7 Ways the 2005 Carter–Baker Report Could Have Averted Problems with the 2020 Election," The Daily Signal, November 20, 2020, https://www.dailysignal.com/2020/11/20/7-ways-the-2005-carter-baker -report-could-have-averted-problems-with-2020-election/.

18. "Post-Election Lawsuits, 2020," Ballotpedia, https://ballotpedia.org/ Ballotpedia%27s_2020_Election_Help_Desk:_Tracking_election_ disputes,_lawsuits,_and_recounts.

19. "Joe Biden Has Been Declared the Winner, Toppling Donald Trump after Four Years of Upheaval in the White House," *Politico*, January 6, 2021, https://www.politico.com/2020-election/results/president/.

20. David Horowitz, "My Former Friends Have Joined the Fascists," FrontPage Mag, May 10, 2021, https://www.frontpagemag.com/fpm/20 21/05/my-former-friends-have-joined-fascists-david-horowitz/.

21. Peter Navarro, "The Immaculate Deception," DocDroid, December 15, 2020, https://www.docdroid.net/QhVNwFw/the-immaculate-deception -121520-1-pdf.

22. Ibid.

23. Ibid., 6.

24. Donald Trump Speech "'Save America' Rally Transcript January 6," Rev, January 6, 2021, https://www.rev.com/blog/transcripts/donald-trump-sp eech-save-america-rally-transcript-january-6.

25. Charles R. Kesler, "After January 6th: The Future of Trump and Trumpism," *Claremont Review of Books* (Winter 2020/21), https://cla remontreviewofbooks.com/after-january-6th/.

26. Brian Naylor, "Read Trump's Jan. 6 Speech, A Key Part of Impeachment Trial," NPR, February 10, 2021, https://www.npr.org/2021/02/10/9663 96848/read-trumps-jan-6-speech-a-key-part-of-impeachment-trial.

27. Madison Hall *et al.*, "510 People Have Been Charged in the Capitol Insurrection So Far," Insider, June 4, 2021, https://www.insider.com/all -the-us-capitol-pro-trump-riot-arrests-charges-names-2021-1.

28. Nexstar Media Wire, "What We Know about the 5 People Who Died during Riot at U.S. Capitol," KTLA, January 8, 2021, https://ktla.com/news/nationworld/what-we-know-about-the-5-people-who-died-during-riot-at-u-s-capitol/.

29. Ibid.

30. Ibid.

31. Kyle Cheney, "Capitol Police Provided More than 14,000 Hours of Jan. 6 Footage to Lawmakers," *Politico*, March 29, 2021, https://www.politico.com/news/2021/03/29/capitol-police-jan6-footage-478439.

32. "Brian Sicknick," Wikipedia, https://en.wikipedia.org/wiki/Brian_Sicknick; Danielle Wallace, "A Month after Capitol Riot, Autopsy Results Pending in Officer Brian Sicknick Death Investigation," Fox News, February 6, 2021, https://www.foxnews.com/us/capitol-riot-brian-sicknick-death-investigation-no-charges-autopsy-results-pending); "The *New York Times* Retracts the Story Asserting Capitol Police Officer Brian Sicknick Was Killed by a Trump Supporter," *Tennessee Star*, February 15, 2021, https://tennesseestar.com/2021/02/15/the-new-york-times-retracts-the-story-asserting-capitol-police-officer-brian-sicknick-was-killed-by-a-trump-supporter/; Matthew Schmitz, "What the Left Wants to Ignore about Slain Capitol Police Officer Brian Sicknick," *New York Post*, January 10, 2021, https://nypost.com/2021/01/10/what-the-left-wants-to-ignore-about-slain-capitol-police-officer/; Joel B. Pollak, "Democrats Cited Debunked 'Fire Extinguisher' Claim in Trump Impeachment Trial," Breitbart, April 20, 2021, https://www.breitbart.com/politics/2021/04/20/democrats-cited-debunked-fire-extinguisher-claim-in-trump-impeachment-trial/.

33. Jon Brown, "'Infamy': Chuck Schumer Compares Capitol Chaos to Pearl Harbor," The Daily Wire, January 6, 2021, https://www.dailywire.com/news/infamy-chuck-schumer-compares-capitol-chaos-to-pearl-harbor; Nick Givas, "Holocaust Survivors Respond to AOC's 'Concentration Camp' Comments in New Video," Fox News, June 23, 2019, https://www.foxnews.com/politics/aoc-holocaust-survivors-respond-to-aocs-concentration-camp-comments.

34. Daniel Greenfield, "The Reichstag Fire of the Democrats," FrontPage Mag, February 8, 2021, https://www.frontpagemag.com/fpm/2021/02/reichstag-fire-democrats-daniel-greenfield/.

35. Ibid.

36. Brittany De Lea, "Black Lives Matter Backs 'Squad' Member's Push to Expel over 100 Republicans from Congress," Fox News, February 1, 2021, https://www.foxnews.com/politics/black-lives-matter-backs-squad-members-push-to-expel-over-100-republicans-from-congress.

37. Cori Bush (@CoriBush), "Expel the Republican Members of Congress. . . ." Twitter, January 8, 2021, 10:30 a.m., https://twitter.com/coribush/status/1347566317168164865?lang=en.

38. "Tell Your Rep(s) to Support Rep. Cori Bush's Resolution," Black Lives Matter, February 1, 2021, https://blacklivesmatter.com/tell-your-reps-to -support-rep-cori-bushs-resolution/.

39. Chuck Ross, "Report: Alleged Chinese Spy Raised Money for Eric Swalwell, Planted Intern in His Office," The Daily Caller, December 8, 2020, https://dailycaller.com/2020/12/08/chinese-spy-eric-swalwell-chris tine-fang/.

40. Tim Hains, "Eric Swalwell Compares Capitol Hill Riots to 9/11, Trump to Bin Laden," RealClearPolitics, January 13, 2021, https://www.realcle arpolitics.com/video/2021/01/13/eric_swalwell_compares_capitol_hill_ri ots_to_911_trump_to_bin_laden.html.

41. Isabel Van Brugen, "Trump Offered to Deploy 10,000 National Guard Troops in D.C. ahead of Jan. 6: Mark Meadows," *Epoch Times*, February 9, 2021, https://www.theepochtimes.com/trump-offered-to-deploy-100 00-national-guard-troops-in-dc-ahead-of-jan-6-mark-meadows_36902 94.html.

42. "Mark Meadows: Trump Offered 10,000 National Guard Troops to Ready Ahead of January 6," KABC News, https://www.kabc.com/news /mark-meadows-trump-offered-10000-national-guard-troops-to-ready -ahead-of-jan-6/.

43. Calvin Freiburger, "D.C. Mayor Refused Trump's Offers of National Guard Aid, Former WH Chief of Staff Says," LifeSiteNews, February 10, 2021, https://www.lifesitenews.com/news/dc-mayor-refused-trumps-of fers-of-national-guard-aid-meadows-says; Prakash Gogoi, "Trump's Offer of 10,000 Troops for Jan. 6 Was Refused," Vision Times, February 13, 2021, https://visiontimes.com/2021/02/13/trumps-offer-of-10000-troops -for-jan-6-was-declined.html; "Trump Offered 10,000 Troops to Protect D.C. on January 6th," Zone News, February 2021, https://zonenews-24 .com/2021/02/11/trump-offered-10000-troops-to-protect-dc-on-january -6th/.

44. Paul Blest, "The Oath Keepers Started Training to Raid the Capitol in November, Prosecutors Say," Vice News, January 28, 2021, https://www .vice.com/en/article/7k9m49/alleged-militia-members-started-planning -capitol-riot-days-after-bidens-win.

45. Jamie Raskin, "Speech on Why Senate Should Convict Trump Transcript: Trump's Second Impeachment Trial," Rev, February 10, 2021, https:// www.rev.com/blog/transcripts/rep-jamie-raskin-speech-on-why-senate -should-convict-trump-transcript-trumps-second-impeachment-trial.

46. Ronn Blitzer, "House Dems Who Challenged 2016 Election Results Escalate Fight with Republicans behind 2020 Challenges," Fox News, January 19, 2021, https://www.foxnews.com/politics/house-dems-chal lenged-2016-election-results-fight-republicans-2020-challenges.

47. Jim Huffman, "The Orchestrated Disruptions of Kavanaugh's Hearings Demonstrated Neither Democracy Nor Free Speech," The Daily Caller, September 18, 2018, https://dailycaller.com/2018/09/18/disruptions-kavanaugh-democracy-free-time/.

48. Eric Lipton, "Officials Criticize Clinton's Pardon of an Ex-Terrorist," *New York Times*, January 22, 2001, https://www.nytimes.com/2001/01/22/nyregion/officials-criticize-clinton-s-pardon-of-an-ex-terrorist.html.

49. "Antifa Protestors Threaten to 'Burn' down Washington, D.C.," ANI News, February 7, 2021, https://www.aninews.in/news/world/us/antifa-protestors-threaten-to-burn-down-washington-dc20210207150821/; "Antifa to 'Burn Down' Washington in Coming Days," We the People Daily, February 8, 2021, https://wethepeopledaily.com/2021/02/08/antifa-to-burn-down-washington-in-coming-days/.

50. "Impeaching Donald John Trump, President of The United States, for High Crimes and Misdemeanors," *Congressional Record* 167: 8 (January 13, 2021), https://www.govinfo.gov/content/pkg/CREC-2021-01-13/html/CREC-2021-01-13-pt1-PgH165.htm.

51. Jim Garamone, "Austin Orders Military Stand Down to Address Challenge of Extremism in the Ranks," DOD News, February 3, 2021, https://www.defense.gov/Explore/News/Article/Article/2492530/austin-orders-military-stand-down-to-address-challenge-of-extremism-in-the-ranks/.

52. David R. Sands, "Space Force Commander Fired for Comments on Marxist Influences in the Ranks," *Washington Times*, May 16, 2021, https://www.washingtontimes.com/news/2021/may/16/matthew-lohmeier-space-force-commander-fired-for-c/.

53. Christopher Rufo, "Critical Race Theory: What It Is and How to Fight It," *Imprimis*, March 2021, https://imprimis.hillsdale.edu/critical-race-theory-fight/; Cathy Young, "The Fight Over the 1619 Project," The Bulwark, February 9, 2020, https://thebulwark.com/the-fight-over-the-1619-project/?amp.

54. Mike Glenn, "Matthew Lohmeier, Dismissed Space Force Commander, Finds Ally in James Inhofe, Mike Rogers," *Washington Times*, May 16, 2021, www.washingtontimes.com/news/2021/may/16/matthew-lohmeier-space-force-commander.

55. Lindsey Burke, "How Biden Aims to Take Critical Race Theory to the Next Level in Your School," The Daily Signal, May 15, 2021, https://www.dailysignal.com/2021/05/15/how-biden-aims-to-take-critical-race-theory-to-the-next-level-in-your-school/.

56. USA 2M, "Tucker Carlson Tonight—5/20/21—Full Show—May 20, 2021," YouTube, May 20, 2021, https://www.youtube.com/watch?v=GHKc4aYeH84.

INDEX